DATE DUE

DE 10 '97			
JY 2 '98			
OC 24 '03			

DEMCO 38-296

PREVENT, REPENT, REFORM, REVENGE

Recent Titles in
Contributions in Psychology

Self-Representation: Life Narrative Studies in Identity and
Ideology
Gary S. Gregg

Hostage: Terror and Triumph
James F. Campbell

From the Other Side of the Couch: Candid Conversations with
Psychiatrists and Psychologists
Chris E. Stout

Counseling in the Asia-Pacific Region
Abdul Halim Othman and Amir Awang, editors

What Wrongdoers Deserve: The Moral Reasoning Behind Responses to
Misconduct
R. Murray Thomas and Ann Diver-Stamnes

Using Bibliotherapy in Clinical Practice: A Guide to Self-Help
Books
John T. Pardeck

Modern Perspectives on John B. Watson and Classical Behaviorism
James T. Todd and Edward K. Morris, editors

Worlds of Common Sense: Equality, Identity, and Two Modes of
Impluse Management
Pauline Nichols Pepinsky

The Five Stages of Culture Shock: Critical Incidents Around the
World
Paul Pedersen

Modern Perspectives on B. F. Skinner and Contemporary Behaviorism
James T. Todd and Edward K. Morris, editors

Chaos Theory in Psychology
Frederick David Abraham and Albert R. Gilgen, editors

Classifying Reactions to Wrongdoing
R. Murray Thomas

PREVENT, REPENT, REFORM, REVENGE

A Study in Adolescent Moral Development

Ann C. Diver-Stamnes
and
R. Murray Thomas

Contributions in Psychology, No. 30
Paul Pedersen, Series Adviser

GREENWOOD PRESS
Westport, Connecticut • London

Library of Congress Cataloging-in-Publication Data

Diver-Stamnes, Ann.
  Prevent, repent, reform, revenge : a study in adolescent moral
development / Ann C. Diver-Stamnes, R. Murray Thomas.
    p. cm.—(Contributions in psychology, ISSN 0736–2714 ; no.
30)
  Includes bibliographical references and index.
  ISBN 0–313–29730–4 (alk. paper)
  1. Judgment (Ethics). 2. Moral development. 3. Reasoning.
4. Punishment. I. Thomas, R. Murray (Robert Murray).
II. Title. III. Series.
BJ1408.5D58 1995
  155.5′1825—dc20   95–16145

British Library Cataloguing in Publication Data is available.

Library of Congress Catalog Card Number: 95–16145
ISBN: 0–313–29730–4
ISSN: 0736–2714

First published in 1995

Greenwood Press, 88 Post Road West, Westport, CT 06881
An imprint of Greenwood Publishing Group, Inc.

Printed in the United States of America

The paper used in this book complies with the
Permanent Paper Standard issued by the National
Information Standards Organization (Z39.48–1984).

10 9 8 7 6 5 4 3 2 1

To

Stephen Paul Stamnes

Contents

Illustrations   xi

Preface   xiii

1 Introduction: The Purpose of the Study   1

   Previewing Key Terms   2
   Previewing Interviews   7
   Conclusion   10

PART I: A Framework for Interpreting Aims   13

2 Two Typologies: (1) Types of Aims and
                 (2) Types of Sanctions   15

   Types of Aims   15
   Types of Sanctions   19
   Conclusion   22

3 Sanction/Aim Relationships   23

   The Nature of Sanction/Aim Structures   23
   A Scheme for Analyzing Causal Relationships   24
   Alternative Patterns of Causal Relations   25
   Conclusion   31

4 Two Aspects of Sanctions and Aims:
                 (1)The Nature of Reality and
                 (2) Moral Value Commitments   33

Conceptions of Reality 33
Moral Value Commitments 36
Conclusion 37

5 Overt Cognitive Sequences and Reasoning Styles 39

Overt Reasoning Styles 42
Conclusion 45

6 Developmental Indicators 47

Stages of Development 47
Differentiation and Interdependence 53
Fanciful Versus Realistic 56
Degree of Rebelliousness 57
Conclusion 58

PART II: Ways of Reasoning About Aims:
          From Child to Adult 59

7 The Nature of the Interviews 61

Interview Goals and Procedures 61
Conclusion 67

8 Proposed Sanctions and Aims 69

Types of Sanctions Recommended 69
Types of Intended Aims 84
Interpretations 92
Conclusion 99

9 Patterns of Causal Relationships:
          Linking Sanctions and Aims 103

Models of Sanction/Aim Connections 103
Interview Results in Terms of the Models 105
Consensus Versus Individuality 108
Conclusion 118

10 Overt Reasoning Styles 121

Pace of Response 121
Reasoning Process 122
Specificity of Recommendations 123
Strength of Ultimate Conviction 123
Interrater Reliability 124
Length of Response 124

Conclusion   129

11 Conceptions of God and the Sanctity of Life   131

Divine Intervention in Human Affairs   132
The Death Penalty—Conditions That Determine Its Proper Use   140
Conclusion   151

12 Views of Imprisonment   153

A Diversity of Opinions   153
Age and Gender Comparisons   164
Conclusion   170

13 Empathy and Sympathy   171

Empathy and Sympathy Defined   172
Comparisons of Empathic Reactions   173
Comparisons of Sympathetic Reactions   177
Conclusion   180

14 Drugs and the Law   183

A Variety of Opinions   184
Attitudes by Age and Gender   189
Adolescent Rebelliousness   192
Conclusion   194

15 Views of Retribution   195

Reasons For and Against Retribution   195
Age and Gender Comparisons   199
Conclusion   201

16 Lessons Learned   203

Hopes   203
Expectations   204
Enlightenment   206
Unfinished Business   208

References   209

Appendix: The Interview Guidesheet   213

Index   219

Illustrations

Figures

9-1. Sanction/Aim Patterns   110

10-1. Estimated Scale Positions of Age Groups on
      Characteristics Contributing to Interview Length   128

Tables

3-1. Sanction/Aim Combinations   26

6-1. Associating Corrective Justice Stages with
      Sanctions and Aims   53

8-1. Sanctions Volunteered in Three Cases of Wrongdoing   70

8-2. Probed Sanctions in Three Cases of Wrongdoing   80

8-3. Agreement on Sanctions within Age Groups   83

8-4. Age Trends in the Choice of Sanctions   84

8-5. Aims Volunteered in Three Cases of Wrongdoing   86

8-6. Probed Aims in Three Cases of Wrongdoing   89

8-7. Agreement on Aims within Age Groups   91

8-8. Age Trends in the Choice of Aims   91

8-9. Students Who Advocated Obeying the Law   93

8-10. Associating Corrective Justice Stages with
      Sanctions and Aims   94

8-11. Differentiation and Expansion   96

8-12. Fanciful Versus Realistic Sanctions ... 98

9-1. Sanction/Aim Patterns in Three Cases of Wrongdoing ... 105

9-2. Separate Sanctions, Separate Aims ... 109

9-3. Sanction/Aim Pairings ... 111

9-4. The Most Popular Sanction/Aim Pairings ... 112

9-5. Age Trends in Sanction/Aim Pairings ... 114

9-6. Agreement on Sanction/Aim Patterns by Age ... 115

9-7. Agreement on Sanction/Aim Patterns by Total Group ... 117

10-1. Interview Time-Length by Age and Case ... 125

10-2. Interview Time-Length by Gender and Case ... 130

11-1. Conceptions of God by Age Level ... 140

11-2. Conceptions of God by Gender ... 141

11-3. Opinions of the Death Penalty by Age Level ... 149

11-4. Opinions of the Death Penalty by Gender ... 151

12-1. Confinement Versus Other Options ... 165

12-2. Who Profits from Imprisonment ... 167

12-3. Perceptions of Imprisonment—Teenagers ... 168

12-4. Perceptions of Imprisonment—Burglar/Killer ... 168

12-5. Suitable Sentence Length ... 169

13-1. Empathic Reactions to Three Cases of Wrongdoing ... 174

13-2. Empathic Reactions Across All Three Cases by Age and Gender ... 176

13-3. Sympathetic Reactions to Three Cases of Wrongdoing ... 178

13-4. Sympathetic Reactions Across All Three Cases by Age and Gender ... 180

14-1. Attitudes Toward the Drug Case by Age ... 190

14-2. Attitudes Toward the Drug Case by Gender ... 191

15-1. Attitudes Toward Revenge by Age ... 200

Preface

The general purpose of the study reported in this book has been to answer the question: "What do people hope to accomplish by the sanctions they would impose on wrongdoers?" A more specific purpose has been to answer this question in relation to people across the age range of 9 to 21, that is, across the stage of life known as adolescence.

The study was conducted in four phases. First, a structured interview was designed for eliciting people's opinions about what consequences should be experienced by the offenders in three cases of wrongdoing. Second, a framework was devised for analyzing those opinions. Third, 136 young people—ages 9, 14, 17, and 21—were interviewed. Fourth, their audiotaped interviews were transcribed and the results interpreted by means of the analytical framework.

As the authors of this work, we are deeply indebted to a variety of people whose assistance made the project possible. First, we are grateful to Humboldt State University for the "Research, Scholarship, and Creative Activity" award, which financed the conduct and transcription of the 136 interviews. Next, we wish to express our appreciation to the graduate students who so ably carried out the interviews and subsequently coded the audiotaped data. The team leaders were Tonya Gray and Karen Wilson. Team members were Scott Carson, Shellye Howard, Linda Lacunza, Michael Van Orden, Carlos Salas, Laura Schlotzhauer, and Barry Tucker.

We particularly wish to thank the 136 interviewees whose enthusiastic participation was essential to the success of the venture.

1

Introduction:
The Purpose of the Study

The investigation reported in this book was designed to answer two questions:

1. What kind of analytical scheme can profitably reveal the nature of people's reasoning about the aims of sanctions they propose for perpetrators of crimes and misdeeds?
2. In the aims that people express, what changes in overt moral-reasoning patterns appear between later childhood and the early adult years?

Our answer to the first question forms the content of Part I: "A Framework for Interpreting Aims." Our answer to the second is found in Part II: "Ways of Reasoning about Aims—from Child to Adult."

For Part I, our quest for a suitable analytical scheme was conducted in two stages. First, we searched through professional and popular writings bearing on the objectives people hoped to achieve by the punishment or treatment they recommended for transgressors. Second, we analyzed the aims that 136 young people, ages 9 through 21, said they would hope to accomplish by sanctions they recommended in three cases of wrongdoing. We combined the results of these two approaches to produce a framework for interpreting aims.

With the analytical scheme in hand, we then sought to answer the question of developmental changes in reasoning patterns by interpreting the interview responses of the 136 youths—more than 30 at each of four age levels (9, 14, 17, 21). Every interview consisted of presenting a respondent with descriptions of three cases of crimes or misdeeds, then asking a series of questions intended to expose that individual's mode of reasoning about the aims of sanctions or treatments for the offenders in each case. Every interview was recorded on audiotape so it could be analyzed in terms of the framework for interpreting aims. That analysis is reported in Part II.

This opening chapter offers two previews of material found in Parts I and II. The first defines a number of key terms that figure prominently in Part I. The second offers a glimpse of one student's interview responses, illustrating the sorts of questions from which the interpretations of Part II have been drawn.

PREVIEWING KEY TERMS

Several words that appear frequently throughout the book have different meanings for different people. To make clear which meanings we attach to those terms, we offer the following definitions and comparisons.

Crimes, Sins, Misdeeds

Crimes, sins, and misdeeds are alike in that all three identify socially unaccept-able acts. However, the three can differ in the contexts of their use or in the degree of harm they imply.

Crimes

For the purpose of this book we have adopted the most common meaning for the term *crime* found in the practice of law, even though we recognize that criminologists do not all agree on what constitutes crime (Matthews & Young, 1992, pp. 11-12). Wrongdoing is labeled a *crime* or *public offense* whenever it involves "an act committed or omitted in violation of a law forbidding or commanding it, and to which is annexed, upon conviction, either of the following punishments: death, imprisonment, fine, removal from office, or disqualification to hold and enjoy any office or honor, trust, or profit within the law's jurisdiction" (Calligan, 1992, p. 3). Stated another way, a crime is any "action or instance of negligence that is deemed injurious to the public welfare or morals, or to the interests of the state and that is legally prohibited" (*Webster's*, 1989, p. 343). Since crimes are violations of obligations due to the community as a whole, they can be punished only by the state rather than by individuals (Carp & Stidham, 1990, p. 135).

Whereas criminal law in the U.S. judicial system concerns offenses against the public (violations of the penal code), civil law pertains primarily to disputes between individuals or organizations. For present purposes, violations of both criminal and civil laws are classified as crimes.

Sins

The term *sin* is not applied in secular settings but, instead, in religious contexts. Sin is a violation of religious or moral principles. "To sin is to do something contrary to the divinely legislated code for proper conduct. . . . [Sin is] an act or state that violates the will of God for communion between himself and man." Sin is thus properly viewed "as the violation of a personal bond with God, [and] not only as a wicked deed" (Pelikan, 1979, p. 3307).

Outside of ecclesiastical applications, the word *sin* is often used informally to describe any act that people find unacceptable: "Polluting the waterways with chemical waste is really a sin" or "Forcing the girl to go without her dinner is a sinful way to treat a child." The 19th-century essayist, John Viscount Morley, linked the secular to the sacred when he declared, "In my creed, waste of public money is like the sin against the Holy Ghost" (Morley, 1948, p. 641).

An act is both a crime and a sin if it violates both secular law and religious dogma. Murder, theft, and bearing false witness at a trial are crimes as well as sins. On the other hand, a motorist's driving a car without an operator's license or a wage earner's intentionally failing to pay income taxes is a crime but not a sin. Worshipping idols, yearning for a neighbor's property, and behaving disrespectfully toward one's parents are sins but not crimes.

Misdeeds

The word *misdeed* is a very general designation that can be applied to any unacceptable act. Therefore, *misdeed* not only can encompass the specialized meanings of *crime* and *sin*, but it can also refer to a wide range of disapproved behaviors that are neither crimes nor sins, such as a pupil consistently failing to do homework, a teenager staying out all night in violation of his parent's orders, and a crowd of hecklers disrupting a politician's public address. In daily conversation there appears to be a tendency for people to use *misdeed* or *misbehavior* when referring to minor infractions in preference to applying the label *crime* or *sin* to fairly inconsequential faults.

Misdeeds can be acts of either commission or omission. Disrupting a politician's speech is an act of commission while failing to file an income tax return is one of omission.

Our purpose in frequently using the term *misdeeds* throughout this book is to accommodate the entire range of disapproved behavior ranging from mortal sins to mere peccadilloes.

Punishment, Reward, Sanction, Treatment

Whereas the terms reviewed in the above section have referred to improper actions, those in the following paragraphs identify general modes of response to such actions.

Punishment and Reward

Punishment has commonly been defined in some such fashion as:

pain, loss, confinement, death, etc., as a penalty for some offense, transgression, or fault (*Webster's*, 1989, p. 1165).

In criminal law: Any pain, penalty, suffering, or confinement inflicted upon a person by the authority of the law and the judgment and sentence of a court, for some crime or offense committed by him, or for his omission of a duty enjoined by law (Black, 1951, p. 1398).

Reward, as the opposite of punishment, has typically been described as:

Something given or received in return or recompense for service, merit, [or] hardship (*Webster's*, 1989, p. 1228).

Although such definitions identify the basic nature of punishment and reward, they fail to recognize an important psychological feature of the two terms—that the proposer of the punishment and the recipient both interpret the action from their own perspectives. When members of a jury recommend a punishment for a felon, they are assuming he will perceive the punishment as painful, or at least as unpleasant. However, this assumption may be faulty, since an event that one person finds painful may be greeted by another with indifference and by a third with delight. In the 17th century, Richard Lovelace in his poem *To Althea from Prison* recognized the importance of an individual's perspective when he wrote:

Stone walls do not a prison make, nor iron bars a cage; . . .
If I have freedom in my love, and in my soul am free,
Angels alone that soar above enjoy such liberty (Morley, 1948, p. 168).

Hence, an intended punishment fails to serve its purpose if the person to whom it is applied does not consider it unpleasant. Likewise, an intended reward is not rewarding unless the recipient deems it so. What a sadist inflicts as pain, a masochist may embrace with pleasure.

Throughout this book we are using the term *punishment* chiefly from the viewpoint of the people who apply sanctions rather than from the perspective of the recipients. The reason we write from the perspective of the punisher is that the opinions we received from the youths we interviewed were collected from the vantage point of people suggesting sanctions and treatments for wrongdoers, not from the position of the people being punished.

Another noteworthy characteristic of punishment and of reward is that the two are not absolute conditions but, instead, are matters of degree. One kind of punishment is intended to be more painful than another and one reward more pleasing than another. On various occasions the penalties for the crime of rape have included death, life imprisonment, 100 lashes with a whip, stoning, and banishment to a remote island. From the viewpoint of either the punisher or the punishee, these acts are not equally offensive. One act will be considered more punitive than another, as determined by the individual value systems of the people involved. John Suckling, another 17th-century poet, acknowledged this relativity of kinds of punishment in his drama *The Tragedy of Brennoralt*:

Death's no punishment: it is the sense,
The pains and fears afore, that makes a death (Morley, 1948, p. 164).

Sanction

The word *sanction* has been used formally in the practice of the law to mean either a penalty for disobedience or a reward for obedience (Flexner, 1987, p. 1698). However, in both the practice of the law and in everyday social relations, people most often use *sanction* to mean only punishment for misdeeds, not rewards for laudatory acts. Freiberg (1987) has reacted to such a narrow use of the word by noting that sanctions provide "a key to understanding the nature and structure of societies and of the power relationships within societies. . . . The debate about sanctions is ultimately a debate about the use of power" (Freiberg, 1987, pp. 223, 225). In our own typology of sanctions and treatments presented in chapter 2 we intend *sanction* to mean either punishment or reward. However, since our study has focused solely on misdeeds and not on good works, the sanctions mentioned throughout the book center chiefly on punishment.

Treatment

A response to wrongdoing that is labeled *treatment* usually means engaging an offender in activities aimed at constructive reform and rehabilitation. "Treatment focuses on the person's mental health, status, or future welfare rather than on the commission of a prohibited act. . . . Punishment imposes unpleasant consequences because of *past offenses,* whereas therapy [or treatment] seeks to improve the offender's *future welfare*" (Feld, 1990, p. 446). Hence, the words *punishment* and *sanction* typically are accompanied by negative connotations, whereas *treatment* tends to convey positive, optimistic affect.

The task of distinguishing between *punishment* and *treatment* in the abstract is relatively simple. However, differentiating between them in daily life is quite another matter, since the two are often intertwined. If treatment is defined as "an action that fosters improved behavior on the part of a wrongdoer," then punishment qualifies as treatment whenever it reduces the incidence of misdeeds in the future. Such a line of reasoning was reflected in 1979 by the State of Washington Supreme Court which ruled that

"sometimes punishment is treatment". . . [thereby upholding the legislature's conclusion that] "punishment commensurate with age, crime, and criminal history does as much to rehabilitate, correct, and direct an errant youth as does the prior philosophy of focusing upon the particular characteristics of the individual juvenile" (in Feld, 1990, p. 448).

Confidence in correctional treatment as a reasonable way to reduce crime has periodically waxed and waned ever since the Progressive Movement in criminal justice first gained serious support nearly 100 years ago. It was around the turn of the century that programs aimed at rehabilitation rather than punishment introduced such judicial practices as probation, parole, indeterminate sentences, and the juvenile court.

All [such programs] emphasized open-ended, individual, and highly flexible policies to rehabilitate the deviant. Because identifying the causes and prescribing the cures for delinquency required an individualized approach which precluded uniformity of treatment or standardization of criteria, a pervasive feature of every Progressive criminal justice reform was discretionary decision-making (Feld, 1987, pp. 474-475).

The most recent wave of reaction against rehabilitation measures occurred during the 1970s, when the ideological dominance of individualized treatment

suffered a swift and devastating collapse. Although the public's belief in rehabilitation was never eroded completely, defenders of treatment were branded scientifically and politically naive apologists for the socially powerful, self-serving human service professions, or curious relics of a positivistic past. Thus, a number of jurisdictions in the United States and Canada embarked on sentencing reforms that undercut the role of rehabilitation in justice and corrections (Andrews, et al., 1990, p. 370).

Social disorder in the 1960s and rising crime rates, coupled with research suggesting that "nothing works," led to disenchantment with correctional treatment. This disillusionment produced legislation requiring determinate sentences based on the nature of the crime rather than on what might be best for the offenders' and society's future as estimated from an analysis of each case individually.

A mild return to confidence in treatment appeared in some quarters during the 1980s, but the debate continued into the 1990s (Lab & Whitehead, 1990; Whitehead & Lab, 1989), with advocates of treatment charging that proponents of punitive justice failed to draw accurate conclusions from research on recidivism. As an example of such charges, a team of researchers (Andrews, et al., 1990) performed a meta-analysis of a wide range of studies describing the effect of treatment programs on the subsequent criminal behavior of program participants. According to the authors, a key error in extracting generalizations from post-treatment criminal behavior has been the tendency to lump all such investigations together without giving sufficient attention to the differences in treatment techniques among programs. When treatment methods are dissected into their constituent elements, the reasons that some programs have reduced recidivism and others have not becomes more apparent. For example, in selecting intermediate targets to be pursued on the way to the ultimate goal of reducing future law breaking, the research team observed that:

The most promising intermediate targets include changing antisocial attitudes, feelings, and peer associations; promoting familial affection in combination with enhanced parental monitoring and supervision; promoting identification with anticriminal role models; increasing self-control and self-management skills; replacing the skills of lying, stealing, and aggression with other, more prosocial skills; reducing chemical dependencies; and generally shifting the density of rewards and costs for criminal and non-criminal activities in familial, academic, vocational, and other behavioral settings. . . .

Less-promising targets include increasing self-esteem without touching antisocial propensity, increasing the cohesiveness of antisocial peer groups, improving neighborhood-wide living conditions without reaching high-risk families, and attempts to focus on vague personal/emotional problems that have not been linked with recidivism (Andrews et al., 1990, p. 375).

Researchers who still question the efficacy of treatment have countered that "our review of a particular set of studies showed that the majority were not effective, but some interventions were effective" (Lab & Whitehead, 1990, p. 414). Thus, the dispute continues over whether it is worthwhile for society to try rehabilitating offenders. And if indeed worthwhile, under what conditions will particular treatment techniques succeed with which kinds of offenders?

It is apparent that the above remarks, focusing solely on formal judicial and correctional practices, relate to no more than a small segment of the treatments for reforming wrongdoers. Far more frequent are the measures that parents, teachers, religious leaders, counselors, friends, and coworkers apply to modify people's unacceptable behavior in daily life. To a great extent, the wide array of any culture's socialization practices are aimed at dissuading the young from misconduct. Thus, the effectiveness of child-rearing practices might be judged in terms of how well the treatments applied to children equip them to satisfy their own needs and at the same time meet their responsibilities toward their society.

Because actions intended to serve as sanctions and treatments can be so intertwined, throughout this book we employ the term *sanction* in an overarching, inclusive manner to encompass treatment as well as punishment and reward. In other words, *treatment* is subsumed under *sanction*.

In the foregoing pages we have discussed a series of key terms that are used throughout this volume. As a further introduction to the book's intent, we next offer a brief sample of one of the interviews on which the contents of Part II have been built.

PREVIEWING INTERVIEWS

As already noted, data for Part II of this volume derived from individual interviews with 136 students regarding three cases of wrongdoing. The cases were those of (1) a nine-year-old girl caught cheating on a test in school, (2) a 16-year-old boy and his 16-year-old girl companion who traded illicit drugs for tickets to a rock concert, and (3) a 23-year-old burglar who killed the woman resident of a house he was robbing. In each interview, the case description was followed by a series of questions designed to elicit the respondent's opinions about four aspects of the incident: (a) the type of misdeed that had been committed, (b) the consequences the wrongdoer should face, (c) the aim that such consequences would be intended to accomplish, and (d) a comparison of these consequences with ones suggested by other respondents.

As a preview of the data base for Part II, the following dialogue between an interviewer and a 14-year-old high-school boy illustrates the sequence of stages in a typical interview. In this example, the boy is considering the last of the three cases.

Interviewer: Here's the case: "In a jury trial, a 23-year-old man was convicted of killing a woman who caught him trying to rob her house in the middle of the night. A police officer who was a witness at the trial of the 23-year-old man reported that the man had also been stealing from other homes over the past several months." —So that's what happened. Do you think the man did anything wrong?

Respondent: Yeah, he stole and he killed.

Interviewer: What do you think should be done about him?

Respondent: I think stealing should be a crime not punished by prison as it is now, but he should give back what he took, or something equal. Like if someone stole a car, and the people didn't get it back for two months, then the thief would have to pay all expenses—like bus transportation—that the people incurred over that period of time. That sort of equals what he took.

As far as killing goes, I think life in prison would be best. I don't believe in the death penalty. Really, the only thing prison should be used for is something serious, like when you kill a person.

Interviewer: How do you think compensating victims for robbery and sentencing killers to life in prison would help? What would be the aim?

Respondent: For compensation? Well, it's like if they steal a whole bunch of money and hide it and they just go to prison, then get out five years later, and they still have the money they stole. So you shouldn't be able to have what you took. Compensating is better than prison.

As for killing, I think life in prison would teach the person not to do it again. Maybe he'll get some time off for good behavior, but I don't think the time in prison should be less than 15 or 20 years. I think life in prison is good punishment for killing, since he took somebody's life.

Interviewer: Okay. Now, some other people we've interviewed had different ideas about the consequences for the robber. I'll read them, and you can decide whether these are as good as yours. Just say whether or not you would agree with these. Here's the first one: "He should be put to death."

I realize you've kind of commented on that already, but would you want to comment a little more?

Respondent: Well, it's really much more expensive to put someone to death than to keep them their whole life in prison, because of all the appeals. I know some people would like to be put to death instead of go to prison because they'd have such a bad life in prison. Life imprisonment is really like taking someone's life away. Besides, I don't believe in capital punishment.

Interviewer: The next suggestion by others is: "We don't have to decide what to do, since God will take care of it."

Respondent: Well, that's sort of a hard one. (*long pause*) I believe in a sort of creator, I don't believe that—if there is a God—that God takes that active a role. It seems that the world isn't perfect, and it never has been. If God fixed things, then everything would be better than it is now. So if we just left it all up to an idea—the idea of God—the world would be much worse. We have to decide for ourselves what to do.

Interviewer: All right. Now, some of the other people we interviewed gave us different kinds of reasons for the consequences they suggested. I'd like to read these to you, and you can decide whether you agree that these aims are as good as the ones you gave—that is, as good as compensating for the robbery and spending time in prison for the killing to teach him a lesson.

The first aim is: "To fix it so the burglar can't rob or kill again."

Respondent: Well, he can always do it again. There's really no way to stop him entirely. (*long pause*) Of course, part of the imprisonment is so he can't kill again. And the robbery—well, unless you put someone in prison for life, and I don't think that's fair—you can't stop him from robbing again when he gets out. Now, I should add something to that—an education process to help stop more robbing.

Interviewer: Okay. The next aim is: "To make him a better person; to reform him."

Respondent: Yeah. I guess that's part of what I just added on.

Interviewer: So the education would be a process of reform?

Respondent: Yeah.

Interviewer: The next one is: "To give the family of the dead woman the satisfaction of having her killer punished."

Respondent: Yeah, I think they would get satisfaction out of his being sentenced to life in prison. I know it would give me personally satisfaction. Some people would probably rather see him dead, but I personally think that life in prison is a worse punishment.

Interviewer: The last aim is: "To make the man do something helpful for the community."

Respondent: Well, I suppose that in certain prisons you work on the roads or you do work in parks and do other stuff that's good. It's all right, as long as there's no contact with the public.

Interviewer: And that's about it. That's the interview. Thanks for your ideas.

Although the detailed analysis of interviews is postponed until Part II, it may be useful at this juncture to note three typical features of interviews that appeared in the dialogue with this 14-year-old high-school student.

First, initially asking people what consequences they would recommend for wrongdoers does not elicit their entire conception of suitable sanctions and treatments. The same is true of asking about the aims they would seek to achieve by their consequences. The fact that the complex configuration of their thoughts about such matters is not revealed in the interviewer's initial open-ended questions about consequences and aims becomes apparent when other alternative consequences and aims are posed for the respondent to consider. For instance, in the foregoing dialogue, the notion of providing learning experiences for the robber was not offered by the respondent until near the end of the interview. Furthermore, the respondent's agreeing with the aims of *providing satisfaction for the victim's family* and of *contributing to the welfare of the community* did not appear in his initial response. We thus might expect that if an even greater variety of possible consequences and aims had been suggested by the interviewer, we would have discovered far more facets of this high-school boy's moral convictions. In summary, the interviews that we conducted with the 136 students revealed only portions of the students' modes of reasoning about sanctions and their aims.

Second, respondents may avoid addressing issues of feasibility in their proposals. For instance, our high-school boy apparently failed to recognize the difficulties of suitably compensating victims for the offenses they suffered. When thieves, before they are caught, have already spent the money they stole, there is a problem of determining how they are going to repay the loss. There is also the question of compensating victims for the anguish or bodily injury they have suffered.

Third, although virtually all respondents are able to suggest sanctions and aims for wrongdoers, and they can offer reasons to support their choices, it cannot be assumed that they come to the task with reasoned, well-balanced answers. Rather, it is apparent that the interview about the case is a learning experience, one in which the respondent engages in a decision-making process, weighing complicated conditions against each other in order to arrive at a reasonable answer. The way the interview is conducted will influence which conditions the respondent includes in producing a judgment of the case. In the foregoing example, the additional sanction and aim options that the interviewer posed served as further conditions which the respondent apparently had not included earlier in arriving at his judgment. Inserting these further variables into the decision-making process likely contributed to some of the inconsistency and revision of opinion that appeared during the dialogue.

CONCLUSION

The purpose of the study reported in this book has been to learn about the overt reasoning of young people between later childhood and the early adult years as they propose consequences for wrongdoers and explain the aims they hope such consequences will achieve. Our investigation was conducted in two stages.

The first stage involved creating a framework within which people's reasoning processes might be interpreted. The framework consisted of (1) a typology of sanctions and treatments for wrongdoers, (2) a typology of aims that such sanctions and treatments are intended to achieve, (3) patterns that respondents' answers to interviews could assume, (4) ways that respondents' answers might reveal their conceptions of reality and their moral values, and (5) several indicators of intellectual development that might be exhibited in the answers participants offered to questions about wrongdoing. The framework is described in Part I.

The second stage involved conducting interviews with more than 30 subjects at each of four age levels—9, 14, 17, and 21. The interviews focused on three cases of misbehavior—a nine-year-old girl who cheated on a mathematics test, two 16 year olds who traded illicit drugs for rock-concert tickets, and a 23-year-old man who killed the woman whose house he was robbing. Part II of the book contains the analysis of the interviews in terms of the framework introduced in Part I.

Part I

A Framework for Interpreting Aims

Our intention in Part I is to describe a multifaceted scheme to use in analyzing the aims that people hope will be served by the sanctions they suggest for perpetrators of misdeeds. This framework is composed of eight major components that offer diverse perspectives from which to view respondents' opinions about cases of misconduct. The description of the framework is distributed over the five chapters that form Part I.

Chapter 2 contains the first two components, each cast in the form of a typology. One typology lists varieties of sanctions. The other lists varieties of aims that sanctions are intended to serve.

A third component, described in Chapter 3, connects the two typologies by identifying relationships that people believe exist between sanctions and their aims. In other words, the chapter addresses the question: Which sanctions and treatments do people believe will achieve which aims?

The fourth and fifth aspects of the framework, found in Chapter 4, concern (1) the way people's conceptions of reality—their view of what the *real world is like*—affect the sanctions and treatments they propose and (2) how their responses to wrongdoing are influenced by their moral values.

Chapter 5 introduces the sixth and seventh components: (1) the sequence in which interviewees describe sanctions and aims when they are questioned about a case of wrongdoing and (2) their overt cognitive styles as seen in terms of the pace of their response, their manner of reasoning, the specificity of their recommendations, how satisfied they appear to be with their final decision about an instance of wrongdoing, and the length of their answers.

The last element of the framework, presented in Chapter 6, "Developmental Indicators," outlines a method of interpreting respondents' opinions about sanctions and aims from the standpoint of several facets of human growth that often have been suggested as useful clues to cognitive development during childhood and adolescence.

The components described in Part I guide the analysis of interviews in Part II.

2

Two Typologies: (1) Types of Aims and (2) Types of Sanctions

Ways that people respond to transgressors and the aims of such responses can be displayed as categories of types. In effect, it is possible to present sanctions (including treatments) and their aims in the form of two typologies useful in comparing the opinions of people who propose consequences for wrongdoers. The typologies provide an analytical framework to apply in the present study for answering the question: How did our 136 interviewees compare with each other in the types of sanctions and aims they recommended in the three cases of wrongdoing that were the focus of the interviews?

Chapter 2 is divided into two sections. The first offers a typology of the aims that sanctions are intended to achieve. The second offers a typology of the sanctions themselves. Neither typology is proposed as being definitive, in the sense of displaying all possible reactions to misdeeds and all possible aims. Rather, the types in each list are limited to ones appearing in the opinions that students offered when reacting to the three cases of wrongdoing used during our interviews. For example, the punishment labeled *put to death* is included in the sanction list because some respondents recommended execution as a penalty for the burglar who killed the householder. However, no sanction labeled *excommunication by religious authorities* appears in the typology because such a response to transgression did not appear in any of the students' answers. (The more comprehensive taxonomies of aims and sanctions from which the material of this chapter was extracted is found in Thomas, 1995.)

TYPES OF AIMS

The following typology of aims has been built from purposes reflected in people's answers to such questions as "What good do you think that sanction would do?" or "How would such a treatment help?" or "What would be your intention in suggesting such a consequence?"

The typology contains 24 aims subsumed under six general categories. The first category, labeled A-1, is a catch-all division intended to reflect widespread societal goals that sanctions are intended to foster. The remaining five categories focus on (A-2) preventing offenders from committing further transgressions, (A-3) improving offenders' life conditions, (A-4) fostering the welfare of the people who propose the consequences, (A-5) promoting the welfare of the victims of misconduct, and (A-6) affecting the lives of people other than the offenders and their victims. Neither the categories nor the aims within them are mutually exclusive. Aims often overlap and are frequently interlinked.

The letter *A* preceding each aim indicates that the item is from the aims typology as distinguished from items in the sanctions typology which are preceded by the letter *S*.

A-1. Fostering Societal Goals

Often reactions to wrongdoing are directed toward promoting general principles deemed desirable for the proper conduct of society. For present purposes, the following aims are of this general nature. They focus on sanctions that are expected to:

A-1.1. Protect society from disruptions.

A-1.2. Maintain tradition—applying a familiar, traditional sanction.

A-1.3. Achieve social retribution—avenging violations of society's rules.

A-1.4. Enforce the law—preventing people from violating the law with impunity.

A-1.5. Match the offense—applying the principle of *lex talionis* by requiring offenders to experience the same offense they committed.

A-2. Preventing Offenders from Committing Further Transgressions

The purpose of prevention may be specific or general. It is specific whenever the intent is to preclude the individual from perpetrating the same unacceptable act in the future. It is general whenever the aim is to reduce the likelihood that the offender will commit any misdeeds in the years ahead.

A-2.1. Incapacitate—removing an offender's opportunity for further trans-gression, usually through executing or incarcerating the wrongdoer.

A-2.2. Disable an instrument used in the offense—removing the means of committing a similar misdeed.

A-2.3. Deter the offender (special deterrence)—discouraging offenders from committing future transgressions.

(Note: Items A-2.4 through A-2.8 are viewed as interrelated instrumental aims which, it is hoped, will contribute toward achieving aim A-2.9—Reform the wrongdoer.)

A-2.4. Diagnose causes—attempting to learn why the offender committed the misdeed.

A-2.5. Generate affect—stimulating an emotional reaction in the offender, such as guilt or shame for committing misdeeds or pride and self-satisfaction for refraining from misbehavior. The emotion is intended to contribute toward the offender's repentance and reform.

A-2.6. Focus attention—encouraging wrongdoers to think about their misbehavior and its consequences. The usual assumption behind this aim is that by inspecting the outcome of their misdeeds they may decide to act differently in the future.

A-2.7. Teach right from wrong.

A-2.7.1. Inform offenders that what they did was wrong, and tell them what proper behavior would be in that situation.

A-2.7.2. Explain to offenders why their behavior was wrong.

A-2.8. Teach accountability—convincing transgressors that they will be held responsible for their actions.

A-2.9. Alter values—convincing offenders to adopt a more constructive set of moral values than those that have led to the present instance of wrongdoing.

A-2.10. Foster alternative behaviors—obliging offenders to adopt morally acceptable ways of fulfilling their needs and desires.

A-2.11. Reform the wrongdoer—changing the offender's stated values and moral behavior. Three levels of reform are identified: (1) avoiding a specific type of misconduct, (2) avoiding many types of misconduct, and (3) not only avoiding misbehavior but actively engaging in constructive moral acts.

A-2.11.1. Specific reformation—the offender improves future behavior in regard to the particular transgression that led to the sanction.

A-2.11.2. General reformation—not only does the offender no longer commit the misdeed that led to the present sanction, but the individual will no longer commit other kinds of misdeeds perpetrated in the past.

A-2.11.3. Character reformation—the treatment brings about a basic change in personality that inspires the offender to become a constructive, responsible member of society.

A-3. Improving the Offender's Life Conditions

Whereas the primary focus of aims under A-2 (Preventing Offenders from Committing Further Transgressions) has been to protect society from wrongdoing, the emphasis of items under A-3 is on improving offenders' lives in ways that enable them to satisfy their needs and desires in a morally acceptable fashion. Hence, the aims in the following list are seen as possibly contributing toward transgressors' reformation.

A-3.1. Reduce the severity of punishment—in a spirit of compassion, lighten the usual penalty in the hope of engendering the goodwill and cooperation of the wrongdoer.

A-3.2. Accommodate for physical and psychological disabilities—adjusting sanctions to recognize physical or mental handicaps that offenders display.

A-3.3. Enhance knowledge, skills, and habits—offering educational opportunities that prepare offenders for a socially constructive and personally satisfying future.

A-3.3.1. General education—upgrading offenders' communication skills (reading, writing, speaking) and general knowledge.

A-3.3.2. Job training—teaching offenders skills needed in specific occupations or in daily activities.

A-3.3.3. Foster self-confidence—helping offenders develop a more positive self-concept

A-3.3.4. Social skills and work habits—improving wrongdoers' techniques of social intercourse and their work attitudes and habits.

A-3.4. Improve social and vocational adjustment—monitoring and guiding offenders' adjustment in social and occupational settings.

A-3.5. Demonstrate concern—showing offenders that someone cares about their welfare and wishes to help them with their problems.

A-3.6. Assist with problem solving—aiding offenders in conquering problems they face.

A-3.7. Obtain help—finding resources to aid offenders in surmounting their difficulties.

A-4. Fostering the Sanction-Proposer's Welfare

The motives behind recommended sanctions frequently reflect the sanction-proposer's self-interest. People who suggest consequences are frequently motivated by a desire to protect society and themselves from harm at the hands of wrongdoers. However, sanction-proposers may also have additional aims that go beyond such protection. The following is of this nature.

A-4.1. Obligate the offender—obliging offenders to respond to the proposer with gratitude and/or respect.

A-5. Advancing the Welfare of the Victims of Misdeeds

Victims are conceived to be of three types—people directly hurt by a misdeed, people harmed indirectly (friends, family members, or colleagues of a direct victim), and society in general.

A-5.1. Compensate victims—making amends for damage done.

A-5.1.1. Specific compensation—recompensing victims for their losses and for physical or mental damage they have suffered.

A-5.1.2. General compensation—indemnifying the community or the society rather than an individual.

A-5.2. Protect potential victims—reducing the chance that the transgressor

will harm or exploit people who might become victims of his or
her misconduct.
A-5.3. Avenge the wrong—achieving retribution by retaliating against the
sources of the misdeed. Vengeance contributes to the victims'
welfare by providing personal satisfaction that the offender has not
escaped unpunished.

A-6. Affecting the Lives of Other People
The term *other people* refers to individuals and groups not directly involved
with an instance of wrongdoing, either as offenders or as recipients of the
misdeed.
A-6.1. Dissuade potential offenders (general deterrence)—warning possible
wrongdoers, other than the offender in the case at hand, that they,
too, will suffer similar penalties if they commit similar offenses.

TYPES OF SANCTIONS

The following typology consists of 17 categories that contain types of
sanctions (including treatments). As the items in the list suggest, the types are
not independent of each other. Instead, they often overlap or form combinations.
For instance, a burglar sentenced to life in prison may not only be incarcerated
but may also, while in prison, engage in constructive work and pursue an
educational program. A high-school student who has sold illicit drugs may be
suspended from school, required to undergo a drug rehabilitation program, and
obliged to contribute 40 hours of community service.

Sanctions are usually directed at the person who has committed the misdeed.
However, in some instances sanctions are applied to other people or agencies
that are thought to have been instrumental in causing an offender to do wrong.
For example, parents may be required to pay for the damage caused by their
teenage offspring's vandalism. The types of sanctions listed below can be
applied either to a transgressor or to others who are considered at least partially
responsible for the transgressor's misconduct.

S-1. Inflicting Bodily Harm
S-1.1. Put to death—intentionally killing someone as a means of administering justice.
S-1.2. Corporal punishment—intentionally causing any degree of physical
pain, discomfort, and/or injury that does not directly result in death.

S-2. Imprisoning and Detaining—requiring an offender to remain in a place of
confinement; this can include structured group care.

S-3. Discharging & Expelling—removing an offender from a place or from a
position of opportunity.
S-3.1. Dismissal—ousting an offender from a position of employment, from

an office of responsibility, or from membership in a group.

S-3.2. Banishment—expelling an individual or group from a particular location for a period of time.

S-3.3. Ostracism—withholding privileges of social contact. (Note: for *ostracism* in the sense of *banishment*, use category S-3.2.)

S-3.4. Suspension—temporarily removing an offender from position of employment, from a post of responsibility, or from membership in a group.

S-3.5. Transfer—moving an offender from one location or position to another. The individual is neither discharged nor suspended and thereby retains the original position and title. The transfer may either include the offender retaining the rights and responsibilities held prior to the transfer or may involve some change of rights and responsibilities.

S-4. Restricting and Altering Rights, Privileges, or Opportunities

S.4.1. Movement limitations—restricting an offender to a given location or declaring particular sites off-limits.

S-4.2. Social contact limitations—proscribing certain social relationships

S-4.3. Activity limitations—proscribing specified activities.

S-4.4. Demotion—reducing offender's official status.

S-5. Censuring and Exposing

S-5.1. Private censure—admonishing the wrongdoer in private (orally reproving the offender face-to-face or over the phone with no witness present, sending the offender a written note of censure, etc.).

S-5.2. Public exposure—publicizing the wrongdoer's misdeed.

S-6. Assigning Labor—requiring the offender to engage in designated work.

S-7. Confiscating Possessions—seizing certain of the transgressor's belongings.

S-8. Imposing adverse appraisals—issuing demerits, verbal criticism, written censure, reduction of mark or grade.

S-9. Monitoring—keeping track of the transgressor's behavior in the community.

S-10. Threatening/Warning—informing offenders of unpleasant consequences they can expect if they commit unacceptable acts in the future.

S-11. Requiring Compensation—offenders endeavor to repay victims in some measure for the damage caused by the misdeed in the form of:

S-11.1. Goods or services.

S-11.2. Apology.

S-12. Proposing Rewards—describing to offenders the desirable consequences they can expect if they refrain from future misdeeds.

(Note: The next two types, counseling and educating, are not distinctly different from each other, in that both represent positive attempts to improve the values, knowledge, and skills of offenders in ways that equip them to satisfy their needs in a socially acceptable fashion. However, it is possible to distinguish counseling from educating in terms of their focus and procedures. Counseling, more often than education, focuses on offenders' immediate problems of personal-social adjustment. Counseling is also more often individualized, whether conducted in one-to-one sessions or in small groups of offenders who experience similar personal-social difficulties. Educating, on the other hand, more often focuses on instruction in knowledge and skills that enhance offenders' ability to communicate efficiently, to understand their world, and to perform well in occupational and avocational pursuits. The following two principal types—S-12 and S-13—are based on such distinctions between counseling and educating.)

S-13. Personal Counseling—conferring with wrongdoers during either group or individual sessions in order to discuss factors associated with their transgressions and to guide them toward more satisfactory personal-social adjustment.

S-14. Educating—providing offenders with organized learning opportunities other than personal counseling.
 S-14.1. Repeating the activity in which the offense occurred so as to discover if the offender can perform without committing a misdeed (retaking a test, doing a job over again, replaying a game, etc.).
 S-14.2. Engaging in a new learning activity.

S-15. Postponing Sanctions—waiting before applying a sanction.
 S-15.1. Investigating offender's background as a basis for stipulating a sanction.
 S-15-2. Delaying the application of a specified sanction.

S-16. Maintaining a Record—keeping a report of the offense for future reference.

S-17. Forgiving—excusing a wrongdoer from paying a penalty.
 S-17.1. Second Chance/Probation—assessing no penalty for the first offense, but administering sanctions for subsequent offenses. Probation is an instance of second-chance policy.

S-18. Delegating Sanction Responsibility—transferring to some other person, group, agency, or supernatural power the tasks of proposing and implementing sanctions.

S-19. Declining to Suggest Sanctions—refusing to recommend consequences
that wrongdoers should experience for their misdeeds on the grounds that:
  S-19.1. The act of which the individual was accused was not an instance of
    wrongdoing (no misdeed had been committed) or
  S-19.2. The authority for assigning sanctions lies elsewhere (courts, athletic
    control board, school principal, parent, God, etc.) or
  S-19.3. There is insufficient evidence on which to base a just decision (needed
    witnesses not available, conflicts in evidence lead to impasse,
    veracity of witnesses questionable, etc.).

CONCLUSION

The pair of typologies outlined in this chapter were generated primarily from
an inspection of the sanctions and treatments suggested during interviews with
136 respondents as they recommended consequences to be experienced by the
principal characters in three cases of wrongdoing. Hence, these are limited
typologies, since they do not include additional types of sanctions and aims that
might be proposed by other respondents for other kinds of transgressions.

Chapters 8 and 9 in Part II describe the way the typologies served in the
analysis of the 136 interviewees' opinions.

3

Sanction/Aim Relationships

Conceptions of sanction/aim relationships are beliefs that people hold about how sanctions can achieve particular aims. The types of beliefs presented in this chapter are those we thought might change between later childhood and the early adult years. The chapter offers a scheme for the analysis of such convictions. The presentation opens with the basic assumption about mental structures on which the chapter's argument is founded. The presentation then continues with (a) a framework for the analysis of causal relationships and (b) alternative patterns of such relationships.

THE NATURE OF SANCTION/AIM STRUCTURES

A necessary assumption underlying the following discussion is this: In people's encounters with the environment, events are not simply recorded objectively in their minds. Rather, the events are interpreted by means of individuals' mental structures that serve as templates or molds which cast stimuli into particular forms that determine the meanings assigned to events. Thus, when two individuals witness a street fight from the same vantage point, the interpretation of the incident will differ somewhat from one witness to the other because their mental structures—their cognitive templates or lenses—are not identical. Such mental structures have been assigned various labels by different theorists. Piaget (Piaget & Inhelder, 1969) called them *schema* or *schemes*. He used the term *assimilation* to identify the process of fitting new stimuli into established schema. Structures as a collectivity were dubbed *the apperceptive mass* by the 19th-century German philosopher Johann Herbart. That mass is composed of a person's entire set of expectations which filter stimuli from the environment and impose meaning on them.

Structures can be divided into different types, such as concepts, processes, values, and more. The type that is of interest in this chapter can be labeled *presumed causal relationships*. A causal relationship is an *if-then* belief that a person holds. In our present context, such a relationship assumes the form of: "If you wish to achieve aim *A*, then impose sanction *Z*." Or, cast another way: "Imposing sanction *Z* will result in (will cause) outcome *A*."

Our contention is that the particular array of presumed causal relationships to which a person is committed serves as the foundation on which that individual bases proposals of sanctions. In the following pages we describe several patterns that such relationships may assume. Those are the patterns to be applied in Chapter 9 for interpreting interview results.

A SCHEME FOR ANALYZING CAUSAL RELATIONSHIPS

Three concepts employed in the following description are *ultimate aims*, *instrumental aims*, and *concomitant effects*.

An ultimate aim is the final or highest-level outcome that someone hopes will result from sanctions. An instrumental aim is an intermediate goal that contributes toward the realization of an ultimate aim. In others words, instrumental aims are steps along the path toward an ultimate outcome. In each of the following examples, the ultimate aim is underlined, while the instrumental aims are printed in italics. The second and third of the examples include instrumental aims, whereas the first contains only an ultimate aim.

> "Putting him in prison at hard labor for life will make him <u>suffer</u>, which is what he deserves for beating the woman to death."
>
> "He needs to go to traffic school so he *learns to drive properly*, and then he won't be a threat to the <u>safety of others</u>."
>
> "Preventing her from hanging around with gang members, and then offering her proper counseling, could make her *change her values* so that she *won't choose the wrong kinds of models* to follow. That could help her *obey the law* so she'll become a <u>constructive member of society</u>."

For convenience of discussion, the outcomes of sanctions can be placed in two main categories, *aims* and *concomitant effects*. Aims are the goals that proposers of sanctions hope to achieve. Concomitant effects are all of the remaining outcomes that result from a sanction.

Concomitant effects can be divided into three types representing their different levels of desirability in the opinion of the person recommending the sanctions: (1) beneficial effects, (2) acceptable effects, and (3) harmful effects. A beneficial effect is one that the proposer is happy about. An acceptable effect is one that the proposer views with indifference—whether the effect occurs or not is immaterial. A damaging effect is one the proposer would like to avoid.

From a different perspective, concomitant effects can be viewed as either inherent or possible. An inherent effect inevitably accompanies a given sanction. Putting felons in prison inevitably restricts their movement and their opportunities for committing crimes in the general community. Furthermore, inherent effects are outcomes that necessarily occur to every person subject to a particular sanction. For instance, every imprisoned felon loses freedom of movement. Possible effects, on the other hand, can occur for some offenders but not for others, depending on the circumstances of the case in question. One drunk driver, as a result of being jailed, may deeply resent the officer who arrested him and may thus seek to retaliate for the arrest. In contrast, a second drunk driver may consider the jail sentence to be justified and may be angry at himself rather than at the officer who apprehended him. As a further example, serious physical injury may or may not result from a teacher slapping a fractious pupil. Thus, injury as an outcome is a possible but not an inevitable accompaniment of corporal punishment.

The above view of causal relationships can now serve as the basis for estimating the process people go through when suggesting sanctions. We presume that in proposing a sanction or treatment, a person (1) has in mind an ultimate aim, (2) may also have in mind instrumental aims leading to the intended ultimate outcome, (3) may or may not consider concomitant effects, (4) may recognize that some concomitant effects are inherent while others are possible, and (5) may estimate how likely—in the particular case at hand—the possible effects will occur. Thus, this sanction-choosing process assumes the form of an algebraic computation in which estimated weightings of positive, neutral, and negative effects combine to yield a judgment of the likelihood a given sanction will produce the desired aim. In other words, the computation suggests the level of probability that the sanction will work as intended This line of logic then leads to a rather obvious principle: The more accurately a person's causal-relationship structures reflect the conditions of the real world in terms of the five steps of the sanction choosing process outlined above, the more likely the aim will be achieved.

From the foregoing argument, we can now generate a scheme for judging the adequacy of people's causal-relationship structures.

ALTERNATIVE PATTERNS OF CAUSAL RELATIONS

Three convenient ways of classifying causal relationships are in terms of (1) which sanctions are presumed to achieve which aims, (2) levels of confidence about how likely those sanctions will produce the desired outcomes, and (3) the complexity of sanction/aim connections.

Which Sanctions Achieve Which Aims

Because the variety of sanction/aim—or cause/effect—relationships that people can hold is seemingly unlimited, it is impracticable here to attempt cataloging all of them. Thus, the examples in Table 3–1, representing eight different people's responses, are not intended to be a definitive list of sanction/aim linkages in people's minds. Rather, the examples are offered only to illustrate ways that:

(a) Sanctions and aims associated in people's minds with a particular misdeed can differ from one person to another (examples 1-2, 3-4, 7-8).

(b) Two people can propose different sanctions in their attempt to achieve the same aim for the same misdeed (examples 5-6).

Table 3-1
Sanction/Aim Combinations

The Misdeed	Sanction (presumed cause)	Aim (intended effect)
1. A 19-year-old youth stabbed two robbery victims to death.	Execute the youth.	Protect society from further misdeeds by that individual.
2. A 19-year-old youth stabbed two robbery victims to death.	Psychiatric treatment for the youth.	Reform the offender so he will lead a constructive life.
3. A 6-year-old boy lied about taking money from his mother's purse.	Give the child a good spanking.	Teach the child that lying can result in pain and humiliation.
4. A 6-year-old boy lied about taking money from his mother's purse.	Explain to the child that lying destroys people's trust, causing them to dislike him and to avoid his company.	Reduce the incidence of lying in the future.
5. A 48-year-old man falsified data on his income tax return.	Require the man to pay a large fine.	Discourage the offender from repeating the misdeed.
6. A 48-year-old man falsified data on his income tax return.	Put the man on probation. and audit his returns over the next five years.	Discourage the offender from repeating the misdeed.
7. A 26-year-old mother was accused of child abuse after her 8-year-old daughter came to school bearing welts received when her mother beat her.	Remove the child from the mother's custody by transferring her to a foster home.	Protect the girl from further battering.
8. A 26-year-old mother was accused of child abuse after her 8-year-old daughter came to school bearing welts received when her mother beat her.	Require the mother to enroll in a course in child rearing and also to engage in counseling sessions.	Teach the mother suitable child-rearing practices.

(c) In some people's minds, the causal relationship associates punishment with the aim, whereas in others' minds the sanction is a positive treatment rather than a punishment connected with the aim (examples 1-2, 7-8).

(d) The aims people hope to achieve in response to the same misdeed can vary in their focus (society, the offender, the victim) (examples 1-2, 7-8).

Levels of Confidence

Comments people offer about their sanction recommendation often reveal that they do not invest every causal relationship with the same degree of confidence.

"Sending the girl to juvenile hall might cure her from using marijuana, but I wouldn't bet on it."

"I think a couple of months in jail rather than paying a fine would more likely keep him from driving recklessly again."

"Putting the kid in a good boarding school—I mean one where they have a strong academic program and proper counselors—stands a good chance of straightening him out. He needs understanding and constructive models among his companions."

In brief, we propose that each causal relationship which an individual harbors is accompanied by an estimate, however imprecise, of the probability that the sanction or treatment will produce the intended result.

Degrees of Complexity of Causal Connections

It is perhaps apparent that at least some of the eight examples we offered above to illustrate sanction/aim connections were oversimplified. That is, in each example the person proposed no more than one sanction to achieve no more than one aim. Under real life circumstances this is often not the case. People frequently view sanction/aim relationships as being far more complex. To illustrate this in some detail, the following paragraphs describe a diversity of cause/effect combinations in terms of their complexity. The types are presented under five categories: (1) singular connections, (2) chains, (3) aim fans, (4) sanction fans, and (5) networks. Each type is accompanied by an example of a rationale a person might offer to qualify his or her causal relationship.

In the illustrative quotations below, SANCTIONS ARE SHOWN IN CAPITAL LETTERS, ultimate aims are underlined, and *instrumental aims are in italics*. The diagrams that accompany the quotations are graphic representations of the several types of relationship.

Singular Connections. A singular connection consists of a single sanction (S) that is intended to produce a single ultimate aim (UA). Each of the eight examples in the above list was of this type. The following quotation illustrates a mother's statement that identifies her presumed causal relationship as involving a singular connection.

"We can TAKE HIS TRICYCLE AWAY FOR A MONTH so he'll <u>learn not to ride it in the street</u>."

$$S \longrightarrow UA$$

Chains. A chain consists of a single sanction that contributes to a single sequence of interlinked instrumental aims (IA) that lead to an ultimate aim. The first example contains one instrumental aim.

"PUT THE FRATERNITY ON PROBATION so as to *prevent them from initiating any pledges for a year.* That should be enough to <u>put a stop to their hazing tactics</u>."

$$S \longrightarrow IA \longrightarrow UA$$

The second illustration depicts a sequence of five instrumental aims that are expected to result in the desired ultimate outcome.

"MAKE A VIDEOTAPE OF HIM WHEN HE'S DRUNK AT A PARTY, THEN SHOW IT TO HIM WHEN HE'S SOBER. That should give him a *good scare* and *embarrass him* enough so he'll *admit he has a drinking problem* Then maybe he'll be willing to *get professional help.* If that all works out, he'll be able to *give up alcohol* and <u>lead a respectable life</u>."

$$S \longrightarrow IA \longrightarrow IA \longrightarrow IA \longrightarrow IA \longrightarrow IA \longrightarrow UA$$

Some students who participated in our study explicitly identified the type of chaining they expected would result from their proposed sanctions. One 14 year old, discussing the case of the 9-year-old girl who had cheated on a mathematics test, explained:

"She should be given an F. That way, she'll think ahead and decide, 'If I copy again, then I'll get an F that'll go on my report card, and then my parents are going to be mad and they'll ground me.' It'll be just like a chain reaction."

Aim Fans. The analogy of a triangular fan is employed here to represent a single aim at the fulcrum with two or more sanctions forming the fan wings.

"<u>The idea is to get him to stop sexually molesting younger kids</u>. To accomplish that, you try three things. You can't put him in jail, since he's only age 16, but you can PUT HIM IN A JUVENILE DETENTION CENTER. There you KEEP CLOSE WATCH OVER HIS BEHAVIOR and you HAVE A PSYCHO-THERAPIST WORK WITH HIM."

Sanction Fans. A sanction fan is the opposite of an aim fan in that a single sanction at the fulcrum is expected to produce two or more ultimate aims (UA), concomitant inherent effects (CIE), or concomitant possible effects (CPE).

> "We can't continue to run the business with young Jones meddling in things he knows nothing about. It's leading to disaster. We'll have to get rid of him. But he can't be fired, since his uncle is still on the board of directors. So I suggest we TRANSFER HIM TO OUR JACKSON HOLE OFFICE. That'll get him out of our hair. He can't do much damage out there, and he'll be able to see how our sales staff spend their days. It also means he can't be here complaining to his uncle all the time (CIE). He might even learn a little humility (CPE)."

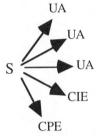

Networks. A network is composed of multiple sanctions linked to multiple aims and effects. Networks vary in their complexity. The simplest type of network consists of two sanctions associated with two aims and/or effects. Networks grow increasingly intricate as they include a greater diversity of sanctions and of outcomes—instrumental aims (IA), ultimate aims (UA), concomitant inherent effects (IEC), concomitant possible effects (PCE). The following examples illustrate two of the many variations that networks or sanction systems can assume.

Case A: The head of an insurance agency is speaking to his sales staff:

> "Ever since we dismissed her, she's been bad-mouthing us around the community. She's even started phoning our clients. There isn't much we can do legally to stop her, but we still have a few options. For one thing, I can *call other insurance agents and warn them about her* so THEY'LL BE AFRAID TO HIRE HER, and then she won't be able to get another insurance job in this town. If she hears I'm doing that, she might just quit attacking us. Then we could *convince our lawyer to phone her* and IMPLY THAT SOME KIND OF LEGAL ACTION IS IN THE OFFING if she doesn't stop spreading her campaign of lies. I can also *report her to her brother-in-law*. He's a decent sort. Maybe he'll be willing to TALK HER OUT OF IT. Then she might stop."

Case A shows that a sanction system can involve a person or agency functioning as an intermediary between the originator of the sanction and the final application of the sanction to the offender. In the above example, there are three such intermediaries—the other insurance agencies, the lawyer, and the brother-in-law. The intent of the irate employer is to pass the baton of sanction responsibility to these three. Since his instrumental aim is to convince the three to impose the sanctions he originated, that aim appears in *italics* in the above description, with the final application of the sanction in CAPITALS. In the following diagram we signify this linking role of intermediaries with the symbol *IA-S* (the intermediary carries out an instrumental aim that leads to a sanction) and identify the sanction originator as SO. Another feature illustrated in Case A is that an intermediary may be expected to contribute toward more than one ultimate aim. The angry employer hoped that his phone calls to other insurance agents not only would prevent the woman from obtaining employment but would also discourage her from continuing to criticize him and his agency.

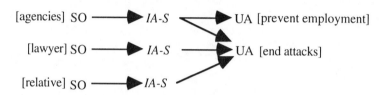

Case B: A judge reads the sentence to be imposed on a man convicted of selling fraudulent bonds to elderly people who had depended on the bonds' ostensibly high yield for financing their declining years:

"First, you are obligated to PAY A FINE of $20,000 as <u>partial indemnity to the public</u> for your offense. Then you will serve a ONE-YEAR-SIX-MONTH SENTENCE in the state prison, which should give you plenty of time to <u>think about the consequences of the crime</u> you committed. Incidentally, it will also ensure that you <u>aren't violating the law</u> for at least a year and a half. When you leave prison, you will be required for a period of three years to REPORT REGULARLY TO AN OFFICER OF THE COURT who will *monitor the way you conduct your life* so as to <u>prevent further offenses</u>. Finally, upon release from custody, you will be required to ENGAGE IN 300 HOURS OF COMMUNITY SERVICE. That service will consist of work at a state-supported retirement home so that in some small measure you can <u>make a positive contribution to the kinds of elderly citizens</u> whose future welfare you've placed in jeopardy."

In Case B, the judge is the sanction originator (SO), but intermediaries actually impose the sanctions (*IA-S*). Only one of the intermediaries—a court probation officer—is specifically identified. The others are recognized only by implication—the court clerk who collects the fine and the prison personnel who supervise the offender's confinement.

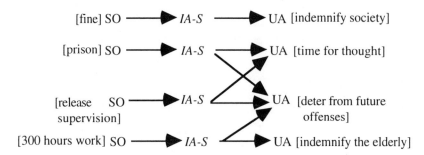

CONCLUSION

In Chapter 3 we have proposed a conception of the mental structures that concern sanction/aim relationships. Our framework for analyzing such relationships contains a variety of components, including sanctions, aims, concomitant effects, and estimates of the probability that an aim or effect will be achieved through the imposition of a particular sanction. We have also suggested that mental structures can vary in their complexity, with the forms and degrees of complexity located under five types—singular connections, chains, aim fans, sanction fans, and networks. This framework is employed in Chapter 9 for interpreting respondents' answers to interview questions.

4

Two Aspects of Sanctions and Aims:
(1) The Nature of Reality and
(2) Moral Value Commitments

Two varieties of belief that help fashion people's judgments of wrongdoing are their conceptions of reality and their moral principles. As demonstrated in the interviews we conducted, when respondents face questions about misdeeds, their answers often reflect their underlying beliefs about both reality and morality. Thus, we concluded that analyzing participants' answers from those two perspectives might prove useful for understanding the likenesses and differences in modes of moral reasoning among age groups and individuals. This chapter describes the manner in which that sort of analysis was applied in the present study.

CONCEPTIONS OF REALITY

In the philosopher's lexicon, people's conceptions of reality belong in the field of ontology, that branch of metaphysics which concerns reality itself as apart from the subjective impressions of the person who is experiencing it. However, one of the knottiest problems confronting philosophers over the centuries has been that of determining what the "real world" outside of a person's mind is really like. Or, indeed, is there actually anything outside the individual's mind that can be considered a "real world," because all knowing and all communication of knowledge necessarily flow through individual minds? Although logicians and theologians have argued this matter at length, no one has come up with a method for producing a universally accepted answer.

Yet, despite this recognition that comprehending reality is dependent on characteristics of the individual experiencer, probably no one operates as a thorough-going solipsist, believing that the only reality is what the individual person imagines, so that there is no "real world out there." Instead, people appear to believe that there is indeed an objective "real world" outside one's body and that each of us holds in our mind a conception—a mental map—of that reality. It also seems generally recognized (at least by people who have thought about such matters) that this conception can differ from one person to another. Indeed, a widely accepted interpretation of children's mental development is that children's notion of reality becomes more accurate as they grow older (Piaget & Inhelder, 1969). Thus, *becoming intellectually more mature* means creating an increasingly accurate cognitive map of "the world out there."

There are at least three approaches people use for judging the accuracy of their own and others' conceptions of reality. One approach involves adult consensus. The greater the number of adults within the society who agree about what is real, the more accurate that conception is considered to be. A second method is by expert opinion. Some people in the society are regarded as more competent —as a result of their experience, position of authority, or skills of investigation— than others. The picture of reality offered by such experts becomes the standard of what the real world is like. The question of who qualifies as an expert depends on the aspect of life under consideration. An occupational title usually identifies the facet of reality in which the expert specializes, as suggested by such titles as medical doctor, theologian, physicist, lawyer, tax accountant, dietitian, plumber, political scientist, historian, and the like. A third method of verifying a version of reality is by precision of prediction. The more often an individual is proven to be correct in predicting the outcome of future events, the more accurate that individual's notion of reality is deemed to be.

For our present purposes, the importance of the foregoing observations is found in the conviction that people do not behave on the basis of objective reality but, rather, they act on the grounds of their particular belief about what is real. A five year old who addresses a letter to "Santa" at the "North Pole" believes that there truly is such a magical person at such a location and that the letter will indeed be delivered to him. A 15-year-old boy asks the school principal to transfer him to a different English class because the boy thinks his present English teacher hates him and intends to make the boy's life miserable. A housewife engages the services of a divorce lawyer because she is convinced that her husband's occasional late nights at the office mean he is involved in an illicit love affair. In brief, people act on the basis of their conception of what is real, whether or not that conception matches either an objective reality or other people's version of reality.

In keeping with this line of logic, we recognize that the sanctions individuals recommend for wrongdoers are founded on those individuals' particular views of the portion of reality relevant to wrongdoing. That portion is the segment of life reflected in the question: "What factors in the world (as I know it) will determine how well a given sanction accomplishes the aims I hope to achieve?" We believe this question is a foundational consideration behind people's suggestions of sanctions. In other words, we contend that people intuitively are applying this question each time they decide whether a potential sanction is realistic. The more that the pertinent factors of the world form a configuration that will accomplish the sanction's aim, the more realistic that sanction is judged to be.

Thus, when people charge that a sanction is unrealistic, they mean it fails to conform to their conception of reality. The mismatch between a sanction and reality can be of two types, the unworkable and the unfeasible. An unworkable sanction is one that can be implemented as the proposer intends, but it will not produce the desired outcome. An unfeasible or impracticable sanction is one that reasonably could be expected to produce the desired outcome if it were applied, but conditions do not permit its implementation. The distinction between the types can be illustrated with comments students offered during the interviews about the three cases of wrongdoing used in the present study.

Unworkable Options

"From what I've seen, kids aren't going to stop cheating just because they hear somebody else got caught at it. So trying to use others as an example won't help."

"Spanking her at school is just going to make her hate teachers and school work. It's not going to make her want to learn what they're trying to teach."

Unfeasible Options

"Several months of intensive one-on-one professional counseling might get those drug-using teenagers to turn their lives around; but that would be very expensive, and nobody's likely to put up that kind of money."

"If the girl has no father and her mother works all the time, it'd be a good idea to put her in a good foster home where she'll get love and proper supervision. But her mother wouldn't go for that even if you found a suitable foster family."

Respondents can consider sanctions to be realistic to different degrees. In some cases, people deem a given option either absolutely 100% workable ("Hanging the burglar makes darn sure he's not going to rob or kill again") or absolutely unworkable ("There's no possible way that assigning the teenagers to do community service—like picking up trash—is going to make them stop using drugs"). In like manner, a potential sanction can be judged either completely feasible ("It's the easiest thing in the world to give the girl a zero on the test answers she copied") or entirely impractical ("You can't execute the man, because in this state the death penalty is outlawed"). However, many times an option is not judged entirely realistic or unrealistic but, instead, considered realistic only to a degree:

"Keeping the girl in after school as punishment for cheating might stop her from doing it again, but I have my doubts."

"From what I've heard, jailing drug users might reform some of them—maybe 10 or 15 percent—but not most of them."

"I think that counseling with the girl to learn where she has difficulty with math has a very good chance of curing her from copying others' tests."

In summary, then, we are proposing that individuals have their personal conceptions of reality, and it is on the basis of these conceptions that they favor certain sanctions and aims over others.

Our discussion has now brought us to the point of considering how such a notion about conceptions of reality might be of use for analyzing students' opinions about sanctions for people who commit misdeeds. We suggest that our effort to understand the underlying structure of people's modes of reasoning about wrongdoing can be enhanced by searching out the beliefs about reality that are implied in respondents' proposals of sanctions for transgressors. In our analysis of interviews in Part II, this search is directed by two questions: What inferences can be drawn about respondents' conceptions of reality from the remarks they make about sanctions and treatments for wrongdoing? What likenesses and differences in such conceptions are found among individuals, age groups, and gender groups?

MORAL VALUE COMMITMENTS

Just as respondents' conceptions of reality can be implied in the sanctions they recommend, so also their moral values can be reflected in what they identify as wrongdoing and in the aims they intend sanctions to achieve. This point is illustrated in the following exchange during an interview with a 21-year-old woman about the case of the 23-year-old burglar.

> *Interviewer*: Did the man do anything wrong?
> *Respondent*: Sure. He stole and killed. Those are both wrong. Killing is the ultimate crime.
> *Interviewer*: What should be done about him?
> *Respondent*: Prison, probably for life, or at least for a long time. He shouldn't be executed, because I don't believe in the death penalty, at least not in this case, because he didn't plan it ahead of time. He was just startled when the woman discovered him, and he just shot her—kind of an emotional reaction, like self defense. But if he'd planned to do it all along, then execution might be okay. He'd deserve it then.

Two aspects of the respondent's moral values that are revealed in her comments are those of principles and conditions. We use the term *principle* here to mean a basic conviction about right and wrong in moral situations. In the case of the burglar, the respondent expressed two such convictions —don't steal and don't kill. The term *conditions* identifies circumstances that determine how the principle is applied in particular situations. Although the respondent has declared killing to be "the ultimate crime," she retreats from a complete proscription of killing by stipulating conditions under which it is admissible. She would permit killing as official punishment for premeditated murder.

In this initial example the interviewee's moral values have been reflected in her explanation of why the transgressor's behavior was wrong. Further values are revealed in the aims she intends for the sanctions she recommended.

> *Interviewer*: What good do you think putting him in prison would do? What might that accomplish?

Respondent: Well, he won't be out on the streets robbing and killing innocent people. It also makes him pay for what he did. I mean, people who commit crimes need to pay some way for harming others. Prison would give him plenty of time to think it over and regret what he did.

Two moral principles to be inferred from these remarks might be phrased as: (1) innocent people have a right to protection from those who might harm them and (2) wrongdoers should suffer penalties for their transgressions.

These observations about the way moral values may be implied in people's responses to wrongdoing suggest a further way that proposed sanctions and aims can be analyzed to enhance our understanding of modes of moral reasoning. The two questions that guide such analysis are: What inferences can be drawn about respondents' moral values from what they identify as wrongdoing and from the aims they intend to achieve by the sanctions they propose for offenders? What likenesses and differences in moral values appear among individuals, age groups, and gender age groups?

CONCLUSION

In this chapter we have contended that clues to people's conceptions of reality and their moral values can be found in the ways they (1) identify instances of moral misconduct, (2) recommend sanctions for such misconduct, and (3) explain the aims they hope such sanctions will achieve. In Part II, the application of this mode of analysis to the contents of interviews is reported in Chapter 11— "Conceptions of God and the Sanctity of Life."

5

Overt Cognitive Sequences and Reasoning Styles

The type of interview we used in this study demonstrated that it is an error to assume that the first answer a person offers to a question about sanctions or aims is that person's entire opinion about the matter. In other words, rarely, if ever, do people's initial responses reveal the entire array of sanctions or aims they would consider appropriate in the case. Realizing this fact prompted us to posit four stages in the sequence of thought that leads to the interview results. We labeled the stages *initial thought, added thought, afterthought,* and *probed thought.*

Initial thought consists of the consequences and aims a respondent expresses when first asked, "What should be done about the offender?" (the consequence) and "What would be the purpose of doing that—in other words, what would that accomplish?" (the aim).

Added thought is a further consequence or aim that a respondent may offer with little or no prompting by the interviewer. The term *little prompting* in this instance means the interviewer follows the initial answer with such a comment as "And that's it?" or "That's what you would recommend?"

Afterthought is an idea about a consequence or aim that occurs later in the interview when the respondent is answering a different type of question. At that juncture, a new consequence or aim comes to mind which the respondent wishes to attach to the initial thought or wishes to apply in revising the initial thought.

Probed thought consists of ideas elicited when the interviewer asks respondents whether they would subscribe to particular sanctions and aims that the interviewer describes.

These four stages can be illustrated by the following segment of dialogue between an interviewer and a 14-year-old girl as they discussed the case of the 23-year-old burglar who had murdered a woman during an attempted robbery. The phrases representing the four stages of overt cognitive sequence are underlined. The interviewer first described the case of wrongdoing, then asked:

Interviewer: "What should be done about the man? What should happen to him?"

Respondent: "<u>Maybe put on trial, maybe put in jail for a little while, and put under counseling.</u>" (initial consequences) "He shouldn't be killed. I don't believe in killing."

Interviewer: "What good do you think your suggestions might do? How might they help?"

Respondent: "Well, in the trial and then in counseling <u>they might find out why he did it.</u>" (initial aims) "Most people are helped with counseling."

Interviewer: "And being in jail?"

Respondent: "<u>That shows him he's done something wrong. And the counseling can help rehabilitate him.</u>" (added aims)

Interviewer: "When we asked some other people about this case, some of them said, 'I don't have to decide what to do about the man. God will know what to do.' What do you think about that?"

Respondent: "Well, <u>yes, that works.</u>" (probed consequence) I don't necessarily believe in God, but there is something up there. And if the burglar knows he did it himself—that he's to blame and it was wrong—then that would help. Because some people believe in God, and then in the guilty part of their mind they feel really bad. And all the time they think, 'What I did was wrong, and I have to correct it.' That might help rehabilitate him."

Interviewer: "All right, now we also asked some other people about the purposes of the consequences they suggested. Here are some other purposes in addition to the ones you gave. Would any of these be ones you would include? Here's the first—to make sure he would not rob or kill again."

Respondent: "<u>Yes, I'd include that.</u>" (probed aim) But it depends on how they would do it. If it means to kill him, I wouldn't agree. But if it means to put him in jail for a little while and in counseling, I'd agree."

Interviewer: "Okay, here's another purpose—to give the family of the dead woman the satisfaction of having the killer punished."

Respondent: "<u>Yes, that would also be part of my purpose.</u>" (probed aim) "Putting him in jail for a while would give them satisfaction. Like, put him in for a couple of—no, not just a couple of years—but like <u>15 years.</u>" (consequence afterthought) "Because if you only put him in for two years, I know the family and the public would be pretty upset, because 24 months isn't a very long time, and this person has killed and robbed. So put him in at least <u>10 years.</u>" (revision of consequence afterthought)

Interviewer: "All right, and now another purpose—to make the man do something helpful for the community."

Respondent: "<u>That I'd include</u>." (probed aim) "After a period of counseling maybe he could <u>help bringing up children and working with old folks</u>." (consequence afterthought)

Interviewer: "Okay, one more purpose—to scare other people who might think they would like to break into houses and steal things."

Respondent: "No, I wouldn't include that, because scaring people doesn't help. Well, sometimes it might work, but I don't think it'd work on many people."

The above interview segment not only illustrates the four varieties of overt thought, but also demonstrates an additional feature that often appears in the remarks respondents offer during an interview. That is, the interview may serve two functions. It may elicit by gradual stages the completely formed opinion about sanctions and aims that a respondent already had in mind when initially confronted with the case. As another possibility, the interview can both (a) evoke some already established beliefs and (b) stimulate a decision-making process—that is, a learning process—through which the respondent generates and organizes additional convictions during the conduct of the interview. It seems likely that the extent of an individual's previous experience with similar cases will significantly influence whether the interview simply reveals an already established set of beliefs or initiates a process of adopting further beliefs. We would estimate that someone with a host of past experience with similar cases—such as a criminal court judge or a defense attorney—would come to an interview with a greater quantity of established convictions than would people who have seldom if ever considered the issue of sanctions and aims for cases of the type at hand—such respondents as elementary school pupils. In other words, the interview would serve more as a learning session for the pupil than for the judge or attorney. This difference between two types of people might be reflected in the degree of consistency among a respondent's replies and in how well that individual adduces a convincing line of logic in support of proposed sanctions and aims. In effect, we propose that individuals who have had more experience would display greater consistency and more persuasive logic in their answers than would ones who have had less experience. In keeping with this hypothesis, we might expect in the present study that older subjects (17 and 21 year olds) would have had more experience—either direct or vicarious—with our three kinds of cases than would younger ones (9 and 14 year olds). We would then expect this difference to be displayed in the extent of consistency and reasonableness of logic of subjects' replies during the interviews. Our test of such a hypothesis is reported in Part II, Chapter 10.

We now turn to five additional features of people's manner of answering questions during interviews, features that may differ across groups and among individuals.

OVERT REASONING STYLES

The term *overt reasoning style* refers to observable aspects of the way people cast their answers in response to interview questions. The five characteristics we adopted to represent reasoning style are labeled (1) pace of response, (2) reasoning process, (3) specificity of recommendations, (4) strength of conviction, and (5) length of response We defined the first four of these in a manner that permits a student's answers to be rated along a four-step scale. The rating procedure yields a score for each characteristic, a score that can be used for comparing individuals, age groups, and gender groups on the four dimensions.

Pace of Response

When an interviewer posed a question, the respondent had the opportunity to reply immediately or to pause a while. Four levels of response pace were defined in terms of the number of seconds it took an interviewee to begin answering a question.

> Level 1. *Immediate.* Not more than two seconds elapse between the end of the interviewer's question and the beginning of the individual's answer.
> Level 2. *3-5 second delay.* About 3 to 5 seconds pass before the person answers.
> Level 3. *6-9 second delay.* Around 6 to 9 seconds pass before the person answers.
> Level 4. *10+ seconds delay.* Ten or more seconds pass before the person answers.

Reasoning Process

The second aspect, called *reasoning process*, focused on an individual's apparent mode of organizing thoughts when formulating answers. This aspect was judged in terms of how a subject explained or defended a decision, such as the decision about why a proposed sanction was desirable or why an aim was unacceptable. The aspect could involve three characteristics: (a) whether the respondent directly listed reasons instead of vaguely groping around for an answer, (b) whether the reasons were placed in a logical order rather than issued in a confusing or random order, and (c) whether the reasons represented logic rather than just intuition. The following example illustrates four different degrees of these variables as they appear in four subjects' answers to a question about why they would recommend that two 16-year-old drug traders contribute community service as a sanction for their misdeed.

> Level 1. *Highly systematic.* "If they do some work, like helping clean up a park or helping in a child-care center, they'll not only be spending their time in something constructive but they'll be giving something back to a society that they've damaged by peddling drugs."

> (*Without hesitation, directly suggests types of activities and the aims they might achieve.*)

Level 2. *Partially systematic.* "Well, I don't know exactly what they should do, but it should be something that's helping others . . . helping society, like maybe cleaning graffiti off walls."

> (*Hesitates a bit, gropes slightly, then offers an aim and a suitable activity.*)

Level 3. *Rather groping.* "It's hard to say, but I should think they should be useful. (*pause*) I guess they could do something around their school. Or would that be too embarrassing? Why not have them do weeding in a park or something."

> (*Initially gropes, questions first option, then proposes another option but fails to show much confidence in it.*)

Level 4. *Very groping.* "Well, it's . . . I'd say . . . Well, that's the kind of thing courts do . . . don't they? I mean couldn't you have kids do that? (*pause*) I'm not sure what you'd have them do, but I just feel that something like that could be done."

> (*Continually unsure, wanders, fails to arrive at a clear solution.*)

Specificity of Recommendations

This variable was judged in terms of how definite respondents were in proposing sanctions and in supporting their suggestions with reasons. The four levels of specificity are illustrated with the following example of sanctions recommended in the case of the burglar who killed the resident of a house he was robbing.

Level 1. *Very specific.* "Put him to death. He killed, so he should lose his life."

Level 2. *Rather specific.* "Sentenced to life in prison. But maybe it wouldn't have to be his whole life. I mean, he might get off in 10 or 20 years if he seems like he's sorry and he has a good prison record."

Level 3. *Somewhat vague.* "He certainly needs to be punished. Probably prison and perhaps a fine if he has any money. It might be good, too, if he somehow could compensate the family of the dead woman. Something like that."

Level 4. *Extremely vague.* "Oh, that's not easy. He's robbed and killed, so likely something kind of drastic is needed, but not really inhumane. I'd say it ought to be something appropriate."

Strength of Ultimate Conviction

This fourth aspect of style concerns an individual's apparent degree of satisfaction with the answer that he or she ultimately offered to a question. In many cases, subjects who were very systematic in their overt reasoning process seemed quite satisfied with their response. But it was also possible for a subject to grope about for an answer, yet ultimately appear convinced that his or her answer was a good one. In addition, there was usually a high correlation between how specific an individual's answer was and how strongly he or she felt about the goodness of that answer. However, sometimes a student who had been quite specific was not really happy about that solution, so in such cases a low correlation obtained between specificity and strength of conviction. The following example illustrates four strength-of-conviction levels for answers to the question of whether the aim of punishing the two 16-year-old drug traders should be to *ensure that the law is enforced.*

Level 1. *Strong conviction, quite satisfied.* "No, just enforcing the law isn't a good purpose. It's really not the point in this case. The point is, what are these teenagers doing to themselves? It's simply not a question of whether the law is enforced."

Level 2. *Somewhat hesitant.* "That's kind of tough. What they did isn't all that bad. Lots of kids try out drugs. And trading drugs for tickets to a concert—so what? But it's true that drugs are illegal, so you have to arrest them. So I guess part of the aim of arresting them is to enforce the law. Yeah, that would be part of it."

Level 3. *Very hesitant, dissatisfied.* "I suppose you could say that it's usually best to enforce the law. But I can think of exceptions, and maybe this is one of them—the two teenagers. But, well, why not? Enforcing the law is probably okay here, though that's really not the best reason."

Level 4. *Can't make a decision.* "You know, some laws are bad laws, so they really shouldn't be obeyed. But, of course, you can't just have people running around breaking laws. You have to have laws or it's chaos. Yet, about the drug laws, I just don't know."

Length of Response

The fifth characteristic of interviews that we regarded as an aspect of style was the length of the answers participants gave to the interview questions. Because each interview was conducted by means of a standard set of questions, the interviewer's contribution to the length of the interview was essentially the same in each of the 136 sessions. The only time an interviewer deviated from the standard protocol was when a participant initially failed to grasp a question so that the question had to be repeated or rephrased. Although this occurred occasionally, particularly with the younger subjects, in general it did not appear to extend the time of the interview significantly. Thus, differences in the amount of time an interview consumed were mainly the result of the respondent's participation, not the interviewer's. The measure for the length of response was the number of minutes consumed by the discussion of each of the three cases of wrongdoing.

Chapter 10 reports the way the foregoing five methods of analyzing style were applied to the 136 interviews.

CONCLUSION

This chapter has offered two approaches to analyzing people's answers about the aims to be achieved by the sanctions and treatments they recommend in cases of wrongdoing.

The first approach, focusing on a respondent's overt cognitive sequence, concerns the order in which an interviewee answers questions about the sanctions and aims that are appropriate in a case of wrongdoing. The approach is founded on the supposition that the initial suggestion a respondent offers is seldom, if ever, a complete representation of that person's notion of suitable sanctions and aims. At later stages of an interview, further sanctions and aims are likely to arise, either as spontaneous afterthoughts or else as beliefs elicited by means of the interviewer asking probing questions.

The second approach addresses the style of respondents' overt reasoning as judged along five dimensions: pace of response, reasoning process, specificity of recommendations, strength of ultimate conviction, and length of response.

6

Developmental Indicators

As noted earlier, a central purpose of this study has been to learn ways in which young people's reasoning about the aims of sanctions and treatments might vary between preadolecence and young adulthood. In order to study potential variations, we needed to identify kinds of dimensions along which changes in reasoning might occur. The dimensions we adopted are explained under the following topics: (1) stages of development, (2) differentiation and interdependence, (3) fanciful versus realistic, and (4) degree of rebelliousness.

STAGES OF DEVELOPMENT

Among theories that picture cognitive development as progressing through a succession of stages, the best-known model is the one offered by Jean Piaget (Piaget & Inhelder, 1969). In one popular version of Piaget's scheme, mental development advances through four principal stages: sensorimotor (birth to about age 2), preoperational thought (about age 2 to 7), concrete operations (about 7 to 11), and formal operational (about 11 to 15). Beyond the mid-teens, thought patterns move from a condition of egocentrism and idealism to a growing recognition that people do not operate solely on the basis of pure logic but that they also are influenced by life's social realities. The following are principal characteristics of the stages:

Sensorimotor Period (Birth–2). The infant advances from performing only reflex actions to finally representing objects mentally and thereby cognitively combining and manipulating them.

Preoperational-Thought Period (2–7). This period is divided into two levels. The first (ages 2-4) is characterized by egocentric speech and primary dependence on perception, rather than on logic, in problem solving. The second (5–7) is marked by an intuitive approach to life, a transition phase between the child's depending on perception and depending on logical thought in solving problems.

Concrete-Operations Period (7–11). In this stage children can perform logical mental operations on concrete objects that either are directly observed or are imagined. An important feature of this period is the child's developing greater ability to recognize which aspects of an object remain unchanged (are *conserved*) when the object changes from one form to another. For example, when a large ball of clay is divided into a series of small balls of clay, the typical preoperational child will not recognize that in this transformation the weight and mass of clay remained the same. The concrete-operations child, in contrast, will understand that weight and mass have been conserved.

Formal-Operations Period (11–15). During adolescence the typical child is no longer limited by what he or she directly sees or hears, nor is he or she restricted to the problem at hand. The adolescent can now imagine various conditions that bear on a problem—past, present, and future—and devise hypotheses about what might logically occur under different combinations of such conditions. By the end of this final stage of mental development the youth is capable of all the forms of logic that the adult commands. Subsequently, further experience over the years of youth and adulthood fill in the outline with additional, more complex concepts so that the adult's thought is more mature and freer of lingering vestiges of egocentrism than is the thought of the adolescent. (Summarized from Piaget & Inhelder, 1969)

In addition to defining stages of general mental growth, Piaget addressed questions of growth in moral reasoning (Piaget, 1932/1948). His study of children's moral decisions led him to propose that such development involves two domains, the *heteronomous* and the *autonomous.* People operating from a heteronomous perspective accord unilateral respect for authorities (such as parents, teachers, the clergy, the police) and for the rules they prescribe. People operating from an autonomous perspective base their moral judgments on mutual regard among peers or equals and respect for the rules that guide their interaction. Whereas heteronomous morality requires obedience to authority and to authority produced rules, autonomous morality is based on reciprocity and equality among peers. Piaget suggested that development in reasoning tended to progress from heteronomous morality to autonomous morality.

> Young children confuse what is just with what is law, law being whatever is prescribed by adult authority. Justice is identified with formulated rules, as indeed it is in the opinion of a great many adults, of all adults namely, who have not succeeded in setting autonomy of conscience above social prejudice and the written law. (Piaget, 1965, p. 317)

Following Piaget's lead, Lawrence Kohlberg (1984) devised the best-known moral reasoning theory to appear in recent decades. He used Piaget's set of general cognitive growth stages as a foundation for erecting a six-stage hierarchy of moral judgments that refined Piaget's original conception of ideal heteronomous and autonomous types. Kohlberg embellished the scheme with his own conceptions and with those of a variety of philosophers and psychologists, ranging from Aristotle, through Kant and Baldwin, to Habermas. He labeled his theory a "rational reconstruction of the ontogenesis of justice reasoning" and not, as people have often assumed, a complete depiction of moral development.

I have always tried to be clear that my states are stages of justice reasoning, not of emotions, aspirations, or action. Our data base has been a set of hypothetical dilemmas posing conflicts between the rights or claims of different persons in dilemma situations. (Kohlberg, 1984, p. 224)

Kohlberg postulated six stages in the development of moral reasoning from early childhood into adult life. The following brief glimpse of the stages in their mid-1980s version suggests several of their distinguishing characteristics. The presentation advances from the earliest levels, indicative of the thinking processes of young children, to the higher levels, which can be achieved by individuals who are intellectually more mature (Kohlberg, 1984, pp. 621–639). Kohlberg linked his scheme to Piaget's stages of logical reasoning by contending that the growing child had to reach a suitable level of logical thought before being able to advance to a comparable stage of moral reasoning. For example, Kohlberg proposed that an individual must be capable of Piaget's concrete-operational thought in order to adopt Kohlberg's Stage 2 (individualistic, instrumental morality) approach to moral judgments. An older child needed to command Piaget's full formal operations thought processes before reaching Kohlberg's Stage 4 (social system morality) (Kegan, 1982, p. 86).

Stage 1: Heteronomous Morality. Kohlberg refers to the perspective at this initial stage as *moral realism* in which a person assumes that moral judgments are so self-evident that no justification is needed beyond simply stating the rule that has been broken. Failing to tell the truth or using an object that belongs to someone else is absolutely wrong and automatically warrants punishment. There are no such things as extenuating circumstances, such as people's intentions or their knowledge of right from wrong. This stage represents Piaget's heteronomous justice—absolute obedience to authority and the letter of the law.

Stage 2: Individualistic, Instrumental Morality. At this second level, the person recognizes that different people can have different points of view toward a moral incident. "Since each person's primary aim is to pursue his or her own interests, the perspective is pragmatic—to maximize satisfaction of one's needs and desires while minimizing negative consequences to the self" (Kohlberg, 1984, p. 626). Thus, the participants in a moral incident seek to negotiate a deal with each other as the instrument for coordinating their efforts for mutual benefit. No general moral principles guide their action, so that each case is handled separately. However, such a pragmatic approach "fails to provide a means for deciding among conflicting claims, ordering or setting priorities on conflicting needs and interests" (Kohlberg, 1984, p. 626).

Stage 3: Impersonally Normative Morality. The notion of justice advances beyond the individual-interest level to a conception of shared moral norms that guide everyone's moral behavior, regardless of the particular situations or particular people involved. In contrast to Stage 1, where rules are handed down by authority, the shared norms at Stage 3 are the result of general agreement about what constitutes suitable social behavior. Individuals operating from a Stage 3 perspective are concerned with playing their social role in a positive, constructive manner, with good compared to bad motives as evidence of one's general personal morality. The guide to action is provided by the golden rule —do unto others as you would have others do unto you. People at Stage 3 are especially concerned with maintaining mutual trust and social approval.

Stage 4: Social System Morality. People at this level look beyond informal, commonly agreed upon rules for individuals' interactions and now encompass the entire social system in their purview of moral behavior. "The pursuit of individual interests is considered legitimate only when it is consistent with the maintenance of the sociomoral system as a whole. . . . A social structure that includes formal institutions and social roles serves to mediate conflicting claims and promote the common good" (Kohlberg, 1984, p. 631). This perspective recognizes a societal, legal, or religious system that has developed codified rules and practices for adjudicating moral conflicts. In some settings, the laws may be ones representing an overarching philosophical or religious conviction embedded in the individual's conscience, a conviction that can be in conflict with the society's dominant legal system. In summary, moral judgments at Stage 4 are founded on legal or religious institutions and belief systems.

Stage 5: Human Rights and Social Welfare Morality. In contrast to accepting the rules of a society as they are already constituted, Kohlberg posits at Stage 5 a perception of morality that people would rationally build into a social system to promote universal values and rights. This prior-to-society viewpoint asks what rules would guide a society that fosters equality, equity, and general welfare for all. Upon answering this question, people are then obligated to make moral choices in keeping with those rules, even when their choices conflict with the society's present codes. Stage 5 provides a concern for the protection of the rights of the minority that cannot be derived from the social system perspective of Stage 4, since "social institutions, rules, or laws are evaluated by reference to their long-term consequences for the welfare of each person or group in the society" (Kohlberg, 1984, p. 634).

Stage 6: Morality of Universalizable, Reversible, and Prescriptive General Ethical Principles. Kohlberg describes this stage as *the moral point of view* which "all human beings should take toward one another as free and equal autonomous persons" (Kohlberg, 1984, p. 636). Such morality is universalizable in being applicable at all times and in all places among all peoples. It is reversible, in that the plaintiff and defendant in a moral incident could exchange places and the decision for resolving the issue would not be affected—a kind of "moral musical chairs" or second order application of the golden rule. Each person understands and respects the point of view of every other person. "General principles are distinct from either rules or rights, first, in being positive *pre*scriptions rather than negative *pro*scriptions (don't kill, don't steal or cheat)" (Kohlberg, 1984, p. 636). One general principle can be respect for human personality or dignity. Another can be benevolence or universal compassion and care. Or moral decisions can derive from a cluster of principles—maximum quality of life for everyone, maximum individual liberty in relation to like liberty for others, and the equitable distribution of goods and services. (Summarized from Kohlberg, 1984, pp. 621–639)

Empirical studies of moral reasoning in a variety of societies have confirmed that people do apply the perspectives of the first five stages in their responses to hypothetical moral dilemmas. However, there remains a question about whether Stage 6 might perhaps be an ideal condition never actually achieved in practice (Colby, Kohlberg, Gibbs, & Lieberman, 1983, p. 5).

An earlier investigation revealed that only about 30% of adults could be classified as having reached Piaget's formal-operations level in logical judgment (Kuhn, Langer, Kohlberg, & Haan, 1977). Thus, not everyone within an age group would be expected to achieve the same level of moral reasoning when facing moral decisions.

In his description of moral reasoning stages, Kohlberg suggests the way three kinds of justice are typified at each stage—distributive, commutative, and corrective. The term *distributive justice* refers to the way desirable assets (honor, wealth) are allotted to people of a society in terms of equality or merit and need. *Commutative justice* concerns issues deriving from voluntary agreements, contracts, and equal exchange. *Corrective justice* aims at repairing private transactions that have been unfair and call for restitution or compensation. Corrective justice also concerns crimes and torts that violate the rights of involuntary participants and thus call for restitution or retribution (Kohlberg, 1984, 621–622). Of these three varieties, the third—corrective justice—is closest to the concerns of our present study and thus can serve as a useful perspective from which to view the results of interviews reported in Part II. As a preparation for that application, in the following paragraphs we draw upon Kohlberg's interpretations of corrective justice for each of his moral-judgment stages (1984, pp. 621–639) and link those interpretations to the content of our typologies in our Chapter 2.

In our initial attempt to link each item in our typologies with a particular corrective morality stage, we discovered that Kohlberg's system and our own scheme were sufficiently different to make a precise stage-by-stage matching unreasonable. However, we could with some degree of confidence identify general tendencies. In other words, we could indicate which sanctions and aims were more indicative of the lower stages and which were more indicative of the upper stages of Kohlberg's hierarchy. The manner in which we performed this matching is illustrated below. First, we summarize Kohlberg's six levels of corrective justice that correspond to his six stages of development in moral reasoning. Then we propose, in the form of two lists, which of the sanctions and aims from our typologies appear more closely associated with Kohlberg's lower levels and which seem more closely related to his upper levels (Table 6-1).

Levels of Corrective Justice

Stage 1: Heteronomous Morality. Corrective justice involves retribution and may be immanent, in the sense that punishment is seen as an automatic consequence of transgression.

Stage 2: Individualistic, Instrumental Morality. Corrective justice can include reference to each individual's needs or intentions as a basis for fairness. One person can see another person's viewpoint and can modify his or her actions in recognition of that viewpoint.

Stage 3: Interpersonally Normative Morality. The relevance of motives is taken into account as well as whether the offender is living up to a shared conception of how a good person acts. Punishment is not warranted if the motive was noble.

Stage 4: Social System Morality. Justice requires impartial application of the law and corrective action to protect society by removing threats to society or by providing ways for transgressors to "pay their debt to society."

Stage 5: Human Rights and Social Welfare Morality. Human rights and social welfare are primary concerns so that retributive punishment is considered unsuitable. It is assumed that, in a reasonably just legal system, adhering closely to legal procedures and consistently applying due process will lead to more equitable decisions than by judging each case solely on its particular features.

Stage 6: Morality of Universalizable, Reversible, and Prescriptive General Ethical Principles. Offenders are viewed as human beings whose dignity deserves respect so far as it is compatible with protecting the welfare of others. If correction includes restricting an offender's opportunities through isolation or monitoring, the purpose is to guard the safety of others and not to inflict suffering or death as a penalty or repayment for immorality. (Summarized from Kohlberg, 1984, pp. 621–639)

Sanctions/Aims Relating to Kohlberg's Levels

Table 6-1 displays those items from our two typologies that conceivably might be associated with stages of corrective justice. Those in the left column are assumed to be indicative of Kohlberg's lower stages and those in the right column more representative of higher stages. Several of the aims are composites of several separate items in the aims typology in Chapter 2. For example, the one entitled "Improve offender's condition" is composed of seven more specific aims (enhance offenders' knowledge and skills, improve offenders' self-confidence, improve work habits, improve social adjustment, show someone cares for them, help offenders conquer problems, and obtain help for offenders).

In a similar fashion, the item "Protect society" is composed of three more specific aims (deter offenders, dissuade others from committing misdeeds, and disable an instrument of offense). From the line of reasoning behind the construction of Table 6-1, we are able to generate the following hypothesis that can be tested with the interview responses reported in Chapter 8.

Table 6-1
**Associating Corrective Justice Stages with
Sanctions and Aims**

Lower Developmental Levels	*Higher Developmental Levels*
Sanctions	
Execute	Counsel (reason, advise, warn)
Impose corporal punishment	Furnish probation, parole
Imprison	Educate (learning opportunities)
Expose publicly	
Banish, ostracize	
Aims	
Achieve social retribution	Improve offenders' condition
Match the offense	Protect society—Incapacitate
Enforce the letter of the law	Protect society—Deter
Revenge, personal	Reform offenders

A significantly higher incidence of left-column sanctions and aims will appear in the sanctions and aims of the youngest respondents (9-year-olds) than in the sanctions and aims of the oldest ones (21-year-olds).

DIFFERENTIATION AND INTERDEPENDENCE

Kurt Lewin (1890–1947) was a German psychologist who immigrated to the United States in the 1930s and subsequently became a distinguished professor in American universities. During his career, he proposed a set of principles that he thought were reflected in the process of child development (Barker, Dembo, & Lewin, 1943). The study reported in this book provides an opportunity to test several of Lewin's principles as they might apply to the sanctions and aims that young people recommend.

In Lewin's system, a person's *life space* consists of all the facts that influence that individual's behavior at a given time. To Lewin, a *fact* is not an objectively verifiable observation from the "real world." Instead, a fact is any aspect of the child's psychological environment that affects the child's behavior or thought, including all aspects that the individual accepts as real or true, whether or not the features can be demonstrated as true by means of objective evidence. Thus, the causal relationship structures that people have in mind are, in this sense, facts. Those structures are the beliefs on which individuals base their proposals about sanctions and treatments for wrongdoers.

Two other terms needed for understanding Lewin's concept of development are region and boundary. A *region* is a fact within the child's life space. Two aspects of regions are of particular importance. One is the *relationship* among two or more regions—they may either be closely connected or be distant from one another. The other aspect is the nature of the *boundaries* between regions. A boundary may be weak, permitting one region to influence the other quite easily, or it may be strong, serving as an effective barrier to the influence of adjacent regions.

In terms of growth principles, Lewin proposed that as children grew up, their regions or clusters of facts develop in several ways—the regions become more differentiated, they expand to encompass more aspects of life, they are linked with each other in complex and interdependent ways, and they become more realistic. If these four principles do indeed apply to the years of adolescence, then we might expect to find the following trends in the sanctions and aims that were suggested by the youths between ages 9 and 21 in the present study.

Differentiation

The principle of differentiation states that as children grow older, their life space becomes more differentiated. This means that regions or facts increase in number and specificity of function. Differentiation occurs as a result of the child's increased experiences in the world and increased capacity to perceive differences between one situation and another.

We may recall that in the present study, each interviewee was asked to judge three different cases of wrongdoing. If Lewin's principle of differentiation did indeed apply to the ages we studied, then we might expect (a) that the number of sanctions and aims proposed by respondents would increase with the age of the interviewees and (b) that the differentiation in the sanctions and aims recommended across the three cases would also increase. In particular, 9 year olds would (a) suggest fewer sanctions and aims and (b) make fewer distinctions from one case to another than did the older respondents.

Expansion

In Lewin's theory, the life space of the child enlarges in terms of both time and space as the years pass. Furthermore, children gain access to increasing numbers of regions of their life space as they grow older.

In applying this principle in the present study, we can hypothesize that there will be greater variability in the elements of older students' answers than of younger students' answers. In other words, older respondents will propose a greater range of sanctions and aims than will younger ones.

Organizational Interdependence

According to this interdependence principle, regions of the life space become increasingly interlinked as the child grows older. Organizational interdependence consists of the arrangement of different regions or facts into hierarchical systems or sequences of actions designed to accomplish a more distant or more complex goal.

Lewin's principle of organizational interdependence and his notion of differentiation are similar to a pair of basic principles of evolution posited by the 19th-century British philosopher Herbert Spencer and later reiterated by the German-born developmentalist Heinz Werner who completed his career in the United States at Clark University. Spencer contended that as individuals develop they become increasingly differentiated in parts and functions and better integrated in the way the parts work together. Werner wrote that:

> We assume that organisms are naturally directed toward a series of transformations—reflecting a tendency to move from a state of relative globality and undifferentiatedness towards states of increasing differential and hierarchic integration. It is this tendency, formulated as "the orthogenetic principle" which serves for us to characterize development as distinct from other types of change over time. (Werner & Kaplan, 1963, p. 7)

In the context of the present study, we propose that interdependence would be shown through older respondents offering more elaborate sanction/aim relationships than would younger respondents. This greater complexity would be displayed in two ways—the kinds of causal relation structures described in Chapter 4 and the intricacy of the arguments adduced in support of a respondent's sanction/aim proposals. Evidence bearing on the above matters is provided in Chapters 8 and 9.

The Nature of Early Adolescence

In writing about adolescence, Lewin suggested that a child's entrance into the teenage years is like an emigrant setting foot in a strange country. The growing child is like the sociologist's *marginal woman* or *marginal man*, moving from the familiar region of childhood into the unfamiliar domain of adolescence. Lewin believed that the adolescent's life space was thus forced into a labile, fluid state by the puzzling bodily changes brought on by puberty, by the youth's growing intellect, and by the new opportunities for social freedom offered by society. In this expansive, labile state, the novitiate would be expected to take extreme attitudes in social judgments and to shift opinions quite readily. In terms of the study reported in the present book, we might expect to find notable differences between the opinions expressed by 9 year olds, who are still in the stage of later childhood, and those expressed by 14 year olds, who are well into early adolescence. More precisely, we would expect to find 14 year olds offering a wider variety of sanction/aim recommendations than do 9 year olds. Furthermore, we would predict that the number of options proposed by 17 and 21 year olds might be fewer than those proposed by 14 year olds on the grounds that by age 17—and even more so by age 21—youths are less labile and more realistic in their opinions. Interview results related to these expectations are found in Chapters 8, 9, and 10.

FANCIFUL VERSUS REALISTIC

If we accept the concept of mental structures (that all stimuli from the world are filtered into the mind through interpretive lenses), then we are obliged to recognize that no one experiences the world objectively as "it really is." In effect, accepting the concept of structures means that we cannot subscribe to *naive realism*. We can, however, assent to *consensual realism*, which is defined as "a description or interpretation of stimuli (in observations of physical events) or of standards (in beliefs about proper values) on which most adults will agree." The term *adults* is used rather than *people* in order to exclude children, whose conceptions of reality are often different from those of most adults. Therefore, for practical purposes, consensual adult beliefs can serve as the criterion for determining the nature of reality. We use this sort of standard because adults, compared to children, are assumed not only to have more mature nervous systems but also to have a richer background of experience, enabling them to distinguish—more accurately than do children—the real from the imaginative.

Attempting to apply our criterion of consensual realism to moral situations is not without its difficulties. This is because achieving consensus among adults for their observations of physical events is easier than obtaining consensus about such moral matters as suitable aims and sanctions. From observing court trials and other moral decision settings, we would propose that adult witnesses to wrongdoing, although they may disagree about certain details of what they saw and heard, are more likely to agree on what happened than they are on (a) what sanctions offenders should face and (b) an appropriate line of reasoning in support of such sanctions. For example, adults who have seen a bank robber shoot a teller to death are more likely to agree on what happened than they are on what punishment or treatment the robber should face. In terms of sanctions, some witnesses may suggest that the robber be executed, others may recommend life imprisonment without parole, and still others may favor 10 to 15 years in prison. However, even though adults' beliefs about moral matters are subject to greater variation than are their reports of physical events, it is still possible to make at least gross distinctions between the realistic and the fanciful in judging sanctions and aims. For example, we may recall that participants in the present study were asked what should be done about the 23-year-old burglar's killing of the woman whose house he was robbing. Here are the recommendations of four 9 year olds.

1. "He should go to jail for a month."
2. "Kill him, because he killed the lady."
3. "Put him in jail for 6,000 years or months."
4. "He should stay in prison for 33 years."

We judge proposals 2 and 4 as being more realistic than 1 and 3 because (a) our own daily life experiences suggest that 2 and 4 have actually been applied in such cases, (b) none of the 17 or 21 year olds in our study recommended such a lenient jail sentence as one month or such an outlandish one as 6,000 years, and (c) present-day law statutes in many jurisdictions would permit proposals 2 or 4 but not 1 or 3. Thus, distinctions among sanctions can be founded on a concept of consensual realism, despite the sometimes clouded, puzzling nature of that concept when it is applied to actual cases.

In summary, both daily observations and theories of human development suggest that, in the above sense of *consensual realism*, children become more realistic as they grow older. Piaget's (Piaget & Inhelder, 1969) discussions of egocentrism picture very young children as often having difficulty differentiating themselves from the environment, and they typically fail to recognize how life must look from other people's perspectives. They also are less capable than most adults in estimating what actions are feasible or prudent in a given situation, frequently because they fail to recognize the complex combination of factors that are likely to influence the outcome of those actions. Lewin and Werner, in agreement with Piaget, also proposed that children grow more realistic with the passing years (Barker, Dembo, & Lewin, 1943; Werner, 1961).

For the sake of the present study, we can imagine a scale ranging from highly fanciful (unrealistic) at one end to highly realistic at the other, and we can try to locate different interviewees' sanction/aim proposals at appropriate junctures along this scale. We then hypothesize that the degree of realism of participants' proposals tends to increase with age. This hypothesis is tested in Chapter 8.

DEGREE OF REBELLIOUSNESS

The years of adolescence have traditionally been pictured as a time of great turmoil involving "serious conflicts and rebellion against one's parents" (Offer & Church, 1991, p. 1148). Anna Freud's (1958, p. 260) description of the adolescent includes such features as "the feeling of oppression by the parents" and "impotent rages or active hates directed against the adult world." However, large-scale longitudinal investigations of adolescent development in recent decades have found the incidence of turmoil and of severe crisis to be rather low (Douvan & Adelson, 1966; Offer, 1969; Offer & Offer, 1968; Offer & Church, 1991).

And although [the youths in these studies] manifested mild forms of rebelliousness, primarily between the ages of 12 and 14, these episodes could in no way be interpreted as serious disturbances. These and other large survey studies of normal adolescents have led clinicians and researchers to realize that the traditional view of adolescence as a highly disturbed state is at best a vast overstatement; at worst, a gross distortion. Perhaps this traditional view reflects the danger of making wide generalizations from a relatively few case histories of disturbed individuals. (Nicholi, 1988, p. 640)

While planning the present study, we recognized that the data we would collect might enable us to perform a modest test of the notion of adolescent rebelliousness. Two ways of conducting such a test could involve (a) determining how far our interviewees' opinions deviated from the opinions of their parents or (b) determining the extent to which interviewees' opinions differed from the dominant opinions of adult society in general. The first of these options was obviously not available in the present study, since we had no information about the beliefs of the parents of our 136 respondents. We were thus obliged to adopt the second approach which we will refer to as *the societal standard.*

For present purposes, we have defined the societal standard as "the appraisal of a given behavior in terms of the adult society's dominant laws, regulations, or widespread customs." Under this definition, the behavior of the principal characters in all three of the cases used in the our study was wrong. That is, most American adults would judge copying other pupils' test answers to be cheating and, as such, immoral. Ingesting illicit drugs or peddling them to others is by definition against the law. So also are burglary and murder. Therefore, adolescent rebelliousness can be measured by the extent to which adolescents disagree with adults in considering such behaviors as wrongdoing.

The results of our testing this adolescent-rebellion hypothesis are reported in Chapter 14.

CONCLUSION

Four types of indicators of development between the years of late childhood and early adult status have been proposed in this chapter. The first type focuses on stages in the development of moral reasoning as postulated by Piaget and Kohlberg. In particular, Kohlberg's proposed phases of corrective justice have been considered appropriate to apply in the present study. The second type involves Lewin's notion of changes in cognitive differentiation, expansion, and organizational interdependence as indicators of development. The third type pictures mental growth as reflecting movement from a more fanciful to a more realistic conception of the world. The fourth views adolescent development from the vantage point of rebellion against the moral standards of adult society. The application of these four perspectives to the data gathered in the present study is described at various junctures in Part II.

Part II

Ways of Reasoning About Aims: From Child to Adult

Part I offered an eight-component framework for interpreting respondents' answers to questions about crimes and misdeeds. That framework provides the structure used in Part II for interpreting interviews that were conducted with 136 young people, ages 9 through 21, regarding three cases of misconduct.

The titles of the chapters that compose Part II and the central questions each chapter addresses are as follows:

Chapter 7: The Nature of the Interviews. Who were the people interviewed, and how were the interviews conducted?

Chapter 8: Proposed Sanctions and Aims. In the order of their popularity, which sanctions and which aims were proposed by respondents in the three cases of wrongdoing? What likenesses and differences in these choices appeared across age groups and gender groups and among individuals?

Chapter 9: Patterns of Causal Relationships—Linking Sanctions and Aims. What varieties of sanction-aim connections appeared in respondents' answers? What likenesses and differences in such connections were found across age and gender groups and among individuals?

Chapter 10: Overt Reasoning Styles: How did respondents compare with each other in their overt manner of reasoning?

Chapter 11: Conceptions of God and the Sanctity of Life: What did students' responses to Case 3 imply about the participants' conceptions of (1) God's role in daily affairs and (2) the propriety of imposing the death penalty on killers?

Chapter 12: Views of Imprisonment: How did respondents perceive the usefulness of detaining and imprisoning offenders for different types of wrongdoing?

Chapter 13: Empathy and Sympathy. In what circumstances did participants appear to emphasize or sympathize with wrongdoers or their victims?

Chapter 14: Drugs and the Law: What did this study reveal about the interviewees' attitudes regarding the use of illegal drugs and the appropriateness of laws governing drug use?

Chapter 15: Views of Retribution. In Case 3, what opinions did respondents express about satisfying the desire of the murder victim's family to see the felon severely punished?

Chapter 16: Lessons Learned. What principal findings derived from this study? What do the results offer for understanding moral development during the years of adolescence? What further investigations of adolescents' moral development might be appropriate?

7

The Nature of the Interviews

Individual interviews served as the means of gathering information about the aims young people intended when they recommended sanctions and treatments for wrongdoers. The purpose of this chapter is to explain the interview procedures and to describe the sample of respondents who took part in the investigation.

INTERVIEW GOALS AND PROCEDURES

The components of the interview method are described in the following sequence: (1) an ideal assessment plan and a practical compromise, (2) the choice of cases of wrongdoing, (3) an assessment problem, (4) steps in the conduct of interviews, (5) the interviewers, and (6) administering the interviews.

Ideal and Practical Assessment Plans

As we sought to devise a method for collecting young people's opinions, we recognized that the cognitive processes involved in people's suggestons of sanctions and treatments for misdeeds are very complex. Past research on decision-making in moral situations indicated that people's notions about suitable consequences for wrongdoing are influenced by a variety of complicated factors, including (1) the nature of the offense, (2) the moral principles that respondents apply to the case, (3) the conditions respondents adopt when deciding how a given principle should be applied, (4) the aims to be achieved by the sanctions, (5) the types of sanctions available at the time, (6) the genetic and environmental influences on people's beliefs about such matters, and more. If we wished to use interviews about cases of wrongdoing to produce a definitive picture of these variables, we would need to:

(a) Interview large samples of respondents who represented varied socio-economic, ethnic, and cultural traditions as well as both males and females of varied levels of intelligence, education, and life experiences.

(b) Include cases representing all possible types of wrongdoing and all likely influential conditions under which these sorts of wrongdoing would take place.

(c) Confront respondents with all possible—or at least all likely—types of sanctions and that could be applied in each kind of wrongdoing as well as all possible—or likely—aims that such consequences would be intended to produce.

To implement such an ideal plan, we would need to pose thousands of different cases to thousands of interviewees. That was clearly impossible. Thus, to render the investigation practical, we fashioned a very limited compromise plan which involved:

(a) Interviewing at least 15 males and 15 females at each of four age levels (9, 14, 17, and 21), with the respondents drawn from within a single county in Northern California.

(b) Presenting interviewees with three cases of wrongdoing that concerned offenders ages 9, 16, and 23.

(c) Asking interviewees to propose sanctions and aims for the offenders in the three cases.

(d) Confronting respondents with two additional potential sanctions and four additional aims in each case, then asking whether they would subscribe to those sanctions and aims.

Because of the restricted nature of this plan, the results reported in Part II do not pretend to furnish an exhaustive description of people's modes of decision making in moral situations. Instead, the results are intended to show how the responses of 136 students to three cases of wrongdoing can be analyzed according to the framework depicted in Part I. The likenesses and differences across age groups, among individuals, and between genders revealed in the present study can serve as tendencies or hypotheses to be tested out in future studies with other types of respondents, other types of misdeeds, and other sanctions and aims.

The Choice of Cases

Each interview session consisted of an interviewer describing three cases of wrongdoing and then asking the respondent a series of questions about the incidents. The following line of reasoning guided the selection of those cases.

Time Restrictions. It would have been desirable to pose a wide diversity of crimes and misdeeds for students to judge in order to reveal the ways different conditions in various cases affected respondents' judgments. However, from our pilot tryout of interviews we concluded that the types of young people participating in the study would, on the average, be willing to concentrate seriously on the task we posed for perhaps no longer than one-half hour. Within such a time period, the number of cases that could adequately be discussed turned out to be three.

Ages of Offenders. A subquestion we wished to investigate was as follows: Do respondents judge offenders who are near their own age in a manner different from the manner in which they judge offenders of other age levels? We sought to approximate the age levels of respondents (9, 14, 17, 21) by making the transgressors in the three instances of wrongdoing a 9 year old in Case A, two 16 year olds in Case B, and a 23 year old in Case C.

The Gender of Offenders. A further subquestion in which we were interested was: Do students tend to judge offenders of their own sex differently than they judge offenders of the opposite sex? To derive at least a hint about the answer to this query, we identified the offender in Case A as a girl, the two transgressors in Case B as a boy and a girl, and the offender in Case C as a man. In analyzing responses, we could then compare the sanctions and aims suggested by the 69 females in our sample with the those proposed by the 67 males.

Types of Wrongdoing. We also wanted the cases to represent three kinds of misdeeds that illustrated different levels of harm. Our purpose in setting such a requirement was to identify ways respondents might differentiate their sanctions and aims in relation to types of transgressions and to the extent of damage done.

A further requirement was that the misdeeds should be ones rather common at the age levels of the offenders so that respondents would find the offenses familiar and realistic. If we had used unusual, exotic transgressions, interviewees might have had difficulty generating relevant sanctions and aims, and they might have been distracted by the surprising and perhaps outlandish characteristics of the acts.

To fulfill these types-of-wrongdoing criteria, we selected the following offenses: cheating in school for the 9-year-old girl in Case A, peddling illicit drugs for the pair of 16 year olds in Case B, and armed robbery combined with murder for the 23-year-old man in Case C.

When the cases were presented during the interviews, they were worded in the following manner:

(Case A) A 9-year-old, fourth-grade girl was caught copying another pupil's answers on a mathematics test. This was the third time in the past two months that she had copied someone else's work and handed it in as her own. Among her classmates, this girl had a reputation for telling lies.

(Case B) A 16-year-old boy and his girlfriend, who was the same age, were arrested for giving illegal drugs to a high-school friend in exchange for tickets to a rock concert. As far as the police could find out, this was the first time the two teenagers had ever given drugs to someone else, but they did admit that they sometimes used illegal drugs themselves.

(Case C) In a jury trial, a 23-year-old man was convicted of stabbing a
woman to death when she caught him trying to rob her house in
the middle of the night. A police officer who was a witness at the
trial reported that the burglar had also been stealing from other
homes over the past several months.

Case Conditions. When people suggest a consequence to be faced by a wrongdoer, their selection of a consequence is usually influenced by conditions
particular to the case at hand. The two conditions we included in our three cases
were the age of the offenders and their history of similar misdeeds. If we had
wished to offer more elaborate depictions of the cases, we could have added such
features as the offenders' socioeconomic status, family background, mental
ability, ethnic origin, reaction to being apprehended (such as acting contrite
rather than antagonistic), and more. However, for three reasons we chose not to
provide detailed descriptions. First, we wanted to learn how readily interviewees
would recommend sanctions or treatments on the basis of no more information
than appeared in the two or three sentences of the case descriptions. Second, we
wanted the portrayals to be brief and simple so they could be easily grasped and
remembered during the interview. Third, we decided that extensive, complex
descriptions would take up time that might more effectively be used by the
respondents' offering detailed opinions about sanctions and aims.

An Assessment Problem

From past experience we recognized that it would be insufficient simply to ask
a respondent, "What consequence would you propose for the wrongdoer, and what
would you expect that consequence would accomplish?" Although such a
question could indeed elicit an answer, that answer might not reveal the entire
complexity of the cognitive lenses through which the individual perceived that
particular case of wrongdoing. In other words, the respondent's answer might
often leave unsaid such additional components of the sanction/aim linkage as
multiple sanctions, multiple aims, and concomitant effects. For this reason, we
not only asked for participants to propose consequences and aims, but we
followed the original question with this sort of query:

> "Often people have more than one purpose in mind for the consequences they
> suggest for wrongdoers. I've got four other purposes listed on this sheet of
> paper. In addition to the suggestion you gave, would you have any of these four
> purposes in mind?" (Interviewer presents the additional options, then asks
> about each option:) "Would that be a purpose you would include? If not, why
> not?"

In suggesting these additional aims, our intention was to help interviewees
bring to consciousness other purposes they hoped to achieve but had not included
in their first answer. Our results suggested that this was true for almost all of

the participants. Nearly every interviewee did add one or more of the aims we listed. However, even when they said they subscribed to our additional aims, we were still left wondering whether those purposes might be ones the interviewees had adopted only at that moment, ones they did not have in mind earlier. In other words, had our suggestion of further aims served to expand their original causal relationship structure so that what we were now assessing was something a bit different than the mental structure they had brought to the interview? This meant that we were faced with the following familiar and apparently intractable problem: The act of evaluating a phenomenon always alters to some degree the phenomenon that the act is designed to measure. In recognition of this problem, our interpretation of results throughout the chapters of Part II has been to qualified with the following caveat:

> The reported results reflect the patterns of sanction/aim structures respondents expressed during the conduct of the interviews; these patterns are likely very similar to, but not necessarily identical to, the ones respondents had in mind prior to the interviews.

Steps in the Conduct of Interviews

The following description of the phases of the interview process is presented in two columns. The left column displays the series of questions posed for respondents to answer. The right column tells the type of information each question was designed to elicit. (The full script from which interviewers operated is reproduced in the Appendix.) The pattern of questions for the three cases was identical. However, the type of wrongdoing, the central characters, and the potential sanctions and aims differed from one case to another. The following example concerns the case of the 16 year olds who traded drugs for rock concert tickets.

The Questions	The Desired Information
Do you think the boy and girl did anything wrong? If so, what was it?	The respondent's belief about what constitutes misconduct in such a situation.
What do you think should be done about the boy? What should happen to him?	Sanctions or treatments considered appropriate for the boy in such a situation.
How do you think your suggestion would help? What good might it do?	The aim the respondent hopes to accomplish by the sanction or treatment.
What do you think should be done about the girl? What should happen to her?	Sanctions or treatments the respondent regards as appropriate for the girl in such a situation.

Other people we interviewed had other suggestions about what to do with the boy and girl. Are these as good as the suggestion you gave? (The options were: send them to a drug rehabilitation center; commit them to juvenile detention hall for six months).	Whether the respondent would subscribe to other specified sanctions. Why or why not?
I have four other purposes here. In addition to the purpose or aim you mentioned, would any of these four be ones you would agree with? (The aims were: make the teenagers stop giving drugs to others; make them do something to help the community; teach them to be responsible; make sure the law is obeyed.)	Whether the respondent would subscribe to other specified aims. Why or why not?

If students failed to explain their reasons for agreeing or disagreeing with a proposed sanction or aim, interviewers asked them why they adopted such a position. Hence, the interviews elicited the participants' explanations of the rationales on which they founded their answers.

The Interviewers

Six interviewers were selected from a pool of interested graduate students enrolled in a fifth-year teacher-preparation program at a university in Northern California. They were chosen on the basis of the high quality of their classwork and their interviewing ability as demonstrated during an earlier class assignment. The six were divided into two groups. Each group's leader took responsibility for contacting principals at local elementary and high schools as well as professors at the university to secure permission to enter classrooms and solicit student participation. One group interviewed 9 and 21 year olds. The other group interviewed 14 and 17 year olds.

Administering the Interviews

In the selected classrooms, the group leaders explained to students that "We are interviewing people of different ages to learn what they think would happen to people who are involved in wrongdoing. If you are interested in this activity, please take one of these permission forms home for your parent or guardian to sign, and bring the form back tomorrow."

This procedure proved successful in attracting subjects who wished to participate in the project, who were able to obtain their parent's or guardian's permission, and who returned the permission forms on time. The sampling process, therefore, involved a large measure of self-selection.

Among the 136, all but five 21-year-olds were currently enrolled in an educational institution. Therefore, because the great majority were students, throughout the following chapters we apply the following terms interchangeably when referring to the 136—*students, respondents, participants, subjects,* and *interviewees.*

The interviewees totaled 136, distributed as follows:

Age	Females	Males	Total
9	18	15	33
14	18	18	36
17	18	16	34
21	15	18	33
Total	69	67	136

CONCLUSION

The interviews conducted with 136 young people, who ranged in age from 9 through 21, were designed to reveal the sanctions they would recommend for the offenders in three cases of wrongdoing. The respondents were also asked what purposes they hoped would be served by such consequences. Audio-recordings of the interviews served as the data to be analyzed according to the framework described in Part I of this volume. The results of that analysis are reported in the remaining chapters of Part II.

8

Proposed Sanctions and Aims

The purpose of this chapter is to identify types of sanctions and aims proposed by the 136 interviewees and to answer a series of questions about their choices. The questions concern the popularity of different choices, the extent to which respondents' recommendations were spontaneous rather than elicited by means of probing inquiries, and the characteristics of the three cases of wrongdoing that appeared to influence the selection of sanctions and aims. The first third of the chapter focuses on sanctions, the second third on aims, and the final third on interpretations of the results.

TYPES OF SANCTIONS RECOMMENDED

For the full sample of 136 interviewees, the following discussion addresses the popularity of different sanctions, individual styles of presenting sanction/aim combinations, and the sequence in which sanctions were proposed. After the results of the entire sample are reviewed, we consider age and gender trends in the participants' proposals.

We may recall that the task posed for each of the 136 consisted of an interviewer first describing a case of apparent wrongdoing, then asking a series of questions about the case. This same process was carried out for each of the three cases. The questions formed two groups. The first group was composed of three open-ended queries about the case under consideration, with participants free to volunteer any sanctions and aims they wished. The second group comprised eight questions—two about specific kinds of sanctions and four about specific kinds of aims, with respondents asked to say whether they agreed or disagreed with each of those options. In brief, the first cluster was designed to draw forth *volunteered* answers, whereas the second group was intended to evoke responses to *probing* questions. The following presentation begins with the volunteered answers, then turns to the probed replies.

Volunteered Sanctions

The initial three questions asked in the interview about each case can be illustrated with Case 1, that of the nine-year-old girl who had copied another pupil's answers on a mathematics test.

Question 1: "Do you think the girl did anything wrong? If so, what was it?"

Question 2: "What do you think should be done about the girl? I mean, what should happen to her?"

Question 3: "You've suggested that (*interviewer repeats consequence the subject suggested*). How do you think that would help? I mean, what good do you think that might do?"

Table 8-1
Sanctions Volunteered in Three Cases of Wrongdoing
(N = 136, in percentages)

Type of Sanction	Case 1 math test	Case 2 drugs	Case 3 rob & kill
Imprisoning, detaining	4	34	82
Personal counseling	16	21	15
Delegating sanction responsibility	35	15	2
Assigning unfavorable evaluation	22	1	
Assigning labor	4	13	4
Requiring task repetition	18		
Executing—put to death			17
Educating	5	10	1
Warning, threatening	5	10	
Limiting activities	7	7	
Confiscating possessions		11	2
Transferring	13		
Allowing probation		10	
Banishing	7	1	
Limiting movement	5	4	
Suspending	3	4	
Investigating offender's background	3	1	3
Limiting social contact	1	2	
Censuring privately	2	2	
Monitoring offender's activities	1	2	
Declining to offer a sanction		4	2
Maintaining a record of the offense			1
Censuring publicly	1		
Requiring compensation for victims	1		4
Ostracizing			1

The obvious objectives of the questions were to discover (1) whether the respondent thought the described incident involved any wrongdoing, (2) what sanctions the respondent thought would be appropriate, and (3) what aims such sanctions would be expected to achieve. Table 8-1 displays the array of consequences the 136 participants volunteered in reply to the second question, the one focusing on types of sanctions. The labels identifying types of sanctions are ones from the sanction typology in Chapter 2. The numbers in the columns represent the percentages of students citing each type of sanction. Within each column the totals exceed 100% because many participants volunteered more than one consequence to be faced by the offender in the case. The following discussion addresses these results for each case in turn.

Case 1: Cheating on a Test

The incident was described to participants as:

A 9-year-old, fourth-grade girl was caught copying another pupil's answers on a mathematics test. This was the third time in the past two months that she had copied someone else's work and handed it in as her own. Among her classmates, this girl had a reputation for telling lies.

The most popular suggestion (35%) was that of delegating to the girl's parents the responsibility for deciding what consequences she should face. That suggestion was often combined with another of the more popular proposals: (a) assigning an unfavorable evaluation in the form of a failing grade on the test (22%), (b) requiring the girl to take the test again (repeat the task, 18%), and (c) talking over the problem with the girl (personal counseling 16%; warning 5%, censuring privately 2%). Other participants recommended teaching the girl how to solve the problems on her own (educating 5%) or investigating the child's background to learn why she had copied (3%).

Some participants would transfer her to another part of the classroom (13%) or limit her activities (7%) and her freedom to interact with classmates (limiting movement 5%, banishing from the others 7%, suspending from class 3%, limiting social contact 1%). No one proposed corporal punishment.

All 136 respondents believed that the girl's act was an instance of wrongdoing, and all 136 were willing to propose consequences she should experience.

One important weakness of statistical summaries, such as the one displayed in Table 8-1, is that they fail to reveal the diverse patterns of the interviewees' reasoning processes that led to those statistics. As a means of compensating for this shortcoming, we offer the following selection of quotations from interviews to illustrate various ways students phrased their answers when asked what they would do about the 9-year-old girl. Each quotation describes the sanctions as well as the aims the respondent hoped would be achieved by those sanctions. (The number in brackets at the end of each quotation identifies the age of the respondent.)

(*Detaining*) "I think she should get held back a grade in school, so she'll stay back and learn, and that will help her know how to do the work herself when she gets into higher grades." [9]

(*Repeating the task, Transferring*) "She should do the test over, and the next time she does a test she should be far away from other people so she can't copy. Then if she can't copy, she'll have to know the answers, and that means she'll have to use her brain, so if they put her a distance away from the others for a while, she'll start learning her math." [9]

(*Limiting activities*) "The girl needs punishment—loss of privileges, like stay in at recess. That way she'll learn if she does something wrong she'll not be able to do something she enjoys very much." [14]

(*Assigning unfavorable evaluation, Assigning labor*) "Give her a couple of demerits and have her copy some stuff out of a dictionary. That'll make her know she did something wrong and she'll stop." [14]

(*Delegating sanction responsibility, Personal counseling*) "Her parents should be notified. Or have her talk with the principal to find out what the problem is. Maybe she didn't understand the math, or she didn't have time to do it, or something else was wrong. That might help her see that she can understand the math, if that's been the problem." [14]

(*Transferring, Delegating sanction responsibility*) "Next time she takes a test they should separate her from the rest of the class so she doesn't copy, and her parents should talk to her about what's wrong with copying. That might teach her not to copy in the future—but then it might not. It depends on how she feels about herself." [14]

(*Detaining, Requiring task repetition*) "She should have a detention for two weeks, and during that time she should be given a quiz every day on math to see if she's really learning it. A lot of people don't like to stay after school so she'll not want to stay in, but when she goes home at night she'll study so she can pass the quizzes and really learn the math." [17]

(*Assigning unfavorable evaluation*) "Give her an *F* on the test. By lowering her grade it would show that what she had done was wrong; and if you do that sort of thing, you get punished for it. Also, her parents should be notified." [17]

(*Transferring, Delegating sanction responsibility, Detaining, Personal counseling*) "They should seat her in a different desk so they can better see whether she cheats next time. And if she cheats again, then report her to her parents. If they didn't do anything about it, then maybe they could enforce something, like she has to stay in at recess if she does it again. But one thing they should do before doing any of those things is to talk with the girl and find out why she did it—like she needed attention or didn't understand the math. Talking to her might show her that someone cares and not just that they are going to punish her. Then if she keeps on cheating, you'd do the other things— change her seat, call her parents—to show there's an authority over her that she sometimes has to obey." [17]

(*Warning, Detaining, Requiring task repetition*) "Give her a warning the first time. The second time she did it, I'd make her stay in at recess time for a week, and she'd have to redo the test. That should teach her it's not right to copy test answers." [17]

(*Requiring compensating apology, Educating*) "She should apologize to the student she copied from. Then they should remedy the problem. If she has trouble with math, make sure she understands the work so she doesn't have to resort to copying. Correct her problem rather than giving harsh punishment. If she apologizes, she'll learn it's incorrect to copy in the first place; and then if she learns how to do her math, she won't have to copy in the future." [17]

(*Delegating sanction responsibility*) "Call the parents and have them tell the girl what she was doing wrong, because a lot of times kids will believe the parents more than they will the teacher. So the child will find out that cheating is wrong and that she should learn to do the math on her own." [21]

(*Transferring, Banishing*) "Since she's copied several times, you've got a problem there. Maybe change her to a different school. Or put her by herself. Somewhat isolate her, but not isolate her to the point of embarrassment, but just make it harder to copy again. That would help her learn that she has to study and do her work herself." [21]

Case 2: Trading Drugs

The drug incident was described in the following way:

A 16-year-old boy and his girl friend, who was the same age, were arrested for giving illegal drugs to a high-school friend in exchange for tickets to a rock concert. As far as the police could find out, this was the first time the two teenagers had ever given drugs to someone else, but they did admit that they sometimes used illegal drugs themselves.

Over one-third (34%) of the 136 interviewees recommended some form of detention or imprisonment for both of the 16 year olds. A recommendation of personal counseling (21%), a group drug education program (10%), or a severe warning (10%) was often combined with detention. A smaller number of respondents (15%) would delegate to the teenagers' parents the responsibility for imposing punishment. Others would assign the offenders to community service projects (13%), put the pair on probation (10%), or confiscate the teenagers' rock concert tickets (11%). Fewer still (7%) would "ground" the pair, restricting their activities by requiring them to stay at home when they otherwise could have been free to socialize with their peers. Four percent would suspend both the boy and girl from school for a period of time.

An additional 4% declined to suggest sanctions because they thought there was nothing wrong with trading illicit drugs for tickets. As one student said, "There was no harm done. It was the kids' own business." The remaining 96% of the participants considered the drug trading wrong, either because "it's against the law" or because drugs are physically and psychologically destructive.

Various ways participants expressed their opinions are portrayed in the following quotations:

(*Imprisoning*) "They should go to jail for about a year or so. Hopefully they won't do it any more. Next time they'll buy their own concert tickets." [9]

(*Assigning labor*) "Like community service. Like picking up litter for a couple of weekends, maybe. That way the next few weekends they couldn't do anything they liked, so the next time they thought about trading drugs they wouldn't do it because they wouldn't want to lose their free time." [9]

(*Imprisoning, Assigning labor*) "Maybe they should go to jail. Or be punished somehow, like I'd make them clean up the road or rake leaves or something like that until they have enough money to pay back the money for the tickets. Then give that money to the sheriff or somebody. That would teach them never to do that again." [9]

(*Imprisoning*) "Jail. They'd find out how bad jail is, and they'd quit drugs because they wouldn't want to go there anymore." [14]

(*Confiscating possessions, Assigning labor*) "They should be fined and then have to do some community activity. That could discourage them from doing drugs. If they're fined they might not have the money, or their parents would have to come up with it, so they'd not want to get caught doing that again." [17]

(*No sanctions*) "I don't think either the boy or girl did anything wrong, so nothing should happen to them. Using drugs is their own affair. Let them go or just take them home to their parents." [17]

(*Delegating sanction responsibility, Educating*) "They are no longer children, so they know what they are doing, and they have to take responsibility for their own actions, especially at age 16. And their parents should be told. Their parents should take action in training them. If I were the parent, I'd ground the kids until they proved that they really have thought about it. I might send to them to a Christian camp for while. The only hope through all this is Jesus and to live for him. When they do things like using drugs, it's really a cry for help. If they have something proper to live for, like for Jesus, then it gives them hope and they no longer act those ways." [17]

(*Delegating sanction responsibility, Allowing probation, Personal counseling*) "I'd notify their parents so they might help, and I'd give the kids probation for a month and talk with them. By talking with them, maybe you could find out why they did it, like maybe they needed money, so you could help them get a job or something. With probation, if anything like that happens again, then they'd go to jail or juvenile hall." [17]

(*Monitoring offenders' activities, Assigning labor, Personal counseling, Allowing probation*) "They should be given drug testing, just to make sure they're clean, and then assigned to community service. Also they should have personal counseling so they understand what's wrong with drugs, and be put on probation for six months." [17]

(*Personal counseling, Educating with new activities, Confiscating possessions*) "I'm not sure the police system or the juvenile hall thing really works. It's been proven so many times that it just encourages kids to do something more drastic. I think both these kids need counseling. They should go into some sort of program. And if they're taking drugs, they should do something to get off drugs, like join some organization where they won't be bored, because that's the reason they take drugs—they're bored. As for a punishment—well, that's sort of difficult—but they need to take a good look at what they're doing. That usually doesn't reform people, I know, but they need somebody to sit them down and talk to them and get them to think. Maybe they should be fined. I don't think locking them in jail is going to work. The fine might pay for the counseling. But the best thing is to get them involved in some kind of big-brother/sister program. They need a project after school and community sponsored things." [17]

(*Investigating offenders' backgrounds, Warning them*) "I guess just question them about where they got the drugs, since somebody must be selling drugs, and find out who it is. They shouldn't be sent to juvenile hall or anything like that. So just talk to the boy and girl to find out where the drugs came from. Hopefully it would help by finding out who was selling drugs to high school students and then put a stop to that. Maybe getting the boy and girl scared a little so they would realize it was illegal and they wouldn't do it anymore." [21]

(*Limiting activities, Delegating sanction responsibility*) "Ground them for a while. I mean, inform their parents, and the parents would probably ground them and scare them. With that punishment, the boy and girl probably wouldn't trade drugs again." [21]

(*Limiting activities*) "They shouldn't get to go to the concert. It probably wouldn't keep them from trading drugs again, but they didn't earn the right to go to the concert the legal way, so it would make me feel better to know they didn't get to go to the concert. You could tell them it's wrong, but I don't think that would do any good. They're 16 years old, so they'll probably just keep doing what they want to do no matter what you tell them." [21]

(*Warning, Threatening, Delegating sanction responsibility*) "Give them a warning for the first time. Put a good scare in them by having the police arrest them, put handcuffs on, take them to juvenile hall a little while, and call their parents to come and get them. Hopefully their parents would really consider it wrong and not just a juvenile prank. That should make them not want to fool with drugs again." [21]

(A detailed analysis of respondents' opinions about the status of illicit drugs in contemporary American society is provided in Chapter 14—"Drugs and the Law.")

Case 3: Robbing and Killing

The interviewer offered this description of the third case:

In a jury trial, a 23-year-old man was convicted of killing a woman when she caught him trying to rob her house in the middle of the night. A police officer who was a witness at the trial reported that the burglar had also been stealing from other homes over the past several months.

The great majority of interviewees (82%) would imprison the offender for an extended period of years. In the opinion of many respondents, the prison sentence should be for life. For some respondents, imprisonment should be accompanied by personal counseling (15%) in an effort to rehabilitate the burglar or by work assignments (4%). Instead of just imprisoning the felon, 17% would put him to death (with 3% first imprisoning the burglar for a period of time before executing him). Two percent declined to suggest sanctions because they could not decide what consequences would be appropriate. An additional 2% said they would leave the decision up to the courts.

Typical ways students cast their views are demonstrated in the following examples:

(*Executing*) "He should get the electric chair, and then he wouldn't be allowed to do those things any more." [9]

(*Imprisoning*) "He should be put in jail for the rest of his life. (pause) Well, not until he dies or anything, but long enough until he learns not to do that any more. Maybe for about five years so he'd see other people in there too who'd done things, and he'd decide to be nice and not steal and stuff." [9]

(*Imprisoning, Personal counseling*} "He should be put in jail—at least 10 years—and put under counseling, because most people who do those things can be helped with counseling. They could find out if there was a reason why he was doing it—like if he just suddenly did it or there was some underlying reason. Putting him in jail will show him that he's done something wrong. There he'll be watched and not be out on the streets. Counseling will help him understand why he was doing these things and maybe get rehabilitated." [14]

(*Imprisoning*) "He should be thrown in jail. Well, he murdered and robbed, so maybe in prison for 20 years. It might teach him that when he gets out not to rob houses any more, because he doesn't want to go to prison again." [14]

(*Imprisoning*) "I'd sentence him for murder and then add some time for burglarizing the houses. I'd probably go for around a three-year sentence. It might make him realize that laws should be obeyed, and when you do that kind of stuff it doesn't pay." [17]

(*Imprisoning, Executing*) "Jail for the rest of his life. But the jails are pretty crowded, so maybe they should just kill him and save money. If he ever got out, he'd probably do it again; and if he's in jail for the rest of his life, it takes money from the taxpayers. so you might as well just kill him." [17]

(*Executing*) "The death penalty. If he's sentenced to death he wouldn't be allowed to kill others, and it would discourage others from doing it. It also means he has to pay the penalty for killing. I'd feel differently if it was self-defense, so there are certain cases in which killing is excusable, but not in this case where he's robbing her house and just kills her." [17]

(*Personal counseling*) "Instead of having the death penalty, I would prefer the man be counseled, if that's possible. It would hopefully correct his behavior. I don't know if that's possible, but that would be the purpose." [17]

(*Personal counseling, Imprisoning*) "He needs to be counseled and needs to have some time in jail. I think human lives are really important and that anyone who takes a life should be put in jail for a while   You know, they're never put in there for very long   He should be put in there for a year or two, not just because he stole, but because he took a life. And if we don't have enough jails, we should make more. The counseling might help him for his motives for doing things like that, and the jail would just make him responsible for his acts." [17]

(*Imprisoning*) "He should go to jail for 10 years for killing the woman, and then one year more for each house he robbed. That would stop him from robbing other people, and obviously he couldn't kill anybody if he's in jail." [17]

(*Executing, Imprisoning, Educating*) "I don't know if execution would be the right thing. In many cases it might be. If he has a series of arrests and he's a violent person and a menace to society, I think some action should be taken to get him off the streets.   Or if he's a real bad person, then get him off the earth. I don't think two wrongs make a right. You should show people that killing is wrong, but I don't think you need to kill him to show other people that killing is wrong. So, well, I don't quite know what to do. (pause) But I think jail, not for a given length of time but (pause) well, there should be a minimum time. But if they're not worthy of coming out, then there should be a series of psychological tests to see if some kind of rehab or education in the jail has worked. Give them some kind of skill and rehabilitate him from his aggressive nature. (pause) But I really do want to say kill him, because he wasted a life and he should pay by giving up his own. Yet if there's hope he might be rehabilitated, then maybe that's what should be done. But he should have a psychiatric evaluation, maybe after 15 years. If he's really a bad guy, keep him in for life. And if he's a particularly nasty guy, like Charles Manson, then kill him." [21]

(*Imprisoning, Personal counseling*) "He should have a punishment. Oh, I don't know what exactly. (pause) Well, he murdered and not in self-defense, and that's pretty big. So I don't know. I think he should go to jail. But murdering is so big. Yet I don't think he should be given one of those sentences for 20 years and out in five years for good behavior. He should have counseling in jail. I think maybe he just got scared and killed her. Either that or he could be psychotic. I think he should be in there a long time and learning. Maybe he's been stealing because he hasn't had work. I guess it's not to reform him in his values or (pause) well, maybe try to change his ideas about society. Gee, I don't really know." [21]

(*Imprisoning, Confiscating possessions*) "They should send him away to prison for a while. It would let him know it's against the law to kill people. Maybe they should take away everything he's got after he gets out of prison.

Somebody's going to have to pay for what happened, so why shouldn't he?"
[21]

(*Imprisoning*) "I'd give him five to 10 years in jail. The immediate purpose
would be to get him off the streets, making the community safer. And the ideal
purpose would be that he would become a better citizen. But then he might just
go before the parole board and say, 'I'm born again. I've found God. I'm sorry I
sinned,' which of course is a crock. I don't believe it." [21]

(*Executing, Imprisoning, Assigning labor*) "Capital punishment. That way
he'll never do it again. Or instead of that, lock him up. But actually instead of
just locking criminals up in jail, I think they should have criminals indirectly
help the community, like cleaning up the place, but under guard. People who kill
somebody should never be set free in the community again, never.   So if this
man has taken a life, he should spend his whole life doing something that helps
people, like community service under supervision instead of just taking up space
in jail for years and years and not doing any good." [21]

(*Imprisoning, Educatiiong*) "I'd put him in prison for 20 years and try to
educate him so he'll become aware that what he had done was wrong and
ultimately that would stop him from doing it again. But even if he is truly
reformed, who's going to hire a murderer after he gets out. Basically his life is
through from here on out." [21]

(*Executing*) "He killed her on purpose, so they should execute him. There's a
sort of contract in society about how people should act, and he broke that
contract, so he's a burden on society. He's old enough where he knows right
from wrong.   And if he's executed, then other people will know that the
punishment is death, so he's not going to be just sitting around in jail a while
and then get out. He'll be an example to others." [21]

Probed Sanctions

After students volunteered sanctions in a case, they were asked their opinion
about the desirability of two other possible consequences. As explained earlier,
prior studies of people's moral reasoning demonstrated that merely asking them
to cite sanctions for an instance of wrongdoing fell far short of revealing their
complete views of such matters. Probing their opinions about other specific
sanctions could provide further information about their beliefs. Although asking
about only two additional sanctions would fail to disclose the entire array of
respondents' views, it could nevertheless divulge at least a small segment of that
array. The sanction options selected for each case were chosen to fulfill two
criteria: First, they should be *realistic* rather than exotic, in that each of them
could be found in the everyday world; in other words, such options should be
ones that might reasonably be invoked—at least occasionally—in situations
involving the age levels and types of misdeeds represented by the three cases.
Second, the selected options should be *varied* in that they should differ markedly

from each other in the kinds of experiences they impose on the transgressors; in effect, the options should represent contrasts in sanction types.

As the interviews demonstrated, the probing strategy not only elicited participants' opinions about the specific sanctions identified in the interviewer's questions, but in some instances the strategy also induced participants to suggest additional consequences for the transgressor in the case. In other words, probing stimulated some students to offer afterthoughts that represented suggestions they had failed to express when answering the original open-ended questions.

Table 8-2 summarizes both the probed and afterthought opinions of the 136 interviewees for the three cases of wrongdoing.

Case 1: Cheating on a Test

In the case of the girl who copied test answers, the two sanctions to which respondents were asked to react were:

> "She should be given a good spanking."
> "She should be warned by the teacher not to cheat and lie again or she then would be in very serious trouble."

If, by chance, a student had already proposed one of these options in answer to the original open-ended question about sanctions, then the following alternative possibility was provided so there would be two probed responses from every participant.

> "She should have to stay after school every day for a week and write 'I will not cheat again' 500 times each day."

This third option was necessary in 30 (22%) of the 136 interviews, in each instance as a substitute for the "warned by the teacher" consequence.

As indicated in Table 8-2, more than one-third (38%) of the interviewees rejected both of the suggested sanctions. However, 34% agreed that warning the girl once again might be a good idea; but the remaining 66% believed that since past warnings had not succeeded, giving another warning would be wasted effort. Nine percent agreed that the girl deserved a spanking; however, all of them stipulated that it was the responsibility of parents rather than school personnel to administer corporal punishment. Eleven percent (half of the 30 who were asked the question) favored keeping the girl after school to write on the blackboard the vow about not cheating.

Eleven additional sanction types were evoked as afterthoughts from 33 participants later in the interview. All of the add-on consequences were types other respondents had originally proposed in answer to the open-ended questions.

Case 2: Trading Drugs

The two principal options to which participants were asked to react in the case of the pair of 16 year olds were:

Table 8-2
Probed Sanctions in Three Cases of Wrongdoing
(N = 136, in percentages)

Type of Sanction	Case 1 math test	Case 2 drugs	Case 3 rob & kill
Accepting proposed sanctions			
Counseling (drug rehabilitation treatment)		54	
Assigning labor (community service)		32	
Warning	34		
Imprisoning (juvenile hall, prison)		18	1
Delegating sanction responsibility (God)			11
Corporal punishment (spanking)	9		
Detaining (kept after school)	11		
Executing (put to death)			10
No probed sanctions accepted	38	21	65
Offering afterthought sanctions			
Assigning labor			4
Delegating sanction responsibility	4	1	
Banishing	4		
Suspending	3	1	
Assigning unfavorable evaluation	4	1	
Monitoring offender's activities	1	3	
Transferring	2	1	
Limiting movement (grounding)	3		
Ostracizing, withholding privileges	1	1	
Confiscating possessions		2	
Limiting activities	1		
Requiring task repetition	1		
Requiring compensation			1
Personal counseling			1
Allowing probation	1		

"They should be put in a drug rehabilitation program that's supposed to make people quit using drugs."

"Both should be put in juvenile hall for six months."

If the participant had already proposed one of these options earlier in the interview, then the following choice was substituted:

"They should each have to give 100 hours of community service, like maybe doing gardening at a hospital or an old-folks home."

Table 8-2 shows that more than half (54%) of the participants favored some form of drug counseling. Nearly one-third (32%) would assign the pair to community service. Only 18% would recommend committing the teenagers to juvenile hall. (Respondents' perceptions of juvenile detention facilities are analyzed at some length in Chapter 12—"Views of Imprisonment.")

The probing technique also drew seven kinds of afterthoughts from 14 of the participants. The afterthoughts included closely monitoring the teenagers' future activities (3%), confiscating their concert tickets (2%), transferring them to different schools (1%), and suspending them from school (1%).

Case 3: Robbing and Killing

The two initial probed choices offered to respondents in Case 3 were:

"He should be put to death."
"I don't have to decide. God will know what to do."

The substitute choice provided for respondents who had originally suggested either of these initial options was:

"He should be put in prison for a year or two."

As indicated in Table 8-2, nearly two-thirds (65%) of the 136 students declined to accept either of the probed options. Eleven percent said that leaving the matter up to God would probably be a good solution; however, several of them felt that the felon should be incarcerated temporarily until God acted. Ten percent were in favor of putting the man to death. When this 10% is added to the 17% who recommended execution in their answer to the original open-ended question, it is seen that over one-quarter of the group—27%—ultimately endorsed the death penalty. (A detailed analysis of participants' replies to both the God and death penalty questions is provided in Chapter 11—"Conceptions of God and the Sanctity of Life.") The option of imprisoning the man for one or two years was accepted by only 1% of the respondents (2 people out of 28 who were presented the third option). Those who rejected the short prison term said that one or two years was too brief a time to represent fair punishment or to protect the public by keeping the killer off the streets.

The probing segment of the interview brought forth only four afterthoughts from 8 respondents. The most popular of these choices (4%) would require the offender to engage in constructive labor while imprisoned.

Age Comparisons of Sanction Choices

As explained earlier, one of our principal motives in conducting this study was to learn what age differences, if any, would be revealed over the years of adolescence in the sanctions and aims the 136 young people recommended when they judged cases of misconduct. Our method of identifying differences consisted of two steps: (a) constructing 18 tables of the sanctions and aims proposed by each age group in terms of the typological categories described in Chapter 2 and (b) inspecting the tables to identify possible age trends. That process prepared us to offer the following pair of observations about sanctions.

1. *Within each age group there was considerable diversity of opinion regarding the sanctions to apply.* An initial question we asked was: To what extent did people within an age group agree with each other on sanctions? The possible answers could range from extreme agreement (all respondents chose precisely the same sanction) to extreme disagreement (no two respondents chose the same sanction). As indicated in Table 8-3, the actual range of selections fell about midway between these two polar positions, at least for the first two cases. In effect, there was notable disagreement within each age group, and the extent of this disagreement was similar from one group to another. Hence, no age trends appeared. However, it is apparent that within every age group there was a higher level of consensus about the consequences the burglar should suffer than there was about suitable sanctions in the other two cases; nearly all respondents concurred that the 23-year-old felon should be either imprisoned or put to death.

2. *Age trends in the choice of particular sanctions were very rare.* Our second question was: What relationship, if any, obtained between age and the number of respondents advocating a particular sanction? In other words, did the number of respondents selecting an option systematically increase or decrease with advancing age? We answered this question at two levels of confidence labeled *an evident trend* and *a possible trend.*

A trend was considered *evident* if (a) the difference between the number of respondents at age 9 and 21 was 9 people or more and (b) the number of people in the two in-between age levels—14 and 17—was at or between those at ages 9 and 21. An example of an *evident trend* is the sanction of "detaining the offender" in the case of the girl who copied test answers. In the probing segment of the interview, the number of respondents who would keep the girl in after school was 12 at age nine, 7 at fourteen, 3 at seventeen, and 2 at age twenty-one.

A trend was considered *possible* if (*a*) the number of 9 year olds choosing an option differed from the number of 21 year olds by at least four people and (*b*) the number at 14 was close to the number at 9, while the number at 17 approximated the number at 21. An example is the sanction of counseling the girl who had copied—1 respondent at age nine, 3 at age fourteen, 10 at age seventeen, and 8 at age twenty-one.

In effect, no statistical tests of significance were applied because the number of respondents that chose many of the options was so small. Our purpose, instead, was simply to identify those choices of sanctions that showed even a slight tendency to change with age and to apply labels to those tendencies, suggesting the degree of confidence we held for their magnitudes. Our criteria were intentionally quite generous, reflecting our attempt to detect any age trends that might exist and enabling us to cast such trends as hypotheses whose validity might be tested with other groups of respondents.

Table 8-3

Agreement on Sanctions within Age Groups

(in the total number of different types of sanctions)

	Age	*9*	*14*	*17*	*21*
	N	33	36	34	33
Case 1: Test Copying					
Combined sanctions (volunteered, probed, and afterthought)		18	17	17	15
Case 2: Drug Trading					
Combined sanctions (volunteered, probed, and afterthought)		15	12	15	10
Case 3: Burglary & Murder					
Combined sanctions (volunteered, probed, and afterthought)		5	7	9	9

Even with such liberal standards of judgment, we found age trends within our sample to be very rare indeed. The total number of volunteered, probed, afterthought, and combined (volunteered+probed+afterthought) sanctions was 130. However, only four of the 130 sanction choices met the *evident trend* criteria and only eight met the *possible trend* standard. Thus, barely 9% of the sanction choices showed even a hint of age trends. Table 8-4 displays the trends for combined sanctions (volunteered+probed+afterthought), which represent the ultimate opinions that participants had expressed by the close of their interviews. As the figures indicate, there were no instances in which their final proposals showed evident trends, and in only three instances did even possible trends appear. Hence, knowing the age of a respondent would be of no help for estimating the sanctions that person would propose compared to the kinds that would be suggested by respondents at some other stage of the adolescent period.

Gender Comparisons for Sanction Choices

The sample of youths participating in the study included 69 females and 67 males. When the sanctions recommended by females and males were compared, only two statistically significant differences were found, even at the .05 level, for either the volunteered or the probed choices. The two instances of a significant difference appeared in volunteered consequences for the burglar who had killed the householder. Whereas 24% of the males would execute him, only 10% of the females would do so (.014 level). Furthermore, 25% of the females but only 4% of the males would provide counseling for the felon while he was imprisoned (exceeds .001 level). These data could be interpreted as support for the proposal

Table 8-4
Age Trends in the Choice of Sanctions
(in numbers of respondents)

Age	*9*	*14*	*17*	*21*
N	*33*	*36*	*34*	*33*
Possible Trends				
Case 1—Counsel the offender	1	3	10	8
Case 2—Imprison or detain	32	20	7	11
Case 3—Delegate sanction responsibility	9	5	1	2

by such investigators as Gilligan (1982) that females are more likely to base their moral decisions on a sense of compassion while males are more apt to found their moral judgments on an objective concept of justice.

However, in the main, the females and males were essentially alike in the consequences they suggested for the offenders in all three cases.

A further question we posed was this: Did interviewees favor their own gender when assigning sanctions? In other words, were females more lenient in the consequences they would impose on female offenders, and were males more lenient in the penalties they would assign to male offenders? The case of the two 16 year olds who traded drugs for concert tickets provided an opportunity to answer this question; the answer was universally "No." All but one of the 136 respondents would assign the same consequence to both the boy and girl. The single exception was a nine-year-old boy who would punish the boy more severely than the girl because "the boy probably did it a lot more than the girl, so he should go to jail for three months. The girl should just have her parents ground her for a while to teach her a lesson."

TYPES OF INTENDED AIMS

As explained earlier, after interviewees had suggested a sanction for a case of wrongdoing, they were asked what purpose that sanction was intended to serve—in other words, what good it would do. Table 8-5 summarizes the 136 participants' intended aims. After offering their suggestions, interviewees were asked whether they might also subscribe to three other specific aims. The outcome of this probing portion of the interviews is presented in Table 8-5. The discussion of the results follows the pattern of the discussion of sanctions.

Volunteered Aims

We may recall that the third question asked of participants during the interview was designed to reveal the aims that they hoped their sanctions would achieve.

Table 8-5 summarizes the results of that inquiry for the 136 respondents. The labels identifying types of aims are drawn from the aims typology in Chapter 2. The percentages of proposed aims exceed 100% because some students included more than one aim in their recommendation.

Case 1: Cheating on a Test

Although 2% of the 136 participants said they could not think of exactly what the purpose of their sanction would be, the remaining 98% suggested a total of 19 different types of aims. Nearly one-third hoped to prevent the girl from copying test answers again (deter = 32%). Ten percent wished to reform the girl. Another 10% wanted to teach her to accept responsibility for her behavior. Nine percent would inform the child of why copying was wrong, and another 9% would seek to diagnose the cause of the girl's misdeed so she could be helped to overcome the temptation to cheat (conquer her problems = 7%). Other respondents would have her tutored in mathematics (enhance knowledge and skills = 7%). In brief, the interviewees hoped to achieve an extended list of aims, many of which were interrelated. The two principal goals were to prevent future cheating and to equip the girl to succeed at mathematics without feeling she had to copy others' work.

Case 2: Trading Drugs

Eight percent of the interviewees declined to cite aims, either because they felt that no offense had been perpetrated by the teenagers or else because they were at a loss to decide precisely what end their proposed sanction should achieve. The remaining 92% suggested a total of 22 types of outcomes they would like to effect.

As in Case 1, nearly one-third of the group (31%) wished to deter the boy and girl from trading drugs again. Thirteen percent hoped to reform the teenagers from using and dealing drugs, 12% wished to generate affect (guilt, shame, fear) that might help prevent further transgression, 12% intended to focus the pair's attention on their deed, whereas 9% wanted to teach the boy and girl to distinguish right from wrong, and 10% wished to make them understand why what they had done was unacceptable. Smaller numbers of participants cited a range of other goals—teaching the youths to be accountable for their behavior (7%), helping them conquer the personal problems that led to drug use (4%), and more.

Case 3: Robbing and Killing

The 2% of students who failed to propose an aim were the ones who had been unwilling to suggest a sanction that the 23-year-old felon should experience. The 98% who did cite aims distributed their choices over 20 types. The intention of nearly half the group (48%) was to incapacitate the man, either by imprisonment or death. In a similar vein, another 19% wanted to deter him from committing further transgressions. Thirteen percent thought their sanction could

Table 8-5
Aims Volunteered in Three Cases of Wrongdoing
(N=136, in percentages)

Type of Aim	Case 1 math test	Case 2 drugs	Case 3 rob & kill
Deter (special—the offender)	32	31	19
Incapacitate	6	2	48
Focus attention on misdeed consequences	6	12	13
Reform (that specific type of misdeed)	10	13	8
Explain why the deed was wrong	7	10	6
Teach accountability (responsibility)	10	7	7
Generate affect	5	12	3
Inform offender of right and wrong	9	4	3
Diagnose cause of wrongdoing	9	3	3
Help offender conquer problems	7	4	2
Deter (general—other people)	1	1	8
Enhance knowledge and skills	7	1	
Improve social adjustment	3	2	1
Reform (general character change)	1	2	2
Require that victims be compensated			4
Require that society be compensated		3	
Obtain help for offender	2	1	
Achieve social retribution		1	1
Enforce the law		1	1
Alter offender's values		2	
Improve offender's self-confidence	2		
Show that the misdeed will not be tolerated	1	1	
Oblige offender to adopt better ways	2		
Avenge the wrong			2
Protect potential victims			2
Maintain tradition		1	
Reduce severity of punishment		1	
Accommodate for a disability	1		
Train for a job			1
Match the offense (eye for an eye)			1
No aim proposed	2	8	2

force him to focus attention on the dire consequences of his deed. Ten percent hoped a reformation might take place, of the specific deeds (8%) or of the man's general character (2%). An additional 8% believed the sanction they proposed would deter other people from robbing and killing. Smaller percentages of respondents distributed their suggestions over the remaining 13 types of aims.

Probed Aims

The final phase of each interview about a case consisted of the interviewer citing four specific aims and asking respondents whether they would want to achieve those aims by the sanctions they had endorsed. An additional option was provided for use with any participants who had already included one of the four in their answer to the original open-ended question about what purpose they hoped their sanction would accomplish. This final probing portion of the interview also stimulated some respondents to offer an afterthought aim they had neglected to include in their original proposal. The results of this phase of the interview are summarized in Table 8-6.

Case 1: Cheating on a Test

The four primary aims posed for respondents in the first case were as follows. (The aims-typology category to which we assigned each quoted statement is identified in the parentheses following the statement.)

"To teach her not to cheat again." (deter offender)

"To show other pupils what could happen to them if they cheated." (deter others)

"To give her a good scare. To make her afraid and ashamed." (generate affect)

"To make her pay for what she has done. When you do wrong, you deserve to be punished." (enforce the law)

However, if the respondent had already proposed one of these options in answer to the original open-ended question about aims, then the following option was substituted for the option that student had offered initially.

"To make the girl want to be a really good person, to really change her personality." (reform)

As shown by Table 8-6, more than half of the participants hoped their proposed sanctions would serve to enforce the rules (60%) and deter others from committing the same offense (58%). Fewer than half wanted to deter the girl from further copying (40%), while one-third hoped the sanctions would improve her character (31%). Seven percent expressed six different afterthoughts. An additional 7% turned down all of the probed consequences.

Case 2: Trading Drugs

The four probed aims in the case of the two 16 year olds were:

"To make them stop giving drugs to other people." (deter offenders)

"To make them do something to help the community." (compensate society)

"To teach them to be responsible for the way they act." (teach accountability)
"To make sure that the law is obeyed." (enforce the law)

The following aim was substituted when any of the above choices had been given by a respondent in the earlier phase of the interview:

"To let everybody know that the boy and girl were using drugs and trading drugs to other teenagers." (expose publicly)

Three-quarters of the interviewees endorsed the aims of teaching the youths to be responsible for their actions (76%) and to make sure the law is enforced (74%). Half of the respondents supported sanctions that would require the teenagers to compensate society through some sort of community service (50%). However, only 16% believed that letting the general public learn of the teenagers' misdeed was a good idea. (The role of empathy in affecting students' beliefs about publicly exposing the misdeeds of young people is inspected at some depth in Chapter 13—"Empathy and Sympathy".) Four percent would add the aim of deterring the youths from further drug dealing.

Of the four types of afterthought expressed, the most frequent was that of wanting the two offenders to express regret and to apologize for their deed (8%).

Whereas originally (Table 8-5) 8% of the interviewees had declined to suggest any aims when first asked about this case, 4% of them accepted one of the proffered aims during the final probing portion of the interview.

Case 3: Robbing and Killing

In the third case, the basic choices among aims were:

"To fix it so he can't rob or kill again." (deter—prevent further misdeeds)
"To teach him to be a better person; I mean, to reform him." (general character change)
"To give the family of the dead woman the satisfaction of having the killer punished." (avenge the wrong)
"To make him do something helpful for the community." (compensate society)

The substitute choice was:

"To scare other men and woman who think they might like to break into houses and steal things." (general deterrence)

Slightly more than half (55%) of the students endorsed the vengeance aim—giving the family of the victim the satisfaction of having the killer punished. Half of the group would like to reform the felon, although many qualified this desire with such a caveat as "at his age I wouldn't have a lot of hope that it would work." The remaining participants rejected such an aim, on the grounds either that the man should be executed and therefore he would not be available for reformation or that it would be futile to try reforming him. Somewhat fewer than half the respondents wanted to compensate society (43%) by having the offender work while in prison. Nearly as many thought the sanction they had recommended might deter others from committing similar crimes (40%). Almost one-quarter of the group intended their sanction as a deterrent, preventing the killer from repeating his transgressions (24%).

Five percent of the group turned down the opportunity to accept any of the probed aims or to suggest additional ones as afterthoughts. Among the several

Table 8-6
Probed Aims in Three Cases of Wrongdoing
(N=136, in percentages)

Type of Aim	Case 1 math test	Case 2 drugs	Case 3 rob & kill
Accepting proposed aims			
Enforce the law (pay for misbehaving)	60	74	
Compensate society (help community)		50	43
Teach accountability (responsibility)		76	
Deter (general—other people)	58		40
Reform (general character change)	31		50
Avenge the wrong			55
Prevent/Deter (special—the offender)	40	4	24
Generate affect (shame, fear)	22		
Expose publicly		16	
No probed aims accepted	7	4	5
Offering afterthought aims			
Generate affect (shame, fear)			1
Obligate offender to express regret or gratitude		8	
Incapacitate			8
Protect potential victims		2	
Enhance knowledge and skills	1	1	
Improve work habits	1		
Inform offender of right and wrong	2		
Explain why the deed was wrong	1		
Improve offender's self-confidence	1		
Reduce punishment severity	1		
Help offender conquer problems		1	
Focus attention (offender thinks about deed)			1
Obtain help for offender			1
Require that victims be compensated			1

afterthought proposals, the most popular was that of incapacitation (removing the felon's opportunities to engage in further wrongdoing) either by executing or by imprisoning him (8%). When that figure is added to the 48% who volunteered such an aim, the total that intended to incapacitate the man reaches 56%.

Age Comparisons of Aim Choices

As in the case of sanctions, age data were used to derive two generalizations about the aims that respondents offered.

1. *Within each age group there was considerable diversity of opinion regarding the aims that sanctions should achieve.* An initial question we asked was: To what extent did people within an age group agree with each other on aims of sanctions? The possible answers could range from extreme agreement (all respondents would chose precisely the same aim) to extreme disagreement (no two respondents would chose the same aim). As indicated in Table 8-7, the obtained range of selections fell about midway between these two polar positions. Thus, there was notable variability in each group—an overall average of 16 different aims—with the extent of variability similar from one group to another and from one case to another. No age trends were evident.

2. *Age trends in the choice of particular aims were very rare but were more frequent than in the choice of sanctions.* A second question was: What relationship, if any, appeared between age and the number of respondents who advocated a particular aim? Stated another way, did the choice of particular aims systematically increase or decrease with advancing age? We answered this question by applying the same criteria of confidence that were used in the search for age trends among sanction proposals—*evident trends* and *possible trends*. The total number of volunteered, probed, afterthought, and combined (volunteered + probed + afterthought) aims was 162. Of this total, five reached the evident level and 13 the possible level. Thus, barely 11% of the entire array of aims displayed even the least hint of age trends.

Table 8-8 shows the five evident trends and the three possible trends for the respondents' final combined judgments (volunteered+probed+afterthought). Among the evident trends, more younger participants than older ones hoped to deter offenders in all three cases from future transgressions (special deterrence). In addition, more younger than older students wished to reform the 9-year-old girl's character and to encourage the teenage drug users to express gratitude for people's efforts to help them avoid further wrongdoing. As for *possible trends*, more younger than older students wished to enhance the 9 year old's math skills, whereas more older than younger ones would make clear to the teenagers why their use of drugs was wrong. In the case of the burglar, a desire for vengeance was more often expressed by younger than by older respondents.

Finally, there was slightly more evidence of age trends in the aims respondents hoped to achieve than there was in the types of sanctions they would

Table 8-7
Agreement on Aims within Age Groups
(total number of different types of aims)

Age	9	14	17	21
N	33	36	34	33
Case 1: Test Copying				
Combined aims (volunteered, probed, and afterthought)	17	18	15	21
Case 2: Drug Trading				
Combined aims (volunteered, probed, and afterthought)	15	14	19	14
Case 3: Burglary & Murder				
Combined aims (volunteered, probed, and afterthought)	12	15	18	16

Table 8-8
Age Trends in the Choice of Aims
(in numbers of respondents)

Age	9	14	17	21
N	33	36	34	33
Evident Trends				
Case 1—Deter offender (special deterrence)	23	15	14	13
Case 1—Reform offender's character	17	11	7	7
Case 2—Deter offender (special deterrence)	25	13	8	2
Case 2—Offender to express gratitude	9	1	1	0
Case 3—Deter offender (special deterrence)	20	4	5	0
Possible Trends				
Case 1—Enhance knowledge & skills	6	2	2	1
Case 2—Explain why misdeed was wrong	1	2	5	5
Case 3—Avenge the wrong	24	19	19	16

advocate. Thus, even though there appeared to be only slight distinctions across age groups in the aims respondents hoped to achieve, there were even fewer distinctions among the sanctions they recommended.

Gender Comparisons for Intended Aims

There were no significant differences between males and females in either the volunteered or the probed aims that respondents cited in any of the three cases. In effect, the two gender groups were essentially alike in the outcomes they hoped to achieve with the consequences they recommended.

Interrater Coding Reliability

As an addendum to the foregoing summaries of sanction and aim choices, we append this note about the reliability of the coding system for categorizing the results of the 136 students' opinions. In coding respondents' answers according to the typologies in Chapter 2, we divided the task by each of us, as coauthors, taking half of the males and half of the females at every age level. At the outset, in order to estimate the amount of agreement about how a given response should be coded, we separately judged a sample of 24 cases involving a total of 210 coding decisions. The two of us agreed in 84% of the decisions. In some instances the difference between our assigning a response involved a distinction between two closely allied aims or sanctions. For example, in a number of instances one of us coded a response as an example of "special deterrence—discouraging offenders from committing further transgressions" whereas the other coded the same response as "teaching accountability—convincing transgressors that they will be held responsible for their actions." When the codes of such closely related items were combined, agreement reached 90%.

INTERPRETATIONS

The purpose of the following section is to propose what the foregoing results may mean in terms of four developmental indicators described in Chapter 6—(1) Piaget's heteronomous versus autonomous morality, (2) Kohlberg's corrective justice theory, (3) Lewin's life-space differentiation and expansion, and (4) fanciful versus realistic views of sanctions.

Heteronomous Versus Autonomous Morality

As explained in Chapter 6, Piaget contended that people who operate from a heteronomous perspective accord unilateral respect for authorities (such as parents, teachers, the clergy, the police) and for the rules they prescribe. People operating from an autonomous perspective base their moral judgments on mutual regard among peers or equals and respect for the rules that guide their interaction. Piaget contended that young children confuse what is just with what is law, law being whatever is prescribed by adult authority, so that younger ones are more likely than older ones to endorse obedience to the law.

Table 8-9
Students Who Advocated Obeying the Law
(in percentages)

The Case	*Age* *N*	*9* *33*	*14* *36*	*17* *34*	*21* *33*
Copying test answers		69	54	56	61
Trading drugs		81	73	71	73

Although the present study was not designed specifically to test Piaget's proposal, at least one item from our aims typology would appear to bear on the heteronomy/autonomy issue. It is the aim of implementing the law, particularly as reflected in respondents' reactions to the enforce-the-law probing question asked in the math-test and drug-trading cases. Even though 9 year olds supported law enforcement in somewhat larger numbers than the participants in the 14-, 17-, and 21-year-old groups, no differences between any pair of groups approaches statistical significance at the .05 level (Table 8-9). Thus, older students did not differ markedly from younger ones in advocating obeying laws. This lack of convincing support for Piaget's proposition might be a function of the age levels represented in the present investigation. If children younger than age nine had been included, perhaps they would have endorsed law enforcement in far greater numbers. In terms of Piaget's cognitive development stages, the 9 year olds in our study were approaching the formal operations period (which might typically begin around age 11) in which they would be expected to engage in more logical independent reasoning than they did earlier in the concrete operations period (ages 7–11). Hence, we could speculate that the somewhat higher percentage of 9 year olds supporting obedience to the law might reflect a lingering heteronomy as they shifted from a dominant heteronomous point of view into the beginnings of a more autonomous perspective. At the same time, the similarity of percentages across ages 14 to 21 might be viewed as evidence that respondents in those age groups were all within the formal-operations period and had thus arrived at a somewhat stable balance between heteronomy and autonomy in their moral reasoning.

In any event, evidence from the present study does not furnish persuasive support for Piaget's proposal, at least across the years of adolescence.

Kohlberg's Corrective Justice Stages

In Chapter 6 we attempted to link Kohlberg's stages of corrective justice to the present study by assigning sanctions and aims to lower and higher developmental levels of Kohlberg's structure. The resulting pattern is shown in Table 8-10.

Table 8-10
Associating Corrective Justice Stages with Sanctions and Aims

Lower Developmental Levels	*Higher Developmental Levels*
	Sanctions	
Execute	Counsel (reason, advise, warn)
Impose corporal punishment	Furnish probation, parole
Imprison	Educate (learning opportunities)
Expose publicly	
Banish, ostracize	
	Aims	
Achieve social retribution	Improve offenders' condition
Match the offense	Protect society—Incapacitate
Enforce the letter of the law	Protect society—Deter
Revenge, personal	Reform offenders

Therefore, (a) if age can be considered an indicator of moral maturity and (b) if we have done an acceptable job of translating his proposal into the patterning of sanctions and aims in Table 8-10, then we will expect more younger respondents to have selected items in the left column and more older ones to have selected items in the right column.

Our analysis of interviewees' choices reveals that among the eight sanctions in the table, only one yielded a statistically significant difference between the youngest group and the two oldest groups. Whereas 72% of the 9 year olds would imprison offenders (combining cases 2 and 3), only 36% of 17 year olds and 42% of 21 year olds would do so. This difference, in keeping with Kohlberg's proposal, resulted primarily from the 9 year olds' willingness to send the teenage drug traders to juvenile hall, while most older respondents were unwilling to do so.

Among the eight aims in Table 8-10, the single significant difference between the youngest participants and the three older groups related to protecting society by deterring offenders (actual and potential law breakers) from misconduct. Whereas 56% of the 9 year olds chose deterrence as an aim, only 25% to 30% of the older groups did so. This outcome does not support Kohlberg's position.

In summary, the results of the present study offer essentially no confirmation of Kohlberg's levels of corrective justice. There are several ways this discrepancy might be rationalized.

First, it is possible, as Henry (1983) has charged, that Kohlberg's hierarchy of moral reasoning stages does not represent a "natural sequence" of development to be expected in every culture. (*Natural development* refers to a predictable series of changes in moral reasoning that will occur in the thinking of a typical person in any society with the passing years as the individual's neural system grows in complexity and his or her life experiences expand.) The stages might represent, instead, a set of values based on a particular philosophical viewpoint deriving from a Western liberal tradition and rationalized from that viewpoint as a hierarchy of moral maturity. In such an event, respondents in our study who were unaware of that tradition would not be expected to reflect it in the types of sanctions and aims they chose.

A second possibility is that the age range we encompassed in our study (9 through 21) was too restricted to reveal the corrective justice changes that would be expected in Kohlberg's typology. Perhaps if younger and older people had participated in the study, Kohlberg's hierarchy would have been confirmed.

As a third option, chronological age over the adolescent years may be a poor indicator of moral development. In other words, Kohlberg's corrective justice may be a reasonable description of levels of moral maturity, but between later childhood and early adulthood such maturity may not be distributed by age. The moral reasoning of some 9 year olds may be as mature as that of some 17 or 21 year olds and vice versa. The great diversity of opinions about sanctions and aims within each age group as reported earlier in this chapter suggests that this possibility might be true.

A final alternative is that Kohlberg's corrective justice stages are indeed correlated with age during the years of adolescence, but our data failed to confirm his hierarchy because the sample of respondents included in the present study did not accurately reflect the composition of the larger population of 9, 14, 17, and 21 year olds.

Lewin's Differentiation and Expansion

In Lewin's theory, with advancing age the regions or facts in a person's life space increase in number and specificity of function. That is, life space expands and its territories become more distinctly different from each other. If Lewin's principle did indeed apply to the ages we studied, then we might expect (a) that the number of sanctions and aims proposed by respondents would increase with the age of the interviewees and (b) that the differences in the sanctions and aims recommended across the three cases would also increase. In particular, younger respondents as compared to older ones would (a) suggest fewer sanctions and aims and (b) would tend to apply the same sanctions and aims across the three cases rather than differentiating sanctions and aims from one case to another.

Table 8-11 addresses this issue. The first two rows show the average number of sanctions and aims respondents volunteered when first asked what should be done about an offender and what purpose that sanction would serve. The averages are for all three cases combined. In agreement with Lewin's principle, the 9 year olds suggested fewer sanctions for the three cases combined (3.91) than did any of the older age groups. The differences between the 9 year olds and the rest

Table 8-11
Differentiation and Expansion
(in arithmetic means)

	Age	9	14	17	21
	N	33	36	34	33
Sanctions volunteered		3.91	4.67	5.24	4.67
Aims volunteered		3.50	3.92	3.97	4.00
Same sanction over 2–3 cases		.81	.64	.32	.55
Same aim over 2–3 cases		.91	.47	.38	.24

are statistically significant beyond the .01 level. However, the difference among the three older sets of students—14s, 17s, 21s—fail to reach the .05 level. Hence, the rather large difference over ages 9–14 is not found across ages 14–21.

The trend for aims displayed in the second row also supports Lewin's proposal but in a slightly more regular fashion, with the average number of volunteered aims increasing with age. Again, the change between ages 9 and 14 is greater than between 14 and 21.

The third and fourth rows in Table 8-11 report the average number of instances in which a respondent chose an identical sanction or aim for two or all three of the cases of wrongdoing. Lewin's principle of differentiation would hold that younger participants, more often than older ones, would apply the same aim or sanction across two or three cases rather than offering a different sanction and aim for each case. The trend of the averages is in keeping with such a prediction. In particular, the number of times the 9 year olds cited the same aims over more than one case is noticeably different (well beyond the .01 level) than among the three older age groups.

(While the general trend for both sanctions and aims fits Lewin's principle, the 17 year olds' sanction choices deviate somewhat from this trend, a finding for which we have no explanation other than a possible sampling deviation.)

In summary, we conclude that Lewin's notion of differentiation and expansion of life space appears to receive some support in our study of youths' moral reasoning, with the greatest change coming in early rather than late adolescence.

Fanciful Versus Realistic Proposals

We suggested in Chapter 6 that distinctions among sanctions can be founded on a concept of consensual realism. In the present context, consensual realism is defined as what most adults—in terms of formal rules or custom—would regard as feasible or prudent in a given situation. Our hypothesis is that among children, realism increases with age. Although the type of data reported in this chapter does not enable us to test that hypothesis with any precision, it still permits us to offer a rough estimate of how well the hypothesis applies to the young people we interviewed.

As for the first case, we estimate that most adults in American society would believe that a 9 year old's copying test answers is not a very serious breach of custom and thus warrants no more than a light penalty or treatment, just enough to discourage future copying. Hence, we would label as *realistic* such sanctions as reporting the behavior to the child's parents, awarding the girl an *F* on the test, keeping her after school to redo the test or to write a self-admonishing statement on the chalkboard, sending her to the principal's office, or the like. In contrast, considerably harsher punishment would be labeled *fanciful* since it would be contrary to the principle of consensual realism. Furthermore, any recommended consequence that could not be carried out because it was unfeasible would be regarded as fanciful as well.

The handling of first-offense drug offenses by police can differ considerably, depending on the conditions of the particular case. Thus, we would consider a variety of sanctions to be realistic for the two teenage drug traders, so long as those sanctions involved moderately light punishment or treatment, such as placing them in juvenile hall overnight or for a few days, remanding them to their parents for disciplinary measures, putting them on probation, requiring that they attend drug education classes, imposing community service responsibilities, or the like. Responses we would label *fanciful* include letting the pair go without any penalty or, at the other extreme, jailing them for several months or years.

In the case of the burglar who killed the householder, consensual realism as reflected in judicial practice would call for a severe penalty. Typically, people would expect the offender either to be imprisoned for an extended period or else put to death. Fanciful consequences for the felon would be ones deemed either too lenient or unfeasible. For instance, suggesting that the burglar have less than a prison term of at least 10 or 15 years could be considered fanciful (regardless of the fact that felons are often released early for good behavior or because prisons are too crowded to keep inmates imprisoned for their entire sentences). As a rule of thumb for conducting our analysis, we have adopted a 10-year sentence as the lower limit for consensual realism in the case of the burglar. Any more lenient sentence than 10 years we regard as fanciful. Any consequence that could not reasonably be carried out is also regarded as fanciful.

Guided by the above line of argument, we classified as realistic or as fanciful the sanctions proposed for the offenders in the three cases by the four groups of respondents (Table 8-12). Whenever a participant would incarcerate the drug traders or the burglar but failed to specify the length of the sentence, the response was listed as indeterminate. Furthermore, whenever a participant could not decide on what sanction to apply, we listed that response as indeterminate.

Table 8-12
Fanciful Versus Realistic Sanctions
(in percentages)

Age	9	14	17	21
N	33	36	34	33
9-year-old test copier				
Realistic	97	97	100	100
Fanciful	3	3		
16-year-old drug traders				
Realistic	61	88	91	86
Fanciful	33	10	3	14
Indeterminate	6	2	6	
23-year-old burglar/killer				
Realistic	39	83	56	71
Fanciful	49	7	12	9
Indeterminate	12	10	32	20

With rare exception, respondents of all ages proposed realistic treatments for the girl who copied test answers. However, in the other two cases, the 9 year olds suggested a higher percentage of fanciful consequences than did members of the other three groups. The difference between the 9 year olds and the older ones is statistically significant at the .07 level in the drug trading case but beyond the .001 level in the case of the burglar/killer. Nine year olds, more often than the older participants, recommended penalties that were unrealistically harsh for the teenage drug users (such as several years in prison) while recommending penalties that were unrealistically lenient for the burglar who had slain the householder (such as one month or one year in jail). The 14% of 21 year olds who offered fanciful suggestions were ones who said the drug traders had done nothing wrong and thus should be set free.

Three observations about the contents of Table 8-12 appear worthy of mention. First is the matter of familiarity. The high level of consensual realism across all age groups for the math test incident likely resulted from all age groups being personally familiar with the kind of infraction that case involved. On the other hand, 9 year olds might be expected to have less personal experience than the older respondents with the use of illicit drugs and thus might be expected to recommend harsher penalties than are typically applied. At the same time, certain of the 17 and 21 year olds appeared to reflect what possibly was considerable experience with drug matters when they suggested that the teenagers' act was either of slight consequence or did not qualify as misconduct— "Trading drugs is no big deal" or "If they want to use drugs, it's their own business; they didn't do anything wrong." As for the burglary incident, older respondents apparently had more vicarious experience with such matters by dint of their paying greater attention to news items about crime and its associated punishment. Thus, a higher proportion of older students recommended more realistic treatment of the burglar than did the 9 year olds.

A second observation concerns the ability to match the severity of sanctions to the seriousness of misconduct. A general rule that seems to be applied in virtually all societies is that the more serious wrongdoing deserves harsher penalties or more drastic treatments. In both the drug trading and burglary cases, 9 year olds were less able than members of the older groups to apply this principle in a consensually realistic fashion. A notable number of 9 year olds recommended too strict punishment for the teenage drug users and too lenient punishment for the burglar.

Third, the greatest difference among age groups in the realistic versus fanciful nature of their suggestions occurred within the four-year space between ages 9 and 14 rather than during the six-year span between ages 14 and 21. If our samples of respondents can be considered at all representative of age groups at large, then the most significant change in reasoning about sanctions occurs at the outset of adolescence, during years 10 to 13, rather than during the middle and late adolescent years. Such an observation, supported by other data reviewed earlier in this chapter, is in keeping with the time of transition from concrete operations to formal operations thought in Piaget's periods of mental growth. It is also in concert with cultural traditions that credit the growing child with achieving adult-like intellectual skills around the time of puberty. At that time children are said to enter "the age of reason," qualifying them to participate in rites of passage into adult institutions—membership in the church, warrior status in the tribe, an occupational pursuit, and possibly motherhood and fatherhood.

CONCLUSION

From the contents of this chapter we have drawn the following generalizations about methods of interviewing, about predicting the sanctions and aims youths will propose, and about generating hypotheses to be investigated.

Interview Methods

The results reported in this chapter strongly confirm our original—and perhaps rather obvious—expectation that asking interviewees only a pair of open-ended questions about sanctions and aims would fail to reveal much about their manner of moral reasoning. In effect, when using interviews as a means of discovering how people think about sanctions and aims, it is not enough simply to inquire: "What should be done about the offender? And what good would that do, that is, what would be your purpose?" It is also necessary to ask probing questions to uncover additional sanctions and aims that respondents would endorse. When applying the probing tactic in the present study, we included a very limited number of additional options for interviewees to consider—no more than two further sanctions and four further aims for each case. Obviously, as demonstrated by the typologies in Chapter 2, a far larger number of alternatives could have been presented if time had permitted. And it seems likely that numbers of such additional possibilities would have been accepted by the respondents, thereby exposing more completely their manner of thinking when deciding on consequences to apply to wrongdoers.

In summary, a detailed understanding of people's modes of reasoning about sanctions and aims would require a very extensive interview that included both open-ended and probing questions, an interview employing far more probing inquiries than we included in the present study. Thus, we recognize that our interviews succeeded in revealing only a segment of the participants' processes of moral reasoning.

Making Predictions

One reason that people peruse empirical research on child development is to improve their predictions about how children are likely to act. We might then ask: "How can the results reported in this chapter enhance the accuracy of predictions about sanctions and aims that youths—from cultural settings similar to that of our participants—would propose for the types of wrongdoing included in the present study?"

In answer, we suggest that the chapter's results might indeed prove somewhat useful. That is, the percentages reported earlier in the chapter can serve as at least rough indicators of what might be proposed by the next adolescents we would meet. For instance, when participants in the present study were asked what should be done about the burglar who killed the householder, 85% said he should be imprisoned and 17% said he should be executed. Thus, in other cases involving a first-offense killing during the course of a crime, we would predict that considerably more adolescents would imprison the offender than would put him to death. In like manner, for cases involving pupils who have submitted a classmate's academic work as their own, we would expect more respondents would shift the responsibility for setting sanctions to parents or to the school principal (35%) than would censure those pupils privately (2%) or suspend them from class (3%). In effect, the percentages in the present study offer at least a modicum of guidance in estimating the decisions about sanctions and aims that can be expected of middle-class American youths in the age range of 9 through 21.

So far we have been speaking of making predictions about adolescents in general, regardless of their age and gender. We may now ask: "Will our estimates become more accurate if we know the age and gender of the youths whose opinions we are trying to predict? In other words, what help can we obtain from this chapter's data on age and gender?" The answer is that the data furnish little or no help, since they offer negligible evidence of differences between age groups or gender groups in proposals of sanctions and aims.

A further aid to prediction can be found in the excerpts from interviews quoted early in the chapter to illustrate participants' modes of presenting their opinions. A marked feature of the quotations was their variegated nature. No two were alike. This idiosyncratic character of students' responses held true for the entire sample of 136 interviewees. Thus, we would predict that if we sought the opinions of other youths about such matters, their opinions would also be expressed in very diverse ways. We would not expect striking similarity among their styles of discourse.

Generating Hypotheses

In the main, our attempt in this chapter to identify significant age and gender changes yielded no more than slight hints of differences. For example, in proposing sanctions in the math test case, more older than younger respondents would offer counseling to the 9-year-old girl. In the drug trading case, more younger than older participants would incarcerate the two teenagers. However, in both of these instances, the number of respondents advocating such sanctions at each age level was so small that the observed differences could not be trusted as representing significant differences within a larger population of youths.

Although more aim proposals than sanction recommendations reflected age differences, again the small numbers of respondents at successive age levels rendered differences unconvincing as indicators of age changes in the broader adolescent population. The differences reflect no more than slight possibilities.

Yet even though the observed differences fell short of statistical significance, we believe they should not be dismissed out of hand. Rather, we consider them proper sources of hypotheses to be tested with larger samples of respondents. In short, we believe the hints are worth following up.

9

Patterns of Causal Relationships: Linking Sanctions and Aims

In the present chapter, the idea of causal relationships as described in Chapter 3 serves as an analytical lens through which the results of the 136 interviews are viewed. Chapter 9 addresses three main questions:

1. How frequently do the various models of sanction/aim relationships appear in the consequences that people propose for wrongdoers?
2. How do different patterns of interview questions influence the picture of people's causal relations beliefs that is revealed during an interview?
3. To what extent do people agree with each other about the causal relations proposals they suggest in cases of misconduct?

The first two questions are treated under the heading "Models of Sanction/Aim Connections." The third question is answered under "Consensus Versus Individuality."

The discussion closes with a summary of six generalizations derived from the results reported in the chapter. The summary also includes comments about how such causal relationship results may help explain the behavior of people who prepare rules and serve on juries and mediation boards.

MODELS OF SANCTION/AIM CONNECTIONS

In Chapter 3, the scheme for analyzing the degree of complexity of people's sanction/aim proposals featured five graphic models. The purpose of the following section is to describe the patterns of sanction/aim linkages derived from the 136 interviews. We begin by recalling the nature of the five models, then describe how frequently each model appeared among respondents' proposals in the three cases of wrongdoing.

The models are defined in the following fashion:

Singular Connections. A singular connection consists of a single sanction (S) that is intended to produce a single ultimate aim (UA).

$$S \longrightarrow UA$$

Chains. A chain consists of a single sanction that contributes to a single sequence of interlinked instrumental aims (IA) that lead to an ultimate aim.

$$S \longrightarrow IA \longrightarrow UA$$

$$S \longrightarrow IA \longrightarrow IA \longrightarrow IA \longrightarrow IA \longrightarrow IA \longrightarrow UA$$

Aim Fans. The analogy of a triangular fan is employed here to represent a single aim at the fulcrum with two or more sanctions forming the fan wings.

Sanction Fans. A sanction fan is the opposite of an aim fan in that a single sanction at the fulcrum is expected to produce two or more ultimate aims (UA), concomitant inherent effects (CIE), or concomitant possible effects (CPE).

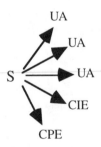

Networks. A network is composed of multiple sanctions linked to multiple aims and effects. Networks vary in their complexity. The simplest type of network consists of two sanctions associated with two aims and/or effects.

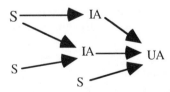

Networks grow increasingly intricate as they include a greater diversity of sanctions and of outcomes.

INTERVIEW RESULTS IN TERMS OF THE MODELS

Table 9-1 summarizes the percentages of interviews that reflected each of the foregoing models. The table shows both of the following:

1. the patterns resulting from the first stage of the interview in which respondents were asked to volunteer a sanction they would recommend for the offender in the case and tell what outcome that sanction would be intended to produce.
2. the combined volunteered, afterthought, and probed answers that represented each respondent's complete reaction to a case. Percentages of volunteered answers appear in roman type, combined answers in *italics*.

The style of interviewing used in the study did not provide for always identifying which of the more complex forms of response might actually be chains rather than networks. Thus, certain of the patterns designated as networks in Table 9-1 may have included some form of chaining that could not be discerned by our method of questioning respondents.

Perhaps the most apparent observation to be drawn from Table 9-1 is that an interview procedure which confronts respondents with only a pair of open-ended questions (What should be done about the offender? What good would that do?) fails to elicit the entire array of sanctions and aims to which respondents would

Table 9-1

Sanction/Aim Patterns in Three Cases of Wrongdoing

(N = 136, in percentages)

Type of Sanction/Aim Pattern	Case 1 math test	Case 2 drugs	Case 3 rob & kill
Singular Connection			
Volunteered	48	51	50
Combined	*1*	*0*	*2*
Aim Fans			
Volunteered	28	26	13
Combined	*4*	*3*	*1*
Sanction Fans			
Volunteered	7	8	23
Combined	*17*	*14*	*47*
Networks			
Volunteered	17	11	14
Combined	*78*	*81*	*50*
No wrongdoing			
Volunteered		2	
Combined		*2*	

subscribe. In other words, by following the open-ended questions with probing inquiries about other possible sanctions and aims, interviewers are able to evoke a variety of additional opinions that respondents hold. Support for this notion appears in the discrepancies between the volunteered and the combined percentages in all three cases. Whereas under the volunteered condition about half of the interviewees suggested only a single sanction that would be intended to achieve a single aim (singular connection), under the probed condition only 0% to 2% suggested a single sanction and single aim. Most participants proposed networks of increasing degrees of complexity.

For each of the three cases, the simplest networks consisted of two sanctions and two aims. The three most elaborate networks for the first case consisted of (1) 6 sanctions and 4 aims, (2) 5 sanctions and 5 aims, and (3) 4 sanctions and 6 aims. Similar highly elaborate patterns appeared in the second case. In the third case the extremes of complexity were only slightly less. For the entire sample of 136 interviewees, the median number of sanction/aim combinations that made up networks in the first case was 2.3 sanctions and 3.4 aims, in the second case 2.8 sanctions and 4.3 aims, and in the third case 2.1 sanctions and 4.1 aims.

We may recall that when each case was presented, interviewees were confronted with two probed sanctions and four probed aims. And because participants so often accepted those options as representing their own views, their sanction/aim connections grew markedly more complex beyond their original volunteered answers. In light of such results, we might presume that if a greater variety of sanctions and aims had been proposed, the number of people subscribing to increasingly complex networks would have been even greater. Thus, it appears that if we hope to estimate with any degree of accuracy an individual's sanction/aim thought processes, we need to conduct a very extensive interview that includes diverse cases of wrongdoing. Hence, the present results offer strong support for two of the propositions posited in earlier chapters—that the sanction/aim causal relationships in people's minds are highly complex and that this complexity will not be revealed if respondents are asked only a pair of open-ended questions about a case of wrongdoing (What should be done about the offender? What good would that do?).

A second observation about Table 9-1 is that, although the singular-connection figures for all three cases are quite similar, the figures for the more complex sanction/aim patterns (sanction fans and networks) of case 3 are notably different from those of Cases 1 and 2. More precisely, Case-3 figures for sanction fans are much larger and for networks are much smaller. In seeking to identify likely causes of these differences, we estimated that some combination of four factors could possibly account for such results. We entitled the factors *sanction tradition, public threat, maturity of judgment,* and *character malleability*. The idea that such conditions might be operating came from comments offered by certain of the respondents during the interviews.

In regard to sanction tradition, we judged that there has been a stronger traditional consensus about what to do with adult burglars and murderers than with math test cheaters and drug dealing teenagers. As shown in Chapter 8, the great majority of interviewees (82%) would imprison the Case 3 burglar, and an additional 17% would execute him. In criminal law, imprisonment and death are the two penalties traditionally applied for such crimes, with the chief aim behind such punishment being that of incapacitating the malefactor and thereby precluding further offenses. In contrast, no tradition of such consensus obtains for academic cheating or teenage drug trading, thereby leaving open a wider variety of sanction/aim combinations that respondents might reasonably propose in the first two cases. By this line of argument we would expect to find a higher percentage of networks for Cases 1 and 2 (78% and 81% respectively) than for Case 3 (50%). But what about the sanction fan figures? By a similar line of reasoning we would suggest that, whereas on the basis of tradition respondents would propose a restricted array of sanctions (imprisonment or death), they still might hold a variety of aims they hoped to achieve in applying a sanction—such aims as incapacitation, revenge, repentance, general deterrence, affect stimulation, and more. In terms of our graphic models, this would result in a high proportion of sanction fans (a single sanction with multiple aims). The figures in Table 9-1 support such an explanation (47% sanction fans for Case 3, but only 14% to 17% for Cases 1 and 2).

A second variable that might enter respondents' mode of reasoning is their fear that the wrongdoer would be a threat to public safety. This fear derives from the principle that the more likely an offender will endanger others, the more important it will be to restrict the offender's freedom. In the first two cases the wrongdoers appeared to pose little or no threat to the general public, so less control over their movements would seem necessary. In contrast, the burglar-murderer was seen as a definite threat, so a more limited set of sanctions (incarceration or execution) would seem reasonable than would be true for the transgressors in the first two cases. Such a belief was reflected in remarks that numbers of respondents offered about the burglar: "You can't let a murderer just run around" or "Lock him up so he can't do it again." No such comments were made about the 9-year-old girl, and only rarely did respondents imply that the teenage boy and girl were a threat to others.

A third possible factor—differences in offenders' apparent maturity of judgment—was occasionally expressed by interviewees in such terms as:

"The girl who copied math answers doesn't understand what that kind of behavior is going to mean for her future. She can't go through life copying other people's work and expect to get anyplace."

"The teenagers don't realize yet the consequences of using drugs and of trading them. They're still just growing up, so they need drug education rather than punishment."

"When you get to be 23 years old, you can't excuse yourself by saying you didn't know any better than to steal and kill. This guy must be a real bad dude who's done it intentionally. He should pay the price."

A fourth variable associated with maturity of judgment can be labeled *character malleability*, in reference to how likely an individual's personality is susceptible to improvement. Some participants' comments reflected the widely held belief that the younger the person, the more malleable the personality.

> "She's only 9, so there's plenty of time to straighten her out."
> "At age 16 the two can still turn their lives around if given proper guidance."
> "If he's stealing and killing by the time he's an adult, I don't have much hope that he will ever reform. I'd say put him away for life."

In summary, the more restricted set of sanctions in Case 3 might result from respondents' beliefs about sanction traditions in felony cases, about the threat an offender poses to the public, and about transgressors' maturity of judgment and character malleability.

CONSENSUS VERSUS INDIVIDUALITY

It is important to recognize that Chapters 8 and 9 offer four different ways to report the extent of agreement among respondents in the aims and sanctions they advocate.

1. The first way appeared in Chapter 8, where individual aims and sanctions were extracted from participants' answers and were reported in separate tables, with no attention given either to which sanctions were intended to produce which aims or to the complexity of the sanction/aim patterns.
2. The second way was offered in the initial section of the present chapter, where the complexity of sanction/aim opinions was reported in terms of several graphic models.

The third and fourth ways are described in the following paragraphs. They are designed to answer two questions:

3. When separate sanction/aim connections are extracted from participants' answers, on how many of these separate linkages do participants agree?
4. To what extent does the overall pattern of one respondent's sanction/aim proposal match the pattern of other respondents' proposals?

The distinctions among these four approaches can be illustrated with the examples of three students' recommendations in the case of the two teenagers who traded drugs for concert tickets. In the following summaries of students' opinions, SANCTIONS ARE SHOWN IN CAPITAL LETTERS (S), ultimate aims are underlined (UA), and *instrumental aims are in italics* (IA).

> **Respondent A:** "LIMIT THEIR ACTIVITIES and MONITOR THEIR BEHAVIOR so as to deter them from further drug use or drug trading and to make sure the law is obeyed. PUT THEM IN A DRUG EDUCATION CLASS to *focus their attention on the consequences of their actions* and to *help them conquer their problems that led to drug use.*"
> **Respondent B:** "PUT THEM ON PROBATION and MONITOR THEIR BEHAVIOR in order to deter them from further drug use or drug trading. WARN

THEM OF THE PUNISHMENT THEY WILL FACE IF THEY CONTINUE TO DEAL IN DRUGS, thus <u>deterring them from further drug use.</u> FORBID THE BOY AND GIRL TO BE TOGETHER AGAIN (limit their social contacts) to *make them sorry for what they did* and thereby <u>deter them from any further misdeeds.</u>"

Respondent C: "<u>Stop them from drug trading</u> by PUTTING THEM IN JUVENILE HALL FOR TWO WEEKS, WARNING THEM OF THE PUNISHMENT THEY WILL FACE IF THEY CONTINUE TO DEAL DRUGS, and thereafter MONITORING THEIR BEHAVIOR. (Whether they use drugs themselves in the future is their own business.)"

The first way to report the extent of agreement among the three respondents is in terms of separate sanctions and separate aims, as in Chapter 8 (Table 9-2).

The second way is in terms of the graphic models. Respondent C's answer is an example of an aims fan (three sanctions to achieve a single aim). In contrast, A's and B's answers represent networks, with A suggesting three sanctions to effect four aims, and B recommending four sanctions to accomplish four aims.

The third way consists of showing how many respondents subscribed to particular pairings of sanctions and aims. In other words, each sanction is linked to an aim it is expected to achieve. From this perspective our three sample respondents' choices can be shown as paired sanction/aim linkages (Table 9-3).

The fourth method involves, first, depicting in graphic form the entire pattern of a person's recommendation and then, second, determining how many people's sanction/aim patterns exactly match those of other respondents. To illustrate, we chart the proposals of Respondents A, B, and C in Figure 9-1.

Table 9-2
Separate Sanctions, Separate Aims

<u>Sanctions</u>	<u>Frequencies</u>
Monitor behavior	3
Warn of future punishment	2
Provide drug education	1
Incarcerate for two weeks	1
Limit social contacts	1
Put on probation	1
<u>Aims</u>	<u>Frequencies</u>
Deter from drug trading	3
Deter from drug use	2
Deter from any misdeeds	1
Enforce the law	1
Focus attention on consequences	1
Generate affect—feel sorry for misdeed	1
Help conquer personal problems	1

It is apparent that the three models do not match each other, thereby graphi-
cally demonstrating how the three respondents differed in their modes of overt
reasoning about sanction/aim causal relations.

Keeping in mind the above distinctions among the four ways of viewing
respondent agreement, we are now prepared to consider how the 136 participants
compared from the perspectives of the third and fourth approaches—separate
sanction/aim pairs and overall sanction/aim patterns.

Figure 9-1
Sanction/Aim Patterns

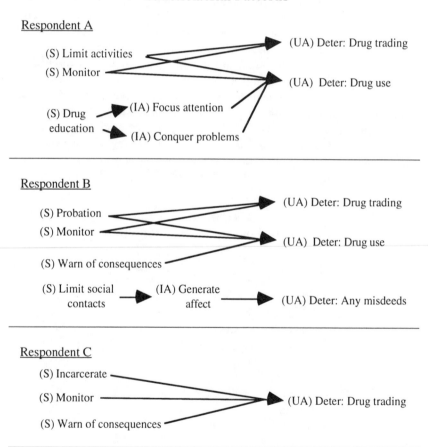

Sanction/Aim Pairs

We posed two questions about the separate sanction/aim pairings. First, how many different pairs appeared in the responses of the 136 participants across all three cases? Second, which pairings were the most popular?

In answer to the first question, the total number of pairs offered by the interviewees was 268. In other words, the participants provided a great many permutations of sanctions and aims. Their opinions reflected far more individuality than consensus. Case 3 elicited the fewest different pairs (152), whereas Case 1 exceeded that sum by 23% (187 pairs) and Case 2 by 63% (247 pairs). In effect, the teenage drug traders attracted the greatest variety of sanction/aim proposals, while the burglar-killer attracted the least. In seeking to explain such results, we drew again on the four factors posited earlier—differences among the three cases in terms of respondents' beliefs (a) about sanction traditions in felony cases, (b) about the threat an offender poses to the public, (c) about transgressors' maturity of judgment, and (d) about character malleability. However, we still need to account for the marked discrepancy between the numbers of pairings in the math cheating case (187) and the drug trading case (247). To do so, we speculated that such a disparity might result from differences in attitudes toward drugs (a) between all of the 9 year olds and certain of the 17 and 21 year olds and (b) within the older groups (14s, 17s, 21s). Whereas all of the 9 year olds condemned both drug use and drug trading, not all

Table 9-3
Sanction/Aim Pairings

Sanction/Aim Linkages	Frequencies
Monitor behavior to *deter from drug trading*	3
Monitor behavior to *deter from drug use*	2
Monitor behavior to *enforce the law*	1
Warn of punishment to *deter from drug trading*	1
Warn of punishment to *deter from drug use*	1
Put on probation to *deter from drug trading*	1
Put on probation to *deter from drug use*	1
Limit social contacts so as to *generate affect (sorrow)*	1
Limit social contacts to *deter from any kinds of misdeeds*	1
Limit activities so as to *deter from drug trading*	1
Limit activities so as to *deter from drug use*	1
Limit activities so as to *enforce the law*	1
Provide drug education to *focus on consequences*	1
Provide drug education to *help them solve problems*	1
Incarcerate for two weeks to *deter from drug trading*	1

of the older participants did so. Furthermore, among those older students who did believe it was wrong to use drugs, some felt such conduct was no more than mildly naughty, whereas others considered it very serious indeed, condemning it as both criminal and sinful. Such a diversity of attitudes regarding drugs within the older groups might reasonably lead to a greater diversity of sanction/aim combinations among older respondents than among younger ones.

Our second question concerned the relative popularity of different sanction/aim combinations. Table 9-4 displays the 19 sanction/aim pairings—out of the total 268—that were proposed across the three cases by 25 or more respondents. The far-right column shows the case—or cases—to which each combination was dominantly applied. Sanction options posed during the probing phase of the interviews are signified by a § sign. Aims posed during the probing phase are indentified by a Δ sign. It is clear that a great many of the most popular choices were ones offered during the probing phase. Such a result appears to support the common-sense notion that bringing specific options to the attention of the inter-

Table 9-4
The Most Popular Sanction/Aim Pairings
(N = 136)

Sanction & *Aim*	Frequency	Dominant Case
Counsel§ to *teach accountability/responsibility*Δ	80	Drugs
Imprison/detain to *reform the specific misdeed*Δ	78	Steal/Kill
Imprison to *avenge the wrong*Δ	72	Steal/Kill
Imprison to *incapacitate the offender*Δ	72	Steal/Kill
Counsel§ to *reform the specific misdeed*Δ	71	Drugs
Imprison to *help/compensate society*Δ	65	Steal/Kill
Imprison/detain§ to *enforce the law*Δ	59	Drugs
Assign labor§ to *help/compensate society*Δ	58	Drugs
Imprison to *deter the offender in the future*Δ	53	Steal/Kill & Drugs
Imprison to *deter other potential offenders*Δ	53	Steal/Kill
Counsel§ to *help/compensate society*Δ	32	Drugs
Detain§ to *teach accountability/responsibility*Δ	29	Drugs
Execute§ to *deter other potential offenders*Δ	28	Steal/Kill
Assign labor to *enforce the law*Δ	26	Drugs
Imprison to *focus offender's attention on misdeed*	26	Drugs & Steal/Kill
Delegate sanction responsibility to *deter offender*Δ	26	Math test
Delegate sanction responsibility§ to *reform misdeed*Δ	25	Drugs & Steal/Kill
Execute§ to *avenge the wrong*Δ	25	Steal/Kill
Execute§ to *incapacitate the offender*Δ	25	Steal/Kill

§=probed sanction   Δ=probed aim

viewees increases the likelihood that respondents will favor those options. However, it should not be assumed that simply offering such choices will ensure that interviewees will agree with them. The discrepancy between the popularity of probed options between the math test case and the other two cases suggests that respondents do not adopt proffered choices indiscriminately. Apparently the probed options for the drug and burglary cases seemed more reasonable to participants than did the alternatives presented in the math test case, since the math test alternatives were accepted rather infrequently.

Age Trends

A comparison of the diversity of sanction/aim pairings across age groups showed that the 9 year olds submitted the fewest types of pairs over the three cases (103 pairs), with the 14 year olds exceeding that total by 70% (175 pairs), the 17 year olds by 52% (156 pairs), and the 21 year olds by 48% (152 pairs). The same ratios were approximated when each of the three cases was viewed individually. These differences invite speculation about why they might occur. Two potential explanations are found among the developmental indicators described in Chapter 6. The two are Piaget's stages of cognitive development and Lewin's concept of life-space expansion and differentiation, especially during adolescence.

According to Piaget's periods of mental development, the 9 year olds in our study would still be in the latter years of the concrete operations stage (ages 7 to 11), whereas the 14 year olds will have advanced well into the formal operations period (age 11 and beyond). Thus, as explained in Chapter 6, a 14 year old should be better equipped than a 9 year old to imagine various conditions that bear on a problem—past, present, and future—and to devise hypotheses about what might logically occur under different combinations of such conditions. A 14 year old should be capable of all the forms of logic that an adult commands. Beyond age 14, further life experiences over the years of late youth and adulthood should fill in the cognitive map with additional, more complex concepts and a greater recognition of the realistic conditions of the world. As a consequence, a 17 year old's—and particularly a 21 year old's—thought should be more mature and freer of lingering vestiges of egocentrism than is the thought of the early adolescent. Using this line of reasoning to interpret the above figures on sanction/aim pairings, we would suggest that the concrete operations stage of cognitive growth of the 9 year olds equipped them with a more restricted perception of sanction/aim options than did the formal operations stage in which the three older groups were found. Thus, the three older groups would be expected to conceive of a greater variety of sanction/aim alternatives. We would also suggest that the wide array of sanction/aim pairings generated by the 14 year olds might well include a greater number of unrealistic (unfeasible, unpopular) options than would the pairings suggested by the 17 and 21 year olds. In other words, the more realistic view of the world found in the two older groups would

Table 9-5
Age Trends in Sanction/Aim Pairings
(in percentages)

	Age	*9*	*14*	*17*	*21*
	N	*32*	*37*	*34*	*33*
Imprison to *deter the offender in the future*		94	46	12	6
Detain to *teach accountability/responsibility*		53	24	3	6
Imprison/detain to *enforce the law*		72	46	24	27

result in a smaller total of pairings than found in the 14 year olds' proposals.

A second potential explanation of the quantity of pairings by age levels derives from Lewin's propositions about life-space expansion and about the nature of early adolescence. On the presumption that the child's mental structures expand and become more differentiated with the passing years, we would expect older respondents in our study to offer a greater variety of sanction/aim pairs. This would account for the reported difference in the number of pairings between 9 year olds and the three older groups. Then the differences among the older groups, with the 14 year olds providing considerably more pairings than did the 17 and 21 year olds, might be interpreted in terms of Lewin's hypothesis about the marked lability of thought and behavior during early adolescence. The somewhat unfettered elasticity of thought in early adolescence would, by the latter teen years, become more controlled and thereby lead to a more restricted range of sanction/aim alternatives among 17 and 21 year olds than among the 14 year olds.

Finally, there is also the possibility that disparities among the age groups appeared because the samples of respondents that participated in our study were not representative of the four age groups in general. In effect, the differences in sanction/aim pairings might be a consequence of sampling bias. Interviewing far larger numbers of youths from the same age groups could help settle this question.

A comparison of how often each of the age groups selected particular sanction/aim combinations shows that in only three instances among the Table 9-4 pairings were there discernible age trends. As shown in Table 9-5, younger respondents reflected greater faith than did older ones in the efficacy of incarceration as a means of deterring offenders, and particularly by teaching youths to be accountable for their behavior. Younger students were also more interested than older ones in using sanctions to ensure that the law is obeyed, an issue we inspect in some detail in Chapter 14. (Differences between 9 year olds

Table 9-6
Agreement on Sanction/Aim Patterns by Age

Age	9	14	17	21
N	33	36	34	33

Instances of Volunteered Pattern Agreement (3 cases)

Case 1: Pattern agreed upon by:

	9	14	17	21
2 respondents	2	1	2	2
3 respondents			1	
4 respondents	1			
Singular, unmatched patterns	25	34	29	29

Case 2: Pattern agreed upon by:

2 respondents	3	1	1	1
3 respondents		1		
6 respondents	1			
Singular, unmatched patterns	21	31	32	31

Case 3: Pattern agreed upon by:

2 respondents	3	5	1	2
3 respondents	1		2	2
10 respondents	1			
13 respondents		1		
Singular, unmatched patterns	14	13	26	25

Instances of Combined Pattern Agreement (3 cases)

Case 1: Pattern agreed upon by:

2 respondents	1			
Singular, unmatched patterns	30	36	34	33

Case 2: Pattern agreed upon by <u>no</u> respondents at any age level.

Singular, unmatched patterns	33	36	34	33

Case 3: Pattern agreed upon by:

2 respondents	3	2	1	1
Singular, unmatched patterns	27	33	32	31

and 14 year olds are significant beyond the .02 level; differences between 14 year olds and either the 17 or 21 year olds are significant beyond the .05 level).

Gender Comparisons

In the math test and drug trading cases, females did not differ significantly from males in the number of sanction/aims pairings they proposed. In Case 1, females offered 108 pairs and males 100. In Case 2 females submitted 148 and males 154. However, in Case 3 the variety of sanction/aim pairs offered by females (124) exceeded that offered by males (99) by 25%.

There were notable gender differences in only three of the most popular sanction/aim pairs. A higher percentage of females (69%) than males (35%) proposed counseling to dissuade offenders from further transgressions in the drug and burglary cases (.001 level). Likewise, 78% of females versus 42% of males advocated counseling to teach accountability in those same cases (.001 level). In addition, more females (60%) than males (35%) would incarcerate the burglar as a means of helping the community, often by requiring the felon to do useful work while imprisoned (.01 level).

Overall Sanction/Aim Patterns

The phrase *overall sanction/aim patterns* refers to the entire array of sanction/aim relationships expressed during an interview, as illustrated in the foregoing diagrams of the opinions of respondents *A*, *B*, and *C*. Our analysis of the 136 participants' interviews was designed to answer a two-part question: How well did the participants' patterns match each other (a) when only their volunteered answers were considered and (b) when their combined volunteered + afterthought + probed responses were compared?

In the attempt to discover the causal relations patterns people apply in cases of wrongdoing, it is useful once again to recognize the importance of probing beyond interviewees' initial volunteered answers about what sanctions to apply and what outcomes those sanctions are intended to produce. This point is illustrated by the contents of Tables 9-6 and 9-7. Table 9-6 shows the extent to which subjects within an age group agreed with each other in the causal relations patterns of their reactions to the three cases of misconduct. Table 9-7 shows the extent of agreement when all 136 participants are compared with each other, irrespective of age.

The figures in the two tables appear to support the following observations. First, there was far more diversity than consensus among respondents, both within age groups and within the entire sample of 136. That is, the number of individuals whose sanction/aim pattern was dissimilar to anyone else's (singular, unmatched patterns) far exceeded the number whose pattern matched that of one or more other participants. This display of individuality in mode of reasoning was considerably more obvious in respondents' combined patterns (volunteered + afterthought + probed) than in their volunteered patterns alone. As noted before, adding afterthought and probed responses to the opinions that interviewees had initially expressed provided a more comprehensive picture of their cognitive processes than did the volunteered answers alone. The combined version thereby accentuated the individualistic nature of participants' styles of thought.

A second observation concerns the extent of agreement across different types of misconduct. Interviewees more often agreed with each other about the burglary

Table 9-7

Agreement on Sanction/Aim Patterns by Total Group

(N = 136)

	Case 1 math test	Case 2 drugs	Case 3 rob & kill
Instances of Volunteered Pattern Agreement			
Pattern agreed upon by:			
2 respondents	11	10	8
3 respondents	4	1	4
4 respondents	1		2
8 respondents			1
12 respondents			1
20 respondents	___	___	_1_
Total respondents with matching patterns	38	23	76
Singular, unmatched patterns	*98*	*113*	*60*
Instances of Combined Pattern Agreement			
Pattern agreed upon by:			
2 respondents	1		9
3 respondents	___	___	_2_
Total respondents with matching patterns	2	0	24
Singular, unmatched patterns	*134*	*136*	*112*

case than they did about the math test and drug trading incidents. For example, in their volunteered proposals, the patterns of 76 participants matched the patterns of one or more other participants for Case 3 but only 38 matched in Case 1 and only 23 in Case 2 (Table 9-7). Even more dramatic are the differences when respondents' combined patterns are compared. The patterns of only two participants agreed in Case 1, none agreed in Case 2, but 24 agreed in Case 3 (Table 9-7). In an effort to explain these results, we turn again to our earlier observation about established traditions in handling the misdeeds represented in the three cases. The consequences imposed for burglary and murder are officially codified in the form of long-established criminal law. Such is not the case for the infractions in the math test and drug trading cases. Thus, we might expect greater agreement on sanctions representing long-accepted societal practice than on sanctions not so deeply embedded in tradition.

In addition to investigating the amount of consensus in overall sanction/aim patterns, we also studied the degree to which respondents' patterns across two cases would match. Our search revealed that there were no matching patterns across Cases 1 and 2, Cases 2 and 3, or Cases 1 and 3. In other words, when two respondents' sanction/aim patterns matched in one case, their patterns did not match in either of the other two cases. Therefore, in no instance did any of the 136 respondents show the same overt line of reasoning as any other respondent over two of the cases. This display of individualism was even more pronounced when students' patterns of reasoning were compared over all three cases.

CONCLUSION

Two types of observations bring this chapter to a close. The first consists of six generalizations that are supported by the contents of the chapter. The second concerns the question of how people reach agreement in daily life situations that call for group decisions about selecting sanctions to apply for wrongdoing.

Observations about Sanction/Aim Relationships

The results reported in this chapter have led us to the following conclusions.

First, learning which sanctions people would propose in a case of misconduct fails to tell anything about the method of reasoning that has led to such a proposal. To discover how people think about imposing sanctions, it is necessary—at the very least—to learn what aims they hope to achieve by the consequences they recommend. Thus, presenting sanctions as separate from their aims, as was done in Chapter 8, is useful in reflecting the quantities of different sanctions and aims that a group may offer, but it is of no aid in revealing the thought processes that have generated the sanctions. In sum, it is important to learn the sanction/aim causal relationships that people have in mind when they recommend what should be done about wrongdoers.

Second, when people recommend sanctions and their aims, rarely if ever is their intention to have a single sanction produce a single aim. Instead, their belief systems about such matters represent complex sanction/aim chains or networks—multiple sanctions to produce multiple outcomes. Evidence from the present study demonstrates that this is true for people age 9 and beyond, and it seems likely true as well for children somewhat younger.

Third, in seeking to learn how people compare in the way they reason about sanctions and aims, it is not sufficient to learn only what they suggest when asked, "What should be done about the offender, and what good would that do?" It is also necessary to probe their reasoning in greater detail to discover if they would subscribe to other sanctions and aims that they did not initially mention but, nevertheless, favor. Only when respondent's thought processes are explored in depth is the individualistic pattern of their modes of reasoning revealed. This point is supported by evidence from both Chapters 8 and 9. Although the method of interviewing that we employed demonstrated some of this complexity of respondents' sanction/aim thinking, it seems apparent that such thinking is exceedingly more elaborate than our data have suggested. That is, the probing portion of our interviews confronted participants with only a few of the many possible sanction and aim options they might have advocated. If more options had been posed, the picture of respondents' sanction/aim thought patterns would certainly have been far more complex.

Fourth, the extent of agreement among people about sanctions and aims decreases as people's thought processes are investigated in greater detail. This matter may seem so obvious that it qualifies as a truism not worth mentioning. However, it still seems useful to note the way that the matter has been illustrated in the four kinds of consensus discussed in the present chapter. Those four involved agreement about (a) separate sanctions and separate aims, (b) types of sanction/aim models, (c) separate sanction/aim pairings, and (d) overall sanction/aim patterns, particularly when volunteered opinions are combined with afterthought and probed opinions. Whereas under the first three conditions there was a noticeable measure of agreement about certain of the sanction/aim choices, under the fourth condition of combined patterns there was almost no agreement. And when the patterns of participants' recommendations over two cases of wrongdoing were analyzed, it was clear that no two respondents agreed exactly in their modes of thought. In short, individualistic decision making rather than group consensus was the dominant characteristic of these youths' overt reasoning processes.

Fifth, age trends in participants' causal relation proposals were rare indeed, involving no more than a very small number of the entire array of sanction/aim pairings and patterns. Out of the 268 pairings expressed by the 136 respondents, only the three reported in Table 9-5 showed a statistically significant change (beyond the .05 level) across age groups. Whereas the diversity of opinions within each age group was great, notable differences from one age level to another were highly unusual. As a result, knowing a respondent's age would be virtually useless as a guide to predicting the sanction/aim causal relationships that such a respondent would propose in a case of wrongdoing.

Sixth, just as there were few age differences in sanction/aim causal relationships, so also were gender differences quite rare. The only notable contrast was the tendency for females, more often than males, to advocate the counseling of offenders in the drug and burglary cases so as to teach them responsibility and dissuade them from further transgressions (.001 level).

Understanding How People Agree in Daily Life Situations

In a host of daily life situations people are expected to reach agreement about consequences to recommend for wrongdoers. The question of agreement is at stake when legislators pass laws, juries decide criminal and civil cases, a state's citizens consider ballot proposals about the death penalty, school faculties establish discipline policies, club leaders vote on what should be done about a member's misconduct, parents punish a recalcitrant child, and the like.

The contents of this chapter suggest that seldom does one person's pattern of reasoning about sanction/aim connections exactly match anyone else's pattern. Not only has this been true for the young people who took part in the present study, but it seems true of other individuals in the same age range. It is probably true as well for adults beyond age 21, since among our respondents the trend—however slight—was for diversity of opinion to increase rather than decrease with advancing age. The question then may be asked: How do people ever come to agree on the sanctions wrongdoers should experience?

Perhaps the most obvious initial answer is that life situations do not require consensus on the entire patterning of people's sanction/aim thought processes. In most cases, people merely need to agree on one or two sanctions, without regard for whatever aims those sanctions might achieve. Thus, in the present study, the information of practical interest would need to be only the extent of respondents' agreement on sanctions reported early in Chapter 8.

An additional answer to the question derives from the analysis of the factors that promote concurrence within a group about what sanctions to recommend. In court trials, evidence about jury members' deliberations shows that a variety of factors can influence the actions jury members will eventually endorse. Those factors include social pressure applied by other jury members, the various individuals' rhetorical skills as they argue the case, their past experience with similar cases, conflicts among their own moral convictions, fatigue, and outside responsibilities (family and occupational demands) that motivate them to end the trial by limiting the amount of deliberation. Such factors can serve to encourage group members to agree on the treatment or penalty to apply even when such a sanction fails to reflect the actual differences of opinion that obtained within the group.

A third answer involves the limitations that may be imposed on the range of sanctions that are permitted in a given case. In a court trial, the law may stipulate which penalties or treatments are allowed for particular infractions. In a school, the rules governing discipline may specify the options from which consequences for misconduct may be chosen. On an athletic team, league policies may prescribe the sorts of actions that can be applied.

In summary, then, in daily life situations the sanctions people recommend, or at least the ones they accept, (a) may not be the ones they would prefer, (b) may not represent the entire array of consequences they would like to impose, and (c) certainly do not reflect the patterning of the way they reason about sanctions and aims. We imagine that sanction/aim reasoning processes—those networks of causal relationships underlying any individual's sanction proposals—are far more complex and individualistic than most people recognize.

10

Overt Reasoning Styles

Chapter 5 described five characteristics of participants' styles of overt reasoning. The present chapter reports age and gender comparisons for those five aspects, with the analyses presented in the following order: (1) pace of response, (2) reasoning process, (3) specificity of recommendations, (4) strength of ultimate conviction, (5) interrater reliability, and (6) length of response. The descriptions of the first four aspects of style do not mention gender comparisons since no significant differences between females and males were found.

PACE OF RESPONSE

As explained in Chapter 5, four levels of response pace were defined in terms of the number of seconds it took an interviewee to begin answering a question.

Level 1. Immediate. Not more than two seconds elapse between the end of the interviewer's question and the beginning of the individual's answer.
Level 2. 3–5 seconds delay. About 3 to 5 seconds pass before the person answers.
Level 3. 6–9 seconds delay. Around 6 to 9 seconds pass before the person answers.
Level 4. 10+ seconds delay. Ten or more seconds pass before the person answers.

Within the entire sample of 136 students, the average (mean) speed of responding to questions in Case 1 was 4.07 seconds, the longest in Case 2 at 4.40 seconds, and the shortest in Case 3 at 3.29 seconds. On the average, males answered as promptly as females.

In each of the cases, 9 year olds on the average were slower in responding than were any of the other groups, a difference most pronounced (.001) in the example of the girl who copied math answers. No systematic age differences appeared across the 14-, 17-, and 21-year-old groups. Thus, the greatest difference in speed of response occurred during the four-year span between 9 and 14. No identifiable change appeared over the six-year span between 14 and 21. This result suggests the possibility that the early years of adolescence produce greater development in young people's ability to respond readily to moral decision questions than do the middle and later teen years.

REASONING PROCESS

In Chapter 5, the four-level scheme for assessing a respondent's overt reasoning style was described as follows:

Level 1. Highly systematic. Without hesitation, directly suggests types of
activities and the aims they might achieve.
Level 2. Partially systematic. Hesitates a bit, gropes slightly, then offers an
aim and a suitable activity.
Level 3. Rather groping. Initially pauses, questions first option, then proposes
another option but fails to show much confidence in it.
Level 4. Very groping. Continually unsure, wanders, fails to arrive at a clear
solution.

For the entire collection of 136 participants, the average (mean) rating for reasoning style in Case 1 fell between the *highly* and *partially systematic* levels (1.69), in Case 2 slightly closer to the *partially systematic* position (1.74), and in Case 3 somewhat closer to *highly systematic* (1.43). The differences between the Case 3 mean and the means of Cases 1 and 2 are statistically significant beyond the .01 level. This result suggests that most respondents offered a somewhat systematic line of logic to support their recommendations in each of the cases but their rationales in the case of the murdered householder were better organized than their reasoning in the math test and drug trading cases. Such an outcome is perhaps a reflection of greater agreement in the society about the seriousness of such felonies as burglary and murder committed by an adult than about the seriousness of drug use among teenagers and of math cheating among children. In other words, respondents may have found it easier to mount a systematic argument in the third case than in the other two, where the conditions may have seemed to them more problematic.

The most noteworthy difference among age groups appeared in Case 1, where 9 year olds, with a mean rating of 2.05, were significantly less systematic (.001 level) than the other three groups, whose scores were much alike (14 and 17 = 1.60, 21 = 1.52). The variability of scores among 9 year olds was also significantly greater (.05 level) than within any of the other three groups. Although the 9 year olds' arguments in Case 2 appeared as well organized as those of the three older groups, in Case 3 the 9 year olds were once again less lucid than the others, particularly less lucid than the 21 year olds (.001 level).

It seems hardly surprising that young adults on the average would present a better justification for their proposals than would preadolescents. However, what we did find of interest was the similarity among the three older groups. Just as in response speed, the notable difference among ages occurred within the four-year span between 9 and 14 rather than across the six-year period between 14 and 21. Such a finding would appear to accord with Piaget's theory, placing children before age 11 in a concrete operations mode of thought and youths after age 11 in a formal operations mode. In contrast to the 9 year olds in our sample, the 14 year olds seemed nearly as well equipped as the 17 year olds and 21 year olds to offer systematic explanations.

The greater variability among the 9 year olds in their reasoning process might be interpreted as an instance of individual differences in the pace of cognitive development, with some 9 year olds already advanced to Piaget's formal operations stage while others were still back in the concrete operations stage.

SPECIFICITY OF RECOMMENDATIONS

The level of specificity of a respondent's proposals in a case was judged in terms of the following four categories:

Level 1. Very specific
Level 2. Rather specific
Level 3. Somewhat vague
Level 4. Extremely vague

In their proposals about what should be done about wrongdoers, 9 year olds were less specific than members of the other three groups for Case 1 (.01 level) but not significantly so for Cases 2 and 3. In each case, the three older groups were similar to each other in the amount of detail included in their suggestions.

STRENGTH OF ULTIMATE CONVICTION

Interviewees' apparent confidence in the solutions they provided in a case were appraised in terms of four levels.

Level 1. Strong conviction, quite satisfied
Level 2. Somewhat hesitant
Level 3. Very hesitant, dissatisfied
Level 4. Can't make a decision

In Case 1, 9 year olds on the average appeared somewhat less confident in their ultimate decisions (.01) than did the other participants in the study. However, Cases 2 and 3 showed no significant differences across groups, with mean scores midway between *strong* and *somewhat hesitant* conviction.

INTERRATER RELIABILITY

As noted earlier, members of the research team listened to the audio-recorded interviews in order to produce a written report of the essence of each respondent's opinions. During this reporting process, team members also assigned numerical scores that were intended to represent the initial four aspects of overt reasoning style explained in Chapter 5. Since making such decisions appeared to depend rather strongly on the subjective judgments of the raters, we sought to determine the extent of interrater agreement by computing Pearson product-moment coefficients on the ratings assigned independently by two team members on 45 case decisions. The resulting interrater correlations were:

> Pace of response = +.76
> Reasoning process = +.39
> Specificity of recommendations = +.26
> Strength of ultimate conviction = +.47

As a result, considerably greater confidence is warranted in the reliability of ratings for pace of response than for the other three variables, with the least reliable involving judgments of the specificity of respondents' recommendations.

LENGTH OF RESPONSE

In the following pages, the length of students' answers are analyzed by age groups and by females versus males. The matter of interrater agreement was not an issue in the judgments of length of response, because the tape recordings provided a precise measure of how long each interview lasted.

Age Group Comparisons

The length of interviews in minutes is reported in Table 10-1 by age groups and by the cases of wrongdoing.[*] The table shows (1) the average (mean) length of an interview for each case, (2) the variability (standard deviation) of interview length within each age group, and (3) the extremes of interview length (shortest and longest interviews) for each age.

For the entire sample of 136 participants, the average length of time used for an interview was 4.70 minutes on the first case (copying test answers), 4.71 minutes on the second case (trading drugs), and 4.51 minutes on the third case (burglarizing and killing). Thus, on the average, each interview segment lasted somewhat under 5 minutes. However, the amount of time was not the same for all age groups. The most apparent difference across ages for the first and second cases was between the 14 year olds and the other three groups—9, 17, and 21.

---

[*] Figures in the tables represent minutes and fractions of minutes on a 100-point scale rather than minutes and seconds. For instance, 3.50 means three and one-half minutes (3 minutes, 30 seconds), not 3 minutes and 50 seconds.

Fourteen year olds spent the least time answering interview questions—just short of four minutes for both cases—whereas the 17 and 21 year olds used over five minutes and the 9 year olds slightly less than five. The difference between the 14s and 17s exceeded the .01 level of statistical significance in the first case and .05 in the second. In the 14 versus 21 comparison, the difference exceeded the .05 level for both cases, whereas the significance levels of the 14 versus 9 differences were somewhat less.

The age comparison picture for the third case was essentially the same as that for the first two, except that the 9 year olds were closer to the 14s than to the 17s and 21s. Still, the 9s spent more time in discussing the case of the burglar than did the 14s.

In an effort to explain this pattern of length of interviews, we listened again to the tape recorded dialogues to learn if attributes of respondents' styles might account for the results. By doing so, we were able to identify four interrelated features that appeared to influence how long an interview would last. We cast the four as scales having polar positions labeled *concise/elaborated, simple/ multifarious, decisive/hesitant,* and *fluent/halting.*

Table 10-1
Interview Time-Length by Age and Case
(in minutes)

Age	*9*	*14*	*17*	*21*
Case 1—copying test answers				
Mean time length	4.79	3.99	5.05	4.95
Standard deviation	2.33	1.31	1.89	2.18
Shortest interview	2.30	2.10	1.70	2.25
Longest interview	10.45	8.00	9.20	13.70
Case 2—trading drugs				
Mean time length	4.51	3.99	5.21	5.12
Standard deviation	1.63	1.59	2.49	1.94
Shortest interview	2.50	1.85	1.60	2.65
Longest interview	8.75	9.00	9.40	11.00
Case 3—burglarizing and killing				
Mean time length	4.05	3.77	5.03	5.17
Standard deviation	1.41	1.31	2.09	2.87
Shortest interview	1.85	2.25	2.15	2.70
Longest interview	7.40	7.65	9.55	15.09

Average difference between each respondent's shortest and longest interview.

Mean difference	2.08	1.01	2.00	2.34
Standard deviation	1.48	.84	1.32	2.13

The meanings assigned to each scale are described below and illustrated with excerpts from interviews about the 9-year-old girl who copied a classmate's test answers. As the excerpts show, a particular answer can qualify as more than one of the four response types.

Concise/Elaborated. Respondents were credited with giving a concise answer if they very briefly told the sanction or aim they would recommend in a case. In contrast, they were credited with giving an elaborated answer if they explained in detail the nature of their proposed sanction or aim, the reasons for their choice, other options they rejected, or the like.

Concise reply
Interviewer: "What about this suggestion? The girl should be given a good spanking?"
Respondent: "No, it's not right to hit children." [14]

Elaborated reply
Interviewer: "What about this suggestion? The girl should be given a good spanking?"
Respondent: "Well, you can't do that at school, but [laughs] that's what my dad did, and with a belt. But the school can't do that, since it's against the law. Of course, if it was in Huckleberry Finn's time, they could do it, and that would be all right with me." [9]

Simple/Multifarious. A simple proposal contained a single, unembellished suggestion about a sanction or aim. A multifarious proposal included more than one sanction or aim, often accompanied by some amplification. This type differs from an elaborated answer in that the multifarious variety includes more than one sanction or aim, whereas the elaborated form involves an extended description of a single sanction or aim.

Simple reply
Interviewer: "What do you think should be done about the girl who copied answers?"
Respondent: "Send her to the principal's office." [9]

Multifarious reply
Interviewer: "What do you think should be done about the girl who copied answers?"
Respondent: "Well, she should be punished—that is, by the teacher. First, when the girl's about to take another test, the teacher should separate her from the one she copied from so she can't cheat. The teacher shouldn't just say, 'You get an automatic *F.*' Instead, she should give the girl a way out, like have her promise not to cheat again and prove it in some way, like maybe spend extra time with the teacher. And maybe the girl should apologize to the student she copied off of, because it's not been fair to that student to be copied from. That way, the girl will learn that what she did was wrong. There are a lot of times in this world where the student doesn't know that it's wrong, so they need to be punished so they realize it's wrong. And if

they keep on doing it, they should get more strict punishment, because if they just go on lying and cheating in their life, the more they do it the easier it gets. So when they're older, it's not going to stop. It's just going to become a bigger problem." [17]

Decisive/Hesitant. Answers were judged as decisive when presented in a prompt, unwavering manner. On the other hand, responses were rated as hesitant when interviewees either paused frequently or for an extended time, changed their opinion, and either displayed little faith in their answers or else failed to reach a conclusion.

Decisive reply

Interviewer: "How about this aim? Is it one you would want to achieve?—To make the girl pay for what she's done. In other words, when you do something wrong you deserve to be punished."

Respondent: "Yes, I believe in that. She deserves some kind of penalty." [14]

Hesitant reply

Interviewer: "How about this aim? Is it one you would want to achieve?—To make the girl pay for what she's done. In other words, when you do something wrong you deserve to be punished."

Respondent: "Well—. [long pause] That's difficult for me to answer, because that's . . . that's how I was taught—if you do something wrong, you should be punished. [pause] What would be a sufficient punishment for . . . for uh . . . . whatever it is that she's done? If, for example, she's copied another student's homework and she should be punished. [long pause] That's a hard one . . . I . . . I don't . . . I don't. . . . First of all, I don't know how to punish her in such a way that she'll not do it again, because she's . . . for whatever reason we're trying to aim for, because she's scared. You know . . . we want to scare her out of doing it, so naturally we'd do something kind of nasty. But punishment isn't going to solve her problem." [21]

Fluent/Halting. An answer was considered fluent if it was well organized, cast in easily understood language, and the respondent appeared to have no difficulty selecting phrases that accurately expressed his or her opinion. An answer was judged to be halting if it was worded in an awkward pattern and the respondent seemed to struggle to find a satisfactory way to explain his or her thoughts.

Fluent reply

Interviewer: "What do you think about this suggestion—that the teacher should warn the girl never to do it again or she would be in very serious trouble?"

Respondent: "No, it's too late for that. The girl's already copied several times. It's now time that the teacher take more direct action—something like a conference with the teacher and the girl's parents to discover what's behind all this." [21]

Figure 10-1

Estimated Scale Positions of Age Groups on
Characteristics Contributing to Interview Length

concise		14	9		17 21		elaborated
simple	9		14		17 21		multifarious
decisive	14 21 17			9			hesitant
fluent	21 17	14			9		halting

Halting reply

Interviewer: "What do you think about this suggestion—that the teacher should warn the girl never to do it again or she would be in very serious trouble?"

Respondent: "I like that."

Interviewer: "All right, why do you like it?"

Respondent: "Well, because . . . (pause) I forget what the question was."

Interviewer repeats the suggestion.

Respondent: "Well, if . . . uh . . . the teacher did warn her . . . she might. . . she might . . . uh . . . she might not do it. [pause] That could teach the girl not to do it." [9]

From our analysis of the tape recordings, we determined that lengthy interviews resulted from elaborated, proliferated answers delivered in a hesitant, halting fashion. On the other hand, short interviews resulted from concise, simple answers delivered in a fluent, decisive manner. Our estimates of the age groups' comparative positions on the scales are shown in Figure 10-1.

Combining data from Table 10-1 with the estimates in Figure 10-1 suggests that 17 and 21 year olds were similar in length of interview as well as in the characteristics contributing to interview length. The 9 year olds were similar to the 17s and 21s in the length of their answers for the first two cases. However, in regard to style, the length of response among 9s was more often determined by a hesitant and halting delivery (diffidence and a need to have questions explained) than by elaboration and proliferation. The 14 year olds, when compared to the 17s and 21s, offered simpler, more concise answers.

In no instance did any respondent spend the same amount of time on each case. Furthermore, there was no consistent pattern within any age group regarding which case—1, 2, or 3—was discussed at greatest length. However, as shown by the bottom entries in Table 10-1, the 9 , 17 , and 21 year olds were similar in terms of the relationship of their shortest and longest interviews. The average for 9s was 2.08 minutes, for 17s was 2.00 minutes, and for 21s was 2.34 minutes. Again, the 14 year olds differed noticeably from the others with the average gap between their longest and shortest dialogues barely more than a minute. In brief, the 14s were the most consistent in interview length from one case to another.

Although the differences between age groups in length of interviews were rather minor, the differences among members within an age group were quite dramatic, as reflected in the standard deviations and the distances between the shortest and longest interviews in Table 10-1. For example, when 9 year olds discussed the first case, their briefest interview was more than eight minutes shorter than their longest interview. Among the 21 year olds' responses to the third case, the most elaborate interview was over 12 minutes longer than the shortest one. And just as the 14 year olds on the average spent less time answering questions than did the other age groups, they also showed less variability within their group, as indicated by smaller standard deviations than those for the 9, 17, and 21 year olds.

In summary, the variability in length of reply and in the style that determined length was far greater within each age group than between one group and another. Consequently, knowing the age of a participant was of little if any use in predicting how long a participant would talk or in suggesting the style in which a respondent's opinions would be attired. For instance, a few 9 year olds were as fluent, decisive, elaborate, and multifarious in their answers as the average 17 or 21 year old, whereas a few 17 and 21 year olds were as halting, hesitant, and simple in their delivery as the less articulate 9 and 14 year olds.

Gender Comparisons

Table 10-2 compares females and males by average length of interview and by variability in length for the three cases of wrongdoing. As the figures indicate, the mean time length for both sexes was identical for Case 1. Although males took slightly longer than females for Cases 2 and 3, the differences failed to reach a .05 level of significance. In contrast, variability among females was significantly greater (.01) than among males for Cases 1 and 2, but not for Case 3.

CONCLUSION

In this chapter, the 136 participants' styles of expressing their opinions were analyzed in regard to pace of response, reasoning process, specificity of recommendations, satisfaction with their ultimate decisions, and length of interview.

In the style analyses, three features deserve mention. First, in several of the aspects of style, 9 year olds on the average were notably different from members of the three older groups. This tendency was particularly obvious in Case 1, where the 9s were slower in responding to questions, less systematic in their reasoning, less specific in their proposals, and less confident in their ultimate decisions. However, in Cases 2 and 3 such trends were either minimal or entirely absent. It is not clear whether the 9 year olds were actually less compe-

Table 10-2
Interview Time-Length by Gender and Case
(in minutes)

Sex	*Female*	*Male*	*Sig. Level*[*]
N	69	67	
Case 1—copying test answers			
Mean time length	4.69	4.69	—
Standard deviation	2.30	1.58	.01
Case 2—trading drugs			
Mean time length	4.53	4.89	—
Standard deviation	2.23	1.76	.01
Case 3—burglarizing and killing			
Mean time length	4.48	4.57	—
Standard deviation	1.98	2.23	—

*A dash (—) indicates that a difference between means or standard deviations did not reach the .05 level of statistical significance.

tent than the older students in answering questions about the math test case or, instead, were initially ill at ease with the interview situation as they faced the first case. Perhaps when they became more accustomed to being interviewed, they were better prepared to perform more in the manner of the older respondents. Second, although in several ways the style characteristics of the 9 year olds appeared different from those of the older students, the distribution of individuals' scores within one group greatly overlapped the distribution of scores in the other three groups. In effect, certain 9 year olds displayed a reasoning style much like the average of one of the older groups. In a few instances, older respondents seemed similar to the average 9 year old. In brief, there were marked individual differences within each group in the students' ways of expressing their opinions. Consequently, as mentioned earlier, knowing the age of a participant would be of virtually no help in predicting how long that person would talk or in suggesting the style in which such an individual would cast his or her opinions.

Third, there were no recognizable differences between females and males in the ways they presented their views.

11

Conceptions of God and the Sanctity of Life

In Chapter 4 we proposed that respondents' answers to interview questions often furnished information about their conceptions of reality and their value commitments. Two of the more dramatic demonstrations of this feature were provided by the interviewees' reactions to a pair of questions about the case of the burglar who killed a woman whose house he was robbing. The questions were as follows:

Interviewer: "Two of the other people we interviewed had different ideas about what should happen to the man. I'll read each of their suggestions, and you can tell me if you think either of these is as good as the suggestion you gave. The first one is: 'He should be put to death.' What do you think about that? How do you like that suggestion compared to your own?"

(*After hearing the respondent's answer, the interviewer asked:*) "Now, what do you think of this second suggestion: 'I don't have to decide. God will know what to do'?"

We interpreted respondents' answers to the death penalty question as a reflection of a moral value, and we regarded answers to the God-will-know question as evidence of beliefs about reality. Compiling the 136 participants' opinions about these two issues enabled us to assemble a pair of analytical schemes that would enhance our understanding of the structure of such beliefs. The purpose of this chapter is to demonstrate the application of those two schemes for the purpose of revealing similarities and differences among individuals and between age and gender groups. The presentation begins with the question about God and then addresses the issue of the death penalty. In discussing participants' beliefs about God and their convictions about the death peanlty, we first survey a variety of individual reaponses, then summarize the responses by age and gender.

DIVINE INTERVENTION IN HUMAN AFFAIRS

As we reviewed participants' replies to the question about God's meting out justice for misdeeds in daily human events, we recognized that the form of a reply often enabled us to draw inferences about the individuals' convictions regarding several matters: (1) the likely existence and nature of a supernatural being that mediated in human affairs, (2) realism versus idealism, and (3) the clarity of respondents' beliefs about such issues. The scheme we devised for analyzing these three variables derived from the following observations.

Characteristics of a Supernatural Being— Omniscience, Omnipotence, and Chosen Role

Reactions to the question about the role of God in the case of the 23-year-old burglar enabled us to estimate what interviewees believed about: (a) whether there indeed is such a supernatural being as God and, if so, whether God (b) is omniscient, (c) is omnipotent, and (d) chooses to assume the role of assessing sanctions for instances of wrongdoing. The way inferences can be drawn about these matters is illustrated with the following excerpts from interviews. In each example, the quoted comment is an individual's reply to the question of whether it is desirable to relegate to God the responsibility for deciding the burglar's fate.

God intervenes. In the answers of people who expected that a supernatural being would certainly apply penalties for misconduct, two varieties of supernatural intervention appeared—the universal and the conditional.

The universal version holds that every instance of misconduct will be met with appropriate consequences. This is an expression of faith in immanent justice—the belief that an inherent feature of reality is that justice is inevitably served. Sometimes people attribute the operation of immanent justice to an impersonal "natural course of events" or "the way things turn out." However, others identify a personalized supreme being or set of spirits (in this case God) as the source of reactions to wrongdoing.

> "Yes, God will take care of the killer, if not immediately, then eventually."
> [17]
> "It's not our right to say what should happen to the man. God will punish him in whatever way is best." [17]

A conditional version of God's intervention contends that only under certain circumstances does a supreme being assume the role of applying sanctions.

> "Well, yes, when it's something like murder—very serious things. God would do that. But I don't think God does anything about little things, like a little child being naughty, maybe stealing a cookie or something. Those things we can take care of by ourselves." [14]

An occasional respondent suggested that God could act to reform an offender, but that it was also necessary for people to take immediate steps to provide the conditions for God's intervention. According to a 14 year old:

"Many people who are put in jail have found God. They realize what they've done and ask for forgiveness and stuff like that, and they kind of become partial friends of the victim's family. They say they're sorry. So the guy should be in prison for a while, and then he'll find God." [14]

A 9 year old observed that even though people could decide what sanctions offenders should experience, it would be better to leave the matter up to God, apparently because God was more competent. Thus, after this child had suggested sending the burglar to prison, he chose to turn the problem over to God.

"God will decide something good for the man to do, like going out to work on the roads or clean up the garbage." [9]

Some participants directly suggested, or else implied, that people served as God's representatives or instruments in administering justice.

"I'm sure God would know what to do, but we're playing a game down here on earth where you've got to follow the rules. You've got to go through the system and serve your time. I mean, when the guy dies later on in life, then let God take care of him. But who's to say that God isn't taking care of him now by our putting him in prison." [21]

Another student proposed that God's decision took the form of instructions issued to those people who are responsible for imposing the sanctions a wrongdoer should face.

"When somebody does something bad, God tells the person who is trying to think of what to do what they should to do about it." [9]

One respondent first proposed that the burglar be sent to jail for three years, but when asked about leaving the matter up to God, he appeared to believe that the task of setting a penalty could be performed either by God or by people in authority.

Respondent: "God will decide something good for him, like maybe having him go work on the roads."

Interviewer: "So you think God could come up with a better punishment than you suggested?"

Respondent: "Yeah. God might keep him in jail a long time and maybe get him a job somewhere and keep him working so he wouldn't do those kinds of things again."

Interviewer: "So you think that God would decide if the man should go to jail, and that the police wouldn't have to do it?"

Respondent: "The police could do it, too. They'd probably put him in jail." [9]

For still another student, leaving the sanction up to God was unacceptable because of the difficulty God would face in trying to communicate directly with transgressors. According to this boy, in order for God to apply a sanction, God would need to explain to the burglar the nature of the punishment that he would be obliged to face. However, there seemed to be no convenient way for God to provide that explanation:

> "The man can't talk with God, so I don't think the man would ever know what God wanted to say about it." [9]

Another interviewee pictured God's dual role as that of equipping humans to solve life's problems and then authorizing people to do so:

> "I believe in God and everything, but I think we're expected to help ourselves. I don't think he'll come down and take over. God gave us brains, and God gave us the authority to make these lives we live. Now it's up to us to deal with them." [14]

An occasional student assumed that God could and would take action, but that God was not infallible, so the consequence that God provided might not be the most suitable. For example, a boy who proposed to imprison the burglar for five years expressed some reservation about leaving the decision up to God:

> "I think letting God decide would be pretty good. It would be just about the same as what I would do. But then, maybe my idea is better, because God sometimes makes mistakes like everyone else. The man should be put in jail. If God just let him free, the man might do it again." [9]

When respondents thus proposed that a supreme being does indeed adjudicate matters of wrongdoing, we can necessarily infer that they also believe there is a God, that God is omniscient (is aware of every transgression), and that God is omnipotent (has the power to produce whatever consequence is deemed suitable).

God could intervene, but doesn't. Some interviewees implied that they believed in an omniscient and omnipotent being, but this God did not allot sanctions and treatments for wrongdoing, at least not in the daily conduct of life. In other words, they assumed that it is not God's responsibility to intercede in mundane judicial affairs.

> "Sure, God could do it, but that responsibility is really left up to us. As they say, 'God helps those who help themselves.' People have to decide what to do with robbers and killers." [14]

Another implied that God might participate by communicating with the wrongdoer. But if the offender was not a true believer and, instead, was a habitual criminal, God would probably not choose to intervene.

> "Leaving it to God would be good. So if the man was very religious, maybe it would work. But maybe God wouldn't even talk to the robber because he's robbed so many times." [9]

God knows. A less common conviction was that there surely is an omniscient being, but such an entity is merely an observer of events and lacks the ability to influence daily affairs. However, some of those who refrained from attributing earthly power to their God contended that the rewards and punishments people earn by their deeds on earth will eventually be assessed on Judgment Day when the deceased begin their life after death:

> "From what I've been told, God knows everything that goes on, and after people die he'll treat them the way they deserve for what they did when they were alive. So this killer will get what he deserves after he's gone—probably some place in Hell." [14]

> "God's not going to punish the guy till after he dies and goes to heaven. In the meantime the guy's going to kill more people if they don't put him in jail. So somebody has to decide what to do with him now." [17]

There is a God. Some respondents appeared to accept the notion that there is a kind of supernatural entity or supreme existent, but they did not assume that such an entity was all-knowing, was all-powerful, or mediated in human affairs.

> "I think there was a God that created the world and got it running, but that doesn't mean there's somebody up there watching everything that goes on. If something's to be done about crime, people have to do it themselves." [21]

The belief that God may function differently at different times in history was reflected in the opinion of a 17 year old:

> "I think God might know what to do, but I don't think there's anything he can do about it. Maybe if we were living in the 1600s or something, everything we did was an act of God, but it doesn't happen any more." [17]

Another student denied that God played a role in adjudicating misconduct on earth, apparently because the task of attending to all instances of misdeeds in the world would be an unmanageable burden.

> "I believe in God and all, but God's not going to make this thing better. There are more people in the world than just that one person anyway, so there's more people to take care of than that one person. Leave it to God? That's really a stupid answer. People have to take care of themselves rather than thinking someone's going to do it for them, so leaving it up to God is a bad attitude." [17]

A 9 year old was unconvinced that God could consistently be counted on to assess sanctions for wrongdoing.

> "God doesn't always fix things like that, so you can't leave it up to him." [9]

A 14 year old expressed a similar view.

> "If God was going to step in any time, he would be helping sick babies or help the Ethiopians, and stuff. There are better things he can do than making something happen to this one man." [14]

Maybe there isn't a God. The answers offered by certain participants implied that they were agnostics. Either they believed that the answer to whether or not there is God is unknowable, or else they thought the evidence presently available to affirm the existence of God is insufficient.

> "You can't take that chance—leaving the robber up to God. Even though some people talk about what God is like, nobody really knows. It's just their opinion. We don't even know if there is such a thing as God." [14]
> "I don't necessarily believe in God." [17]
> "It's true that you could leave it up to God, but there might not be a God and there might not be a Devil. So the man really should be sent to prison." [21]

There is no God. By direct admission or by implication, some participants indicated that they did not believe in God, or that at least they did not believe in a personalized being who influenced life's events. On these grounds they rejected the option of delegating to God the responsibility to punish the burglar.

> "I'm an atheist. Our law system, not a God, has to deal with killers." [21]

A 14 year old professed to being an atheist, while still averring that there was some sort of supernatural existence "up there." She further noted that if she did believe in God, such a God would not be omnipotent.

> "I don't believe in God, so—well, I believe there's something up there, you know, but I don't believe in it like a god. But even if I did believe in God, I don't think that God has the capability to kill the burglar. Even the Greeks believed in gods. They had lots of them, and they had three gods—three sisters—who could take your life whenever they wanted to, but the Greeks still had jails and stuff. So even if you do believe in a god, I think you can't let this guy who's killed somebody go free. Something has to be done short of killing the burglar." [14]

Indeterminate conception. Sometimes interviewees' answers failed to reveal what those individuals believed about God's existence, traits, and role in adjudicating instances of wrongdoing. The following are remarks that rendered a participants' convictions about such matters indeterminate.

> "Why would anyone make a suggestion like that? It's just a cop out. People have to decide what to do about the crime." [21]
> "I don't know about that. I'm not really a bible fanatic." [17]

Since such replies did not fit any of the above defined categories, an additional type of answer labeled *indeterminate conception* was required to accommodate unclear and ambiguous opinions.

In summary, the answers students offered to the question of leaving the killer's fate to God often reflected an aspect of their views of reality. Their answers furnished clues to their beliefs about the presumed "real" existence and nature of a personalized, supreme power that takes action in cases of misconduct.

Realism Versus Idealism

Respondents' answers also suggested that some viewed the question of super natural influence from a realist perspective, while others replied from an idealist viewpoint. In the present context, a realist perspective holds that God exists (or fails to exist) in the real, objective world outside the perceiver's mind. In contrast, an idealist perspective assumes that God exists as an idea in the perceiver's mind, whether or not there "really is a God out there."

Most of our participants addressed the case of the burglar from a realist vantage point. In other words, their responses focused on the issue of whether there was *really* a God in the *real* universe who might apply sanctions to offenders.

"I think God can give us hints about what we should do, but he doesn't take direct action himself." [14]

"There are times that I'm sure God does punish people. I've known of criminals who weren't caught by the police but they still had something awful happen to them." [21]

However, a few participants expressed an idealist view. For instance, one 14 year old disagreed with the proposal that the burglar's fate be left up to God:

"Because maybe the man who robbed and killed doesn't believe in God, so he'll just go out and do it again. Unless he believed in God, he wouldn't care about it. Killers aren't very religious." [14]

"If he didn't believe in God, I'd say don't leave it up to God. But if the man did believe in God, then I'd say to go with that. I'd make him spend some time in jail, like a month or week to see if he believes in God, and if he does and it goes into his mind what to do with him, then he'd just do it." [17]

The implication here is that any effect which God—solely as an idea—will have on an offender's feelings or behavior must be entirely a function of the characteristics attributed to God in that offender's mind. For instance, one commonly accepted idea of God portrays the supreme being as exceptionally punitive and vengeful. If the burglar embraces such a belief, he may well expect that evil will befall him in the coming days or that, following his death, he will be consigned to eternal suffering in hell. The fear and misery generated by such an expectation could serve as punishment for his misdeeds and might deter him from further transgression. However, from an idealist's perspective, if the burglar does not believe in God, or if the God of his conception is not punitive and vengeful, then leaving the burglar's fate up to God could not be expected to prevent the felon from future wrongdoing. Hence, the idealist would say that it is the wrongdoer's conscience, rather than an actual supernatural being, that imposes penalties.

Responding from an idealist vantage point, a 21 year old appeared to feel that leaving the matter up to God might have been appropriate in the past but was not appropriate today.

"The 20th century is a godless century. You can't leave it up to something people don't believe in." [21]

Not all of the students answered in a way that would warrant their being identified as either a realist or an idealist. For instance, as another student struggled with the question, he vacillated between the two positions—God as an objective reality versus God as an idea in people's minds.

"Hmm. That brings up so many questions. Is there a God? There must be a higher power out there. Is that power going to take action? I don't think so, since the higher power is worried about bigger things than one human killing another human. If God is in our mind—and I believe that's where God is. I mean, God is a human creation, because we don't know what the cosmic, universal being is. We label it *God*. We need to believe that God will take care of us, and things are going to be okay. If God is in our mind, then it's going to be on the robber's mind and conscience, and he'll always know he's got blood on his hands. But then he'd have to believe in God. No, we can't leave the decision up to God. We do have to decide what to do with the man. It's up to us. Of course, God's here, God's everywhere, but he gave us our minds, and we have to use our minds, so it's our right to decide what to do about the man who killed the woman." [21]

In brief, interviewees' replies could be seen as representing either a realist or an idealist perspective toward the role likely to be played by supernatural sources of sanctions.

Clarity Versus Confusion

We also recognized from the form of participants' answers that some of them held clearly defined opinions about the issue at hand, whereas others seemed rather confused. Thus, we concluded that their expressed beliefs might be located along a scale ranging from substantial clarity and precision at one end to great confusion at the other. The following response is one we would place near the great clarity end of the continuum.

"God knows what to do, and probably he'll do it. But as they say, sometimes God waits a long time to do his job. You might think the robber will be punished by God sooner or later, but it might be later rather than sooner so in the meantime the guy can go out and rob and murder again. So the guy should go to prison to keep him from doing it again." [14]

In contrast, consider another answer that we believe qualifies for the confused end of the scale.

"Leave it up to God? Yes, that's good. Umm. That's probably better than my idea of putting him in prison. (pause) Yeah, I. (pause) You can appeal to God for blood guilt. But it depends on how. (pause) Well, you can't let people just wander around. That's why we have a system in our country. You can't let people who've done something wrong just wander around. There has to be someone to decide what the punishment should be, so robbers don't think. (pause) It's not something that can be taken lightly. It can be taken care of, I guess. (pause) I don't know exactly. God will know what to do, but there has to be some decision made about what the man's punishment should be, because otherwise there'd be a bunch of crazy people walking around our world. There has to be some decision made." [14]

A young woman appeared to recognize that her reasoning was a bit muddled when she remarked:

"Well, if you're religious in that sense, then you can believe what you want. (pause) It's kind of true in a way in my own way of thinking about God taking care of it, although I don't necessarily believe in God but. . . . (long pause) Now that's a funny statement. It kind of makes me laugh." [21]

Summarizing Respondents' Conceptions of God

Tables 11-1 and 11-2 offer two summaries of the interviewees' conceptions of God as reflected in the case of the 23 year old burglar. Table 11-1 presents respondents' opinions by age level and Table 11-2 by gender. The figures in the two tables appear to support the following conclusions.

First, there was far more diversity than consensus among the 136 participants in their beliefs about the existence and characteristics of a supreme being who might impose sanctions for such offenses as burglary and murder. Furthermore, there were no consistent trends in terms of diversity as associated with either age or gender. In other words, variability of conviction within each of the age and gender groups occurred in relatively equal measure, with every group including some share of orthodox believers, of partial believes, of agnostics, and of atheists. With one exception, there were no statistically significant differences across age or gender groups in regard to any of the types of belief about a supreme being. Although more females (60%) than males (44%) believed that God existed as a real being, the difference did not reach significance at the .05 level. Likewise, the observed difference between the percentage of females (19%) and males (25%) whose belief about God was indeterminate fell short of statistical significance.

The one exception is observed in how lucidly interviewees described their beliefs. Older students (ages 17 and 21) generally explained their convictions with greater clarity and internal consistency than did younger ones (ages 9 and 14) (Table 11-1). In particular, the way older respondents declared that they did not believe in God suggested that their disbelief was of a thoughtful variety, arrived at after considering the issue at some length. The fact that some identified themselves as atheists—not simply as doubters or nonbelievers—indicated that they were aware of how their position would be cast in theological terms.

Table 11-1
Conceptions of God by Age Level
(in percentages)

	Age	*9*	*14*	*17*	*21*	*All*
	N	*33*	*36*	*34*	*33*	*136*
God's Existence						
God exists:						
As a real being		55	39	65	52	53
Only as an idea		9	6		15	7
God's existence doubtful		3	11		3	5
Don't believe in God		3	22	9	18	13
Belief indeterminate		30	22	26	12	22
Clarity versus Confusion						
God's Role						
God applies sanctions:						
In offender's lifetime		15	3	3		4
After offender's death		12	8	23	24	17
God does not punish						
wrongdoers		30	36	65	49	45
Clarity versus Confusion						
Clearly stated opinion*		52	64	94	91	75
Partially clear opinion		6	11			4
Confused opinion		42	25	6	9	21

*Difference between ages 9/14 and 17/21 statistically significant beyond .001.

THE DEATH PENALTY — CONDITIONS THAT DETERMINE ITS PROPER USE

The following discussion is designed to achieve two ends. The first is to use a particular punishment, the death penalty, to illustrate in some detail our earlier contention that people's answers to questions about wrongdoing can furnish clues about their moral values. The second purpose is to show how respondents' conceptions of the death penalty have influenced their decisions about whether or not to execute the man who killed a woman while burglarizing her house.

Table 11-2
Conceptions of God by Gender
(in percentages)

	Sex	*Females*	*Males*	*Both F & M*
God's Existence	N	*69*	*67*	*136*
God exists:				
As a real being*		60	44	53
Only as an idea		6	9	7
God's existence doubtful		5	5	5
Don't believe in God		10	16	13
Belief indeterminate		19	25	22
God's Role				
God applies sanctions:				
In offender's lifetime		7	3	4
After offender's death		16	18	17
God does not punish wrongdoers		50	40	45
Clarity versus Confusion				
Clearly stated opinion		69	81	75
Somewhat confused opinion		6	3	4
Very confused opinion		25	16	21

* Chi square for God as a real thing = 2.95 with p .086; does not reach .05 level.

Clues to Moral Principles

The clues appear most obviously in (1) the acts that respondents regard as misdeeds and (2) the aims they hope to achieve by sanctions and treatments they recommend.

A key assumption underlying this analysis is that each moral value comprises two components—a moral principle and a description of conditions that govern the application of that principle. The term *principle* means an unembellished statement of what is right or—in its reciprocal form—what is wrong. The most familiar list of moral principles in Western societies is perhaps the biblical set of ten commandments that Moses presented to the people of Israel. The commandments ordered Israelites to refrain from worshipping any gods other than Jehovah, carving idols of gods, using God's name lightly as in cursing, working on the Sabbath day, dishonoring their parents, killing, stealing, lying about others, committing adultery, or yearning for their neighbors' possessions (*Holy Bible,* 1611, Exodus, chap. 20). In modern times, Gert (1970) derived a somewhat similar set of principles by means of a rational analysis of human social behavior: don't kill, don't cause pain, don't disable, don't deprive others of freedom or opportunity, don't deprive others of pleasure, don't deceive, keep your promise, don't cheat, obey the law, and do your duty.

The term *condition* in the present context means a circumstance that influences when and how a principle will be applied to a particular event that involves morality. The presumption here is that rarely if ever is any moral principle exercised unconditionally in every life situation to which that principle could apply. One typical condition is *knowledge of right and wrong,* meaning the capacity of people to understand the implications of an offense they might commit. Hence, young children are often forgiven transgressions for which their elders would be punished, on the grounds that the young have not yet reached "the age or reason" and therefore have inadequate knowledge of right and wrong. Another condition is the offender's *intent.* A person who breaks a jewelry store window by accident is subject to less stringent sanctions—or perhaps none at all—than a person who smashes the window in a robbery attempt. There are many other conditions as well, such as the mental state of the transgressor at the time of the misdeed, the motive behind the act (hunger, greed, self-defense, revenge), the wrongdoer's socioeconomic or ethnic status, information about the offender's general character or reputation, and more.

This notion of principles and conditions can be used in constructing an analytical scheme for comparing our 136 respondents' opinions about the death penalty. The scheme is divided into three steps. The first consists of determining whether a respondent does or does not recommend that the burglar be executed. The second involves identifying the conditions under which the respondent considers the death penalty justified. Third is the rationale adduced in support of the first two steps. Depicting each interviewee's answers in terms of these steps can contribute to comparisons of individuals so as to understand how they are alike and are different in the bases for their moral judgments.

It is well beyond the scope of this chapter to provide a detailed analysis of principles behind each of the 136 students' comments about the death penalty. However, the manner in which such analysis is performed can be illustrated with the following ten examples showing how individuals' principles, conditions, and rationales can be compared. Studying the ten examples enables us to recognize a vital characteristic of the respondents' recommendations. First, we should note that none of ten students would advocate executing the 23 year old burglar. All would place him in prison. However, it would be an error to assume that the ten respondents' recommendations were all founded on the same pattern of moral reasoning. As the following sketch of their views demonstrates, no two students based their decision on precisely the same combination of principles, conditions, and rationales. In effect, the respondents' agreement about not executing the felon derived from ten different modes of thought. Hence, what on the surface would appear to be a high degree of consensus in the group (don't kill the murderer), on closer analysis shows marked individualism and diversity in the interviewees' moral values and modes of logic.

1. A 14 year old disagreed with the suggestion that the burglar be executed: "I don't think anybody should be killed. It's a human right not to be killed no matter what they do. Wrongdoers should be punished, but not killed."

(*a*) The principle: Do not kill.
(*b*) Conditions: None—unconditional application of the principle.
(*c*) Rationale: The right not to be killed is inviolate.

2. Another 14 year old first agreed with the death penalty, but promptly changed her mind: "You should put him to death, you know. Oh, but— If you— I don't know exactly. But I don't think death's the answer. That's pretty harsh. I know that sometimes they say a life for a life, but I don't know. It depends on how he felt about it and if he was really repentant enough or whatever. I don't really know. Instead of death, prison for a long time is better."

(*a*) The principle: Kill only under certain conditions.
(*b*) Conditions: The degree of an offender's contrition for committing the act.
(*c*) Rationale: People who repent deserve less severe punishment.

3. A 9 year old said: "He only killed one person. That means they shouldn't put him to death unless he killed at least five people."

(*a*) The principle: Kill only under certain conditions.
(*b*) Conditions: The extent of damage in terms of the number of victims.
(*c*) Rationale: A single victim is not sufficient to warrant execution.

4. A 17 year old vacillated while deciding whether the burglar should be put to death, or even whether anyone should ever be executed. She appeared to struggle with the dilemma of trying to reconcile two incompatible moral principles: "No, he shouldn't be put to death. His act wasn't that extreme. Well, yes, it was extreme, in that he did kill someone. But even so, I think the death penalty should be used only in extreme cases where the same crime has happened at least several times before. But really, death is too extreme. Also, we don't really have the right to take that life. Um—I really don't think that punishment should be used at all. But I can understand its being used in extreme cases."

(*a*) The two principles: (1) Do not kill. (2) Kill only under extreme circumstances.

(*b*) Two conditions: (1) Unconditional condemnation of the death penalty. (2) Kill only after several repetitions of the crime of murder.

(*c*) Rationales: (1) No one has a right to take another's life, even as punishment for a crime. (2) Although a single victim is not sufficient to warrant executing an offender, multiple victims provide that right.

5. A 14 year old proposed that the penalty imposed for murder might depend on the relationship between the murder victim and the person who is recommending the penalty: "I don't believe in capital punishment. You have a message here that it's not right to kill people. Then if you execute that person, it's not right, since it's saying '*You* can't kill people but *we* can kill them.' I mean, I know that if I was part of the family, I'd probably want him dead. But as an outsider, my morals say don't kill somebody. I can never see taking somebody's life."

(*a*) The principle: Never kill, except possibly for personal revenge.

(*b*) Conditions: If you are a member of the murder victim's family, execution may seem warranted.

(*c*) Rationale: It is illogical to use killing as a punishment for killing. However, the emotional distress suffered by family members may qualify them to seek revenge for the loss of their loved one.

6. The notion that offenders should be treated equally before the law was suggested by a 14 year old: "Well, criminals these days are doing stuff like raping a lot of people, and Jeffrey Dahmer was eating people, and those criminals don't get a death sentence, so I don't think this guy should be put to death for just that one crime."

(*a*) The principle: Evenhanded justice.

(*b*) Conditions: None stipulated.

(*c*) Rationale: A less serious crime does not warrant a more severe consequence than more serious ones.

7. The belief that execution is too light a punishment for the combined crimes of burglary and murder was reflected in a 9 year old's recommendation that "The man should have to suffer, not just be put through a quick death. He should go to prison for 33 years. When he got out, he'd be too old to have the energy to do those things again."

(*a*) The two principles: (1) The amount of suffering offenders experience should be commensurate with the seriousness of their crime. (2) Future crimes can be prevented by reducing offenders' ability to transgress.

(*b*) Conditions: None stipulated.

(*c*) Rationales: (1) Imprisonment can provide the suffering offenders deserve, whereas sudden death does not. (2) Lengthy prison sentences can so debilitate offenders that they will lack the ability to commit crimes after their release.

8. A 9 year old would first incarcerate the burglar for two years. "And if he hurts somebody in jail, in his jail cell, like killing someone, I'd give him the electric chair."

(*a*) The principle: Kill only under certain conditions.
(*b*) Conditions: Committing another murder while imprisoned for murder.
(*c*) Rationale: A relatively mild sanction for a first offense should be followed by a harsh sanction for further misconduct.

9. A 17 year old agreed to have the burglar executed "because in the Bible it says that if someone takes a life, their life should be taken. Actually, I think it depends on why they did it. If it's self-defense, then that's different."

(*a*) The principle: Kill except under certain conditions.
(*b*) Condition: An individual kills in self-defense.
(*c*) Rationales: (1) The Bible is a proper guide to action. (2) People have a right to defend themselves, even if defending themselves requires killing an attacker.

10. Another 17 year old would not execute killers unless they committed a specified multiple number of murders. "No, don't apply the death penalty until after he's killed more than three. Maybe he was just scared. I know I would be if someone snuck up on me while I was robbing their house."

(*a*) The principle: Kill only under certain conditions.
(*b*) Condition: Execution is not warranted until three murders have been committed.
(*b*) Rationale: Whenever a person kills fewer than three people, there may have been extenuating circumstances in those killings, such as the killer had not plotted ahead of time to commit murder but, rather, was simply frightened into the act on the spur of the moment by being startled. However, after three murders, the felon's actions can no longer be excused as fortuitous, so execution is warranted.

The marked variability among the above examples is typical of the extent of diversity found throughout all 136 respondents' opinions about executing the burglar. A lesson illustrated by these examples is similar to one identified in Chapter 9, where the summarized evidence about sanction/aim linkages led to the conclusion that

Learning which sanctions people would propose in a case of misconduct fails to tell anything about the method of reasoning that has led to such a proposal. To discover how people think about imposing sanctions, it is necessary—at the very least—to learn what aims they hope to achieve by the consequences they recommend.

In view of the manifold patterns of moral principles, conditions, and rationales in our ten examples, we are now prepared to offer an addendum to the lesson from Chapter 9.

To discover how individuals think about imposing sanctions, it is also necessary to learn what moral principles and conditions underlie the values on which they base their sanction decisions and to learn the rationales they offer in support of their position.

The method of analysis illustrated above is useful in summarizing the ways people combine sanctions, principles, conditions, and rationales, a summary that renders the beliefs of different individuals conveniently compared. However, this mode of displaying the elements in such a condensed form fails to reveal the individualized pattern of reasoning that each person has followed in generating the elements. This matter of personal reasoning styles can be demonstrated with the following segments from interviews with six representative participants.

First is a 9 year old who was indecisive and groped for suggestions as he tried to accommodate new considerations that came to mind during the conversation.

9 year old: "The man should go to jail for a long time or get the electric chair."

Interviewer: "How long should he be in jail if he was sent there."

9 year old: "I don't know. If he was behaving better, and they let him go out every day and he could be doing things—like almost every other day or about every other week—and he doesn't do anything wrong and he doesn't do anything wrong in jail, I'd probably let him go."

Interviewer: "How would you decide if he ought to go to jail or ought to get the electric chair?"

9 year old: "Well, killing somebody isn't that good. (long pause) If I had kids and my daughter or son killed somebody, I'd disown them. I'd say they weren't my kids. Make them move out. If they stole something, I'd make them take the stuff back and go to jail."

Interviewer: "What good would it do if he went to jail."

9 year old: "If he got the electric chair, it would teach him. Well, it wouldn't teach him anything because he'd be dead. But if he had the electric chair he wouldn't be killing anyone again."

Interviewer: "Now you think the electric chair is better than jail."

9 year old: "I think jail is better. And if he hurts somebody in jail, in his jail cell, like killing someone, I'd give him the electric chair."

Interviewer: "You'd put him in jail a year or two? "

9 year old: "Yes, he deserves it for what he did."

Interviewer: "Earlier you said you would put him in jail for a long time, but two years is not so long. Which would you do?"

9 year old: "About two years, because he probably wouldn't do stealing or killing any more if he got out."

Interviewer: "You said that putting him in jail would teach him not to do it again."

9 year old: "It would teach him not to steal anymore, but he probably would kill some more people when he got out."

Interviewer: "Putting him in jail a long time would keep him from stealing and killing again."

9 year old: "Yes."

Interviewer: "What about the aim of giving the family of the dead woman the satisfaction of knowing he was punished."

9 year old: "I'd let them decide what to do with him. If they thought it was really bad, they might put very heavy things on his legs or something. But that's too horrible. So they should just decide how long he stays in jail or have him do some work."

Next is a 17 year old who initially suggested that the murderer be jailed for one or two years and given counseling.

17 year old: "That's because I think human lives are really important, and I think that anyone who takes a life should be put in jail for a while, even though they never are put there for very long. And if we don't have enough jails, we should build more."

Interviewer: "Some other people we've interviewed thought the man should have the death sentence. What do you think about that?"

17 year old: "Yes, that could be done, because in the Bible it says that if someone takes a life, their life should be taken. Actually, I think it depends on why they did it. If it's self-defense, then that's different."

A third respondent proposed solitary confinement for the burglar, then distinguished the crime from others on the basis of the offender's intent.

21 year old: "When this burglar committed the crime, he was probably scared and didn't know what he was doing. He needs to be punished, he needs to change, and solitary confinement would do that. Now, when you compare that to someone who goes into a bank, robs the bank, kills a teller, and starts killing other people—multiple—then I'd jump straight to the capital punishment, because he's reduced his victims to objects instead of people. Once you've done that, you've become inhuman."

A fourth interviewee rejected the death penalty out of her faith in basic human nature.

17 year old: "No, don't kill him, because anyone can change. It's like saying, 'You are like this, and you can't change since there's no good in you.' And I believe there's good in every single person, somewhere—maybe it's very, very deep, but still, you know, there is good in every person. His problem could be something in his past, the way we've treated him or something else. We shouldn't say, 'You're hopeless,' because people can be helped."

Another student who would also try to reform the felon was not so confident that it would work.

> *21 year old*: "I don't think he should be put to death without first being given a chance at rehabilitation and to repent for what he has done. I don't think the death penalty is too harsh if he doesn't choose to change. It's an option to be applied if he doesn't choose to reform."

A sixth respondent recommended the death penalty, then added her convictions about a role to be played by God.

> *17 year old*: "I think God will decide where the killer will go after he dies, depending on if the man accepted God. If just before he died he decided that Jesus is God, then the man will go to heaven. But if he didn't accept God, then he'll go to hell. I mean, it doesn't really matter about what he actually did on earth. What matters is whether or not he accepts God. So I think that we should deal with things on earth, and afterwards it's what God will do."
>
> *Interviewer*: "But you believe the man deserves the death penalty."
>
> *17 year old*: "Yes, God will decide in the end. But when we are on earth, God's put some government officials in charge of us, so the officials need to deal with it, too. But if you want, you can pray about it. God may tell you what he wants you to do Maybe he'll give you wisdom for each day and each case."

In summary, students' modes of reasoning about executing the 23 year old burglar were individualistic and notably varied in complexity.

Comparing Groups' Views of the Death Penalty

Finally, we can use a compilation of the students' opinions in Case 3 to answer the following question: What likenesses and differences were found among age groups and between gender groups in the sanctions, moral principles, and conditions that respondents advocated when deciding whether the burglar should be executed? Data bearing on this question are summarized in Tables 11-3 and 11-4.

In Table 11-3, the initial section ("Execute in order to") lists the percentage of students at each age level who would put the burglar to death as dictated by (a) the moral principle of matching the punishment to the felon's offense ("Those who kill deserve to be killed"), (b) the principle of incapacitating the offender ("Eliminate the chance the offender will murder again"), or (c) some other reason ("The man might get killed by other inmates of the prison anyway" or "It costs too much to keep murderers in prison for life"). As the figures in Table 11-3 show, there are no consistent trends across age groups in the percentage of respondents applying these principles, and none of the differences between pairs of age groups approaches statistical significance at the .05 level.

The next two sections of the table ("Execute only if" and "Execute because of conditions in this case") show the percentages of students who would put a killer to death only under specified circumstances. The most frequently cited condition was that of committing multiple murders. The next most frequent was planning the murder ahead of time rather than committing it spontaneously in a sudden flood of such an emotion as fright. Other reasons included: Execute "if the victim was a child" or "if the victim was hacked up or dismembered" or "if it wasn't in self-defense." Although more younger than older respondents applied the multiple murders principle, the differences between the age groups failed to reach a .05 level of significance.

At each age level, more than half of the students would endorse the death penalty, at least under certain circumstances. No percentage difference between

Table 11-3
Opinions of the Death Penalty by Age Level
(in percentages)

Age	*9*	*14*	*17*	*21*	*All*
N	33	36	34	33	136
Execute in order to:					
Match the offense	9	3	12	6	7
Incapacitate	18	8	6	9	10
Other reasons		3	6	6	4
Execute only if:					
Multiple murders	30	22	18	12	21
Premeditated murder		14	15	6	9
Other conditions	9	6	6	6	7
Execute because of					
conditions in this case			6	9	4
Total favoring execution					
in at least some cases	*67*	*56*	*68*	*55*	*61*
Don't execute because of:					
Compassion	30	28	21	33	27
Easy way out	3	14			4
Other reasons	3	3	6	6	4
Total never favoring					
execution	*33*	*44*	*27*	*39*	*36*
Can't decide			6	6	3

any pair of age groups approached statistical significance (.05), nor did the percentages form a consistent trend from younger to older respondents.

The next section of Table 11-3 shows the percentages of students who would not endorse the death penalty under any condition. The most common principle (compassion) underlying such a position was that no one had the right to end a life as a way of administering justice: "I consider the death penalty inhuman" or "Only God has the right to take a life." A far smaller number believed death was the "easy way out" for those who had committed heinous crimes; imprisonment accompanied by hard labor would cause a murderer the suffering he deserved. A few supported their decision with some such principle as the *opportunity for compensation* ("If he's killed, he can make up for the crime he committed") or *a chance to reform* ("He might reform in prison, but he can't reform if he's dead").

Finally, several 17 and 21 year olds were so torn by the dilemma of resolving conflicting moral principles that they were unable to suggest a sanction they considered just.

In summary, the diverse attitudes toward execution were distributed so evenly across the age groups that knowing a respondent's age would be of no help in estimating what that individual's opinion of the death penalty would be. A younger student would be as apt to endorse a death sentence for a murderer as would an older student. Likewise, a younger student would be as likely to reject execution as would an older respondent, and all age groups based their decisions on the same array of moral principles.

Table 11-4 portrays gender comparisons in the same fashion as age comparisons. Whereas no statistically significant differences appeared between any age groups, such was not quite the case with gender comparisons. The total percentages of respondents favoring execution in at least some circumstances was 51% among females and 72% among males, a difference reaching a .01 level of significance. The same level of significance obtained for the difference between the females (46%) and males (25%) who would not endorse execution ("Don't execute"). However, it is useful to recognize that not all of the anti-execution advocates supported their position with the same rationale. The numbers of females (33%) and males (21%) who appeared motivated by compassion or a belief that it was not their right to kill are not significantly different even at the .05 level. More females (7%) than males (2%) rejected the death sentence because they thought it was "the easy way out" in comparison to life in prison.

In light of these results, consider again Gilligan's (1982) hypothesis that females' moral judgments are based on compassionate caring, and males' decisions are founded on on objective even handed justice. At first glance, it might appear that Gilligan's proposal is well supported by the results in Table 11-4. However, this impression is weakened somewhat when the moral principles for adopting an anti-execution position are recognized. Not everyone who rejected the death penalty did so out of compassion for the offender.

Table 11-4
Opinions of the Death Penalty by Gender
(in percentages)

Sex	*Females*	*Males*	*Both M & F*
N	*69*	*67*	*136*
Execute in order to:			
Match the offense	4	10	7
Incapacitate	8	12	10
Other reasons	3	5	4
Execute only if:			
Multiple murders	16	25	21
Premeditated	9	9	9
Other conditions	10	3	7
Execute because of			
conditions in this case		8	4
Total favoring execution			
in at least some cases	*51*	*72*	*61*
Don't execute because of:			
Compassion	33	21	27
Easy way out	7	2	4
Other reasons	6	3	4
Total never favoring			
execution	*46*	*25*	*36*
Can't decide	3	3	3

CONCLUSION

The central purpose of this chapter has been to demonstrate how answers to our interview questions could reveal something about respondents' conceptions of reality and about the nature of their moral values. Although we used a question about God's role in adjudicating wrongdoing as the means of eliciting young people's notions of "what is real and true," we could have demonstrated students' beliefs about reality equally well with any number of the other questions we asked during the interviews. In a similar way, we could have demonstrated how values are reflected in participants' replies by using questions other than the one about the death penalty. Doing so would have provided further evidence of the complex, individualistic nature of the interviewees' modes of moral reasoning. Among the 136 participants in this study, no two were precisely alike in their conception of a supreme being's intervention in earthly moral matters, nor did any two offer quite the same rationale to buttress their position on the death penalty. In effect, the conclusions at the close of Chapter 9 about the markedly idiosyncratic character of moral thought over the age range 9 to 21 are clearly supported by the contents of the present chapter.

However, even though respondents universally displayed individual modes of overt reasoning, subgroups of the sample of 136 participants did agree on certain issues, such as particular sanctions to impose, basic moral principles, and some conditions governing the application of those principles. For instance, more than half of the 136 interviewees, regardless of age or gender, believed that the death penalty was an appropriate sanction for murderers under particular circumstances. Furthermore, 21% felt that killing several victims was the condition warranting the execution of a murderer. Another 27% rejected execution because of their unconditional regard for human life, and smaller percentages of interviewees agreed on other aspects of the death sentence issue, as shown in Tables 11-3 and 11-4.

We were disappointed in our effort to identify significant differences between age groups in attitudes about God's imposing sanctions for wrongdoing and about the death penalty as a proper punishment for murder. In effect, the same range of beliefs found at one age level was found in similar amounts at the other age levels. However, the two older groups (17 and 21) were significantly clearer in explaining their beliefs about God's role than were the younger respondents (9 and 14).

The analysis of gender groups also revealed the same varieties of attitudes about God and the death penalty among females and males. However, significantly (.01) more males than females would execute murderers under certain circumstances. The results thereby furnished at least modest support for Gilligan's (1982) claim that females are more apt than males to apply the moral principle of compassion when proposing sanctions for wrongdoers.

12

Views of Imprisonment

In two of our three cases of wrongdoing (teenage drug users and the 23-year-old burglar), respondents faced the option of committing the offenders to a penal facility. They could voluntarily propose such a sanction when they were first asked what should be done about the transgressors in each case. Subsequently, in the case of the 16 year olds, interviewees were asked specifically if the two teenagers should be sentenced to six months in juvenile hall.

The opinions that the 136 participants voiced about incarcerating the offenders provides insight into their beliefs about the role of penal facilities in present-day U. S. society. The dual purpose of Chapter 12 is to analyze those beliefs in terms of (1) the diversity of opinions represented within the total sample of 136 participants and (2) likenesses and differences of beliefs across age groups and gender groups. The first part of the chapter inspects the diversity of views. The second part compares respondents' opinions by age and gender.

A DIVERSITY OF OPINIONS

The range of different viewpoints displayed within the total sample is described in the following pages under four headings: (1) what labels identify penal facilities, (2) whose welfare is served by imprisonment, (3) how imprisonment is perceived, and (4) what length sentence is appropriate.

What Labels Identify Penal Facilities

During the 20th century, places for incarcerating lawbreakers have been referred to by a variety of both formal and informal terms. Formal designations have included *prison, penitentiary, jail* (sometimes spelled *gaol* in Britain), *penal facility, detention center, penal colony, reformatory, juvenile hall, school for delinquents, rehabilitation center,* and *correctional institution.* Informal labels have been even more numerous—*the big house, inside, up the river, doing time, the lockup, the pen, the clink* (after a London prison of that name), *the bastille* (after a Parisian fortress that served as a prison until destroyed during the French Revolution), *the hoosgow* (from the Mexican/Spanish *juzgado*), *the calaboose* (after the Spanish *calabozo*), *the jug, the tank, the hot house, the joint,* and *the slammer.*

Official distinctions are frequently drawn among the formal designations. In the United States the word *jail* is applied to facilities maintained by a smaller governmental unit (village, town, city, county) for offenders serving sentences of not more than one year and for people who have been arrested and are awaiting trial. The word *prison* identifies an institution maintained by a larger governmental unit (state, nation) to house felons serving sentences of more than a year. A *juvenile hall* is a place for youths under age 18 who have broken the law or else for those who have not broken the law but have been removed from an unsatisfactory home situation. *Reformatory* is a term created in the 19th century to designate an institution in which lawbreakers were not simply to be punished but, rather, were to be educated and counseled in ways that might turn them into law-abiding citizens. However, within reformatories there has always existed a conflict between punishment and treatment. Over the early decades of the 20th century, "This system of organized conflict between the treatment and punishment reactions also spread rather quickly to state prisons, so that it is now difficult to draw a line between state prisons and state reformatories so far as methods are concerned" (Sutherland & Cressey, 1970, p. 489).

In the present study, we wished to discover which words respondents would use in referring to penal facilities and to see how accurately those words reflected official distinctions among such terms as *jail, prison,* and *juvenile hall.* Our analysis of the 136 interview records showed that all 136 participants used formal rather than informal terms when referring to places for incarcerating lawbreakers. No respondent used such slang terms as *joint, lockup,* or *slammer.* Perhaps the participants thought slang was unsuitable for the serious nature of our research project.

To determine how closely interviewees' uses of words for penal facilities matched official terminology, we adopted the standards noted above. Jails are for adults who have committed minor crimes (misdemeanors) that warrant sentences of less than one year. Prisons are for adults convicted of serious crimes (felonies) that call for imprisonment exceeding a year. Juvenile halls or juvenile detention centers are for youths under age 18 charged with various degrees of law breaking. When we applied these criteria to assessing interviewees' suggestions about incarcerating the 23-year-old burglar and the 16-year-old drug users, we obtained the following results. Among the 96 respondents who used the term *jail* in their sanction recommendations, only 8% accurately applied it to mean confining an adult for less than a year. The remaining 92% used *jail* to mean either locking up the burglar for more than a year (63%) or detaining the teenage drug users (29%). In effect, a majority of our 136 interviewees employed *jail* in a generic sense to mean any form of official incarceration. Of the 45 people who used the word *prison* in their sanction proposals, 96% applied it in its accurate sense of long-term confinement of an adult. Only 4% (two 9 year olds) inaccurately applied *prison* to the detention of the 16 year olds. All 22 of the respondents who voluntarily used the term *juvenile hall* accurately applied it to the 16-year-old drug users.

In summary, none of the 136 participants used slang terms when identifying a place of imprisonment. Nearly all who used the words *prison* and *juvenile hall* applied these terms in their technically accurate meanings. On the other hand, a substantial majority used *jail* in an inclusive, technically inaccurate sense to mean any place of confinement or punishment. In comparing subgroups of respondents, we found no statistically significant differences by age or gender in the technical accuracy of the terms used.

Whose Welfare Is Served by Imprisonment

When interviewees considered the option of imprisoning an offender, the rationale they offered in support of their decision often indicated whose welfare they had uppermost in mind. Some focused primarily on the well-being of the offender, hoping to direct the transgressor into a more constructive way of life. Others focused on the safety of the general public, using prison to keep wrongdoers off the streets. Some centered attention on the stability of the social system, on the importance of maintaining a lawful society. Still others were concerned about both the offender and the law-abiding public, hoping to achieve a solution that would enhance the welfare of wrongdoers and at the same time protect the public from danger. The manner in which these various objects of attention were expressed is illustrated by the following excerpts from interviews.

The Offender's Welfare

By far the most frequently mentioned way that confinement might improve an offender's welfare was in the lesson imprisonment could teach about the consequences of wrongdoing.

In the case of the teenage drug users, typical expectations of what good would be accomplished by confining them in juvenile hall included teaching them (a) to avoid future punishment, (b) to give up drugs, (c) to stop peddling drugs to others, (d) to realize the seriousness of using drugs and trading them, and (e) to accept responsibility for their own behavior.

(a) "Juvie would make them behave better. Kids don't like to be locked up." [9]
   "It'll show them what jail is like, and they won't want to go back." [9]
   "Makes them think about what they've done. It wouldn't do any good if they got off too easy. They'd realize that they could spend a lot of time in jail if they did it again." [21].
   "They'll see that drugs aren't worth going to jail for." [21]

(b) "They won't do drugs again and won't get addicted, so then their life will be better." [14]
(c) "It'll teach them right from wrong—selling drugs is wrong." [14]
(d) "They'll recognize that doing drugs is really a serious problem." [17]
   "They'll know that drugs isn't something to be joked about." [17]
   "They find out it's wrong and that society won't take it lightly if they continue drugs in the future." [21]
(e) "Educate them that they are responsible for their actions." [21]

The great majority of respondents who recommended a period of confinement for the teenagers intended the experience to improve the youths' lives by teaching them a lesson. However, the aim of most interviewees who would imprison the 23-year-old burglar was to protect the public by preventing him from roaming about. But a small number of respondents also wanted incarceration to foster the felon's well-being by (a) effecting a positive change in his character or at least (b) influencing his future behavior.

(a) "Prison would make him think about what he did and maybe change him." [17]
(b) "It'll teach him not to do it again when he gets out." [14]

The Public Good

Beliefs about how imprisonment should affect the community's welfare often differed from one interviewee to another. For instance, a respondent's motive could be to protect the public from harm, to minimize the cost of dealing with transgressors, to avenge the wrong that society suffered, or to deter other potential wrongdoers by the example of confining malefactors.

Protect the Society. The most frequently mentioned purpose was that of promoting public safety.

Attempts to rehabilitate inmates can either emphasize the aim of improving life for the inmates or of protecting other people from the offender's committing further misdeeds. The following opinion from a 21 year old centers on the second of these goals; this proposal also includes the prison population as part of the public that should be protected.

> "I'd like to see jails take more of a reformatory attitude. In this case, we can lock him up, but can we ever feel safe letting him out on the street again? So I think reforming him would be a good aim if the jail sentence was something less than life. But even if he is in there for life, reform him so that at least he behaves okay in the prison and is not causing more problems there." [21]

Save Money. An economic motive can underlie either a preference for execution over imprisonment or a preference for imprisonment over execution. Which of these alternatives was chosen by a respondent depended on that interviewee's conception of the comparative costs of the two options—imprisonment and execution. One 21 year old had an economic motive for imprisoning rather than executing the burglar who had killed the householder.

"Putting murderers on death row? Bad idea. They never get killed, and it costs much, much more to keep a person on death row than to keep them in for life. To go through all the legal actions and appeals to impose the death penalty costs millions of dollars and takes years. And all the while the criminal is sitting in jail anyway, so it's cheaper just to put them in for life. Hopefully they could get rehab while in prison, but that never happens." [21]

A contrary opinion about cost was offered by a 17 year old who said:

"Keeping a criminal in prison costs taxpayers enormous amounts of money every year. So putting a murderer away for life is a great burden on taxpayers. Since locking a killer up for his whole life is like taking his freedom away— really taking his life away—it makes better sense to execute him in the first place and save all that money." [17]

Avenge the Misdeed. A desire to impose punishment as an instrument of vengeance was reflected in a student's admission that:

"My gut reaction would be to throw the bastard in jail and throw away the key. But to try to be reasonable about it, maybe a prison sentence is the only reasonable method of punishment. The trouble with prison is that he'd be locked up with baby killers and all kinds of other interesting people. I don't know if attempts at rehabilitation would be effective at all. If he doesn't value another person's life by the time he's 23, he's never going to, and you can't expect to rehabilitate a thief. Well, actually, if I had my way, everybody who'd done something like rape or murder would have the same thing done to them in exactly the same way. That doesn't solve the problem, but it sure would feel good. So I'd go with capital punishment. At least that would protect society." [21]

Other participants who would punish the 23-year-old burglar in a spirit of revenge said they favored life imprisonment over the death penalty because "death would be the easy way out."

"He's got to suffer for what he did. Spending the rest of his life in prison at hard labor gives him plenty of time to think. Executing him would be letting him off too easy." [17]

Deter Others. Although some respondents believed that imprisoning the burglar might prevent potential law breakers from committing similar crimes, a larger number thought the example of the burglar's punishment would have little or no effect as a deterrent to others.

"If people know the man personally, yes, they might think that could happen to them. But if they don't know him, they really don't care." [17]

Concern for Both the Wrongdoer and the Public

Although the notion of using imprisonment to reform wrongdoers appealed to many interviewees, some viewed this possibility with a great deal of skepticism.

"Reform is the ideal motivation, I think.   But I guess I have doubts about whether that really happens in our society with the options available.   I don't think putting lawbreakers in jail reforms them or turns them in to better persons. I just think it protects other people." [21]

Others who expressed concern for both the wrongdoer and the public despaired of finding an acceptable alternative to imprisonment.

"I don't think jail helps anyone personally.   But with the resources we have, there seems to be nothing else we can do.   You know, a lot of these 'help centers' aren't really there to help people.   Still, maybe he should be sent to jail a while. Since it was manslaughter, and no one should kill anyone, so I suppose jail for the rest of his life would be best.   That wouldn't solve anything for him, but it would get him away from society.   I certainly wouldn't want him in my neighborhood.   That would ensure that he wouldn't kill innocent people.   He could kill someone in jail, but that's another story.   It would be a punishment, though I don't see how punishing him would help anything.   But after they kill someone, they shouldn't just be able to—oh, I don't know." [17]

A few respondents puzzled over the conflict between removing transgressors from society while, at the same time, attempting to socialize them to function as constructive members of society.

"Ideally rehabilitation is what I'd like to see done.   The only problem with rehabilitation is that the only way to know someone is rehabilitated is to let that person out.   The treatment would have to be a combination of prison and rehabilitation.   First, you have to incarcerate these kinds of people for a period of time until they were felt no longer to be a threat to society.   Perhaps a kind of cross between a prison and a university.   The aim would be to protect society from this individual, while at the same time trying to make this individual a functioning member of society.   (laugh) But those two things kind of contradict each other, since if you're protecting society from him, at the same time you're shutting him out of the society into which he should be integrated." [21]

Certain participants suggested that prison inmates could serve a positive social function by dramatically portraying the dangers of prison life as a means of dissuading potential wrongdoers from committing misdeeds.

"I know there are some programs that have volunteer inmates who are willing to speak to youths and tell them how awful prison is.   It's a program called 'scared straight.' Kids grow up thinking the mafia and gangs are great, so I think scare tactics work.   So in prison he could be useful as an example to prevent others from committing crimes." [21]

How Imprisonment Is Perceived

Respondents' perceptions of the conditions and effects of imprisonment were often reflected in what they said about sentencing the 16 year olds to juvenile hall or committing the burglar to prison.   In the following paragraphs, the typical range of viewpoints about juvenile hall is displayed in the first set of quotations, and the range of opinions about prison is reflected in the second set.

The Effect of Juvenile Hall

Detention facilities for juveniles were seen by interviewees in three principal ways—as having a constructive influence on delinquent youths, as having no effect at all, and as being harmful.

Positive Influence. A 17 year old believed that a few months in juvenile hall would convince lawbreakers that society regarded their misconduct as a grave error which could lead to even more severe consequences if they were caught again in misdeeds.

> "Sending them to juvenile hall would make them realize they are not just joking when they are fooling with drugs. It might not make them stop using drugs, but it would make them take drugs more seriously. They realize they broke the law and they have to face consequences. What happens to them as a minor is not anything as bad as what would happen to them as an adult. Juvenile hall isn't any thing like being in jail." [17]

A 14 year old thought of juvenile hall as a place in which youthful offenders receive a constructive combination of discipline and personal guidance.

> "I kind of agree with that because in juvenile hall they help with counseling and they won't let you do practically anything. They have strict rules. They show you what you can do, and if you don't do it you get in trouble. It'll help them get counseling, and they'll be able to get off drugs. It can show them that there are different ways of living and that what they are doing right now is wrong, but they may have grown up with it. But they can find a better way of life." [14]

Little or No Effect. An older student relied on her conversations with delinquent acquaintances for deciding that the punishment received in a juvenile facility was so mild that it had no influence on inmates' future behavior.

> "I've had friends who've been in juvenile hall before, and they say it's taken just like a slap on the hand; so they've continued to commit the same crime for which they'd been sent to the hall in the first place." [21]

For other reasons, a second student also felt that time in juvenile hall would leave the youths unchanged.

> "No. Don't send them there. Juvenile hall doesn't do anything for anyone. They'd just find a bunch of new connections, that's for sure. I don't think juvenile hall is good for things like that They're not going to learn anything and they'll not stop doing drugs. They're just going to see a whole bunch of other people who are doing the same thing that they are, and that's not a good positive way to teach anyone." [21]

Negative Influence. Some respondents predicted that several varieties of unwelcome outcomes could be expected from sentencing youths to a juvenile facility. One result could be that newcomers would be physically harmed by the existing inmates.   For that reason, a 17 year old, who first believed time in juvenile hall would be appropriate, subsequently rejected the proposal.

"That seems kind of reasonable, but six months is a very long time for a first offense. Actually, using juvenile hall for inappropriate behavior really sucks. I'd hate to put that on someone for their first offense.   When I was in eighth grade we were having a big thing about drugs, and we had to take a tour of juvenile hall.   Basically the policeman said it was to scare us, like, 'We'd better not see your face around here again.' I'd never want to end up there. He told us about kids taking their beds apart and using pieces of bed springs to stab other kids—terrible things like that." [17]

Another cited his observations of acquaintances as the basis for his adverse opinion of juvenile detention:

"I've seen people come out of juvenile hall and they didn't seem to be changed much. If anything, they even did drugs worse. I really don't think that works." [17]

Still another youth criticized what she believed to be an absence of constructive counseling and a lack of individualized treatment of offenders in detention centers.

"What I've heard of juvenile hall is that it brings in people who've done so many different crimes that it's almost like a militarized jail with physical and emotional punishment that's really not an understanding approach as to why the person committed the crime. It's not specific to the particular crime. So juvenile hall just holds people a while and then sends them out not understanding why the crime was wrong in the first place. I just heard last night that 70% of the people who've been in jail will return, so obviously that way of dealing with the problem is not working, and I'm sure juvenile hall isn't that much different." [17]

The Effect of Prison

As in the case of juvenile hall, respondents often differed in the effect they believed a prison sentence would have on the present fate and the future behavior of such an inmate as the 23-year-old felon. Many thought prison would contribute to his becoming a law-abiding citizen. Others believed prison would have little or no effect on his future behavior. A few said imprisonment would be destructive.

Positive Influence. Respondents suggested three interrelated ways imprisonment contributed toward changing lawbreakers into law-abiding citizens—by instilling fear of future imprisonment, by teaching inmates to obey the law, and by reforming their moral values, life goals, and skills.

Faith in the deterrent effect of prison life was expressed by a 17 year old as:

"Put him into prison, put him to work, and give him time to think about it. But I don't agree with rehab in prison. I don't think it helps anybody's mind, but that's the option we have in today's society. There should be other forms of helping people. Maybe psychological, maybe a work camp where they actually do good work. I think that if he spent 10, 20, or 50 years working hard in prison, when he got out he wouldn't kill people again, because he wouldn't want to go back. In America we connect liberty and life; so if you don't have freedom, you don't have life. Give me liberty or give me death, right?" [17]

A 21 year old believed imprisonment might teach offenders to obey the law in the future by convincing them that they would likely be caught and punished. However, he held a dim view of the ability of prisons to alter offenders' values and skills.

"Putting him in prison removes him from society and lets him be involved with other people who have done such things. He'll realize he can't get away with such things. It's really hard to change people. The way the prison system operates now, you can't expect him to reform. The prison system could change and help reform people, but I don't think it's possible with the way prison systems work now. You're just like a number there. They just don't care about you. I know that it could be better than it is now, but I don't see it happening." [21]

A more optimistic view of imprisonment was offered by a younger student.

"Maybe put him in jail for a little while and put him under counseling, because most people who do such things can be helped with counseling. And find out if there's a reason why he did that. Being in jail he'll understand that what he did was wrong. And counseling may help him understand why he did it, and he may be rehabilitated." [14]

Little or No Effect. The nature of imprisonment, as envisioned by numbers of interviewees, convinced them that little or no improvement could be expected in criminals' behavior as a result of their confinement.

A 21 year old found fault with both the likely influence of prison on inmates and the great cost of keeping them locked up.

"I feel that prisons are just a waste. I don't think that punishing people for crimes is helping anything. Something else should be done. We spend so much money on them, and they're living in awful conditions, so I don't see how sending them to prison is going to help them out, because obviously people who go to prison have problems. If there was some kind of a place to go where they could be enlightened to change their ways, and do something like community service to help people out instead of just sitting there. If I'd murdered someone, I don't think being sent to jail would help me out at all." [21]

A youth who seemed to think that present-day prisons held little hope for reforming inmates described the conditions of imprisonment that he believed were needed.

"You could put the killer in jail until he knows he's done wrong and wants to change. But he needs to have counseling in jail, to have someone there to talk with and to grow with. He needs positive encouragement, a motivator in his life, someone just to help him. A lot of the problem in our society is that we just give them punishment. We don't give them a better way out. We don't help them; we don't tell them how to be optimistic. We have mostly a negative society. They just tell people who do wrong that 'You can't do that.' And when you say 'You can't,' a lot of the time that's the reason people keep on doing it. We must remember that we all make mistakes and we can all change." [17]

Negative Effect Three types of destructive results of prison life mentioned in interviews were inhumane living conditions, undesirable models of behavior, and a lack of constructive counseling and guidance for inmates.

In regard to inhumane conditions, one student's bleak view of prison life led her to object to sending the burglar to prison, even though she felt some sort of confinement would be necessary. After she unsuccessfully grappled with the problem, her inability to settle on a convincing means of reforming the felon induced her to envision a natural course of events that would result in the man's eventually experiencing suitable consequences. In effect, the girl retreated to placing her faith in the notion of immanent justice.

"Prison won't help the person. He might have a bad time there. You hear horror stories about what goes on in prison, and no one should have to submit to that. You should be able to make people repent for what they do, but you can't get them to repent by putting them in jail. Jail just makes them more uncomfortable. But you still have to confine them someplace till they grow or change, but you can't be sure they'll change. I believe people are basically good and have a basic sense of morals that can surface if they're in a constructive environment. And I don't think you have to punish a person to make sure they obey the law. The way I see it, people who do things wrong don't necessarily get their just deserts at that time but it comes back to them later. If you steal someone's wallet, you may not be put in jail at that time; but eventually if you keep doing it, something will happen to you. I like to think about it as a universal concept like if you do something immoral it's going to get back to you, but you don't really know why or when. So, to avoid that consequence, you should try to behave in a moral manner." [17]

What Length Sentence Is Appropriate

Respondents' suggestions that offenders be imprisoned displayed a wide range of differences in opinions about what period of confinement would be appropriate. Both cases—the drug traders and the burglar—showed a striking difference between the shortest and longest sentences proposed. For the two teenagers, the shortest was for one day and the longest for 15 years. For the burglar, the shortest was for a few months and the longest for the man's entire lifetime. (We set aside one 9 year old's recommendation that the killer be confined for 6,000 years.)

Interviewees' explanations of the logic behind their proposals made clear that recommendations for similar lengths of sentence often resulted from rather different lines of reasoning. Consider, for example, these three proposals of short sentences for the burglar.

"He should be put in jail for one or two years and counseled. I think human lives are really important, and I think that anyone who takes a life should be put in jail for a while, even though they never are put there for very long. And if we don't have enough jails, we should build more." [17]

"If this is his only killing, then I don't think it warrants capital punishment. What I would do would be to sentence him to solitary confinement. I think solitary confinement is one of the most effective punishments. For how long? Well, I wouldn't go over a year. I think he would go insane with solitary confinement for more than several months. The reason I'd put him in solitary rather than just in prison is because there are too many distractions in regular prison life. They can use exercise equipment and mingle with the other prisoners. What they really need is to come to grips with what they've done. If you put them in solitary confinement, then sooner or later they're going to think about what they did. Using solitary in that way would also help clear out the prisons. Afterwards the man needs to meet with the judge and understand that if he commits such crimes again, capital punishment will be warranted." [21]

"Jail, definitely. Put him in prison, probably for life. Possibility of parole if he goes through some program. The prison system as it is isn't very good, because when people come back out of prison they're back into society. And basically, a lot of them do something wrong to get caught, to go back, because they don't know how to live any more in society. So I think that in the prisons there needs to be some kind of—not necessarily job development because that could take jobs from people outside—but some sort of developmental program that helps prepare them to get back into society so they can be more normal citizens. I want to take back what I said about life, because a shorter sentence might be just right for him. It depends on the individual. A year might even do it. So it should be life with the possibility of parole depending on his progress in some kind of developmental program." [17]

Numbers of respondents said the sanction they chose was influenced by the way prison sentence lengths are actually administered. When asked about putting the killer in jail for two or three years, a 21 year old said:

"No, I don't like that one, but that's what happens. They get a prison sentence of 25 years to life, with a parole chance maybe in 17 years. But because of the overpopulation in jails, within the first three years they get out on good behavior and they're back out on the streets again. Not only can they kill again, but it's not fair to the family of the murder victim." [21]

Other participants also expressed disappointment with the operation of the criminal justice system.

"I would sentence the burglar to death, because he killed a woman when he was committing a major crime. I wouldn't be so much for the death penalty if I had more faith in our judicial system; because if they're sentenced to life in prison, it seems like they're really not sentenced for life since it's possible for them to get out. So, the way things are, the only way I can think to make sure the person won't get out is to have them killed. If, when people were sentenced in court for a given time—like life or 60 years—and you could count on their actually being there for that time, then that's an alternative for the death penalty. But that's not how it is right now, so that's why I think the death penalty is a good tool for protecting society." [17]

"I don't want to say a jail thing, because when you say he's going to go to jail they always get out early, and then they can kill other people, too. But I don't like the electric chair thing either, because it's kind of scary. So I think he should be in jail and not let out at all. If there's a chance he would kill somebody again, I don't think you should take that chance. If he's in jail, he can't kill or rob people—well, I guess he could, but it's not that important there." [14]

"How many years he should get in prison depends on where he would be. Like if he's in a minimum-security prison then, say, five years. But if he's in a worse place that has gangs and guys that rape other guys, then maybe it should be about four years—a shorter time because it's a harder punishment to be there." [14]

Summary

The observations offered in Chapters 9 and 11 about the extent of individual differences among students in their moral reasoning are further supported by the present chapter's interview excerpts. Among the young people participating in our study, widely diverse opinions were expressed about the nature of the justice system and the desirability of incarcerating teenage drug traders and adult burglars who commit murder.

AGE AND GENDER COMPARISONS

The remainder of the chapter reviews likenesses and differences across age levels and genders in relation to four issues: (1) the confinement of offenders versus other options, (2) whose welfare is served by imprisonment, (3) how imprisonment is perceived, and (4) what length sentence is appropriate.

Confinement Versus Other Options

Table 12-1 displays the percentages of interviewees at each age level who recommended some form of detention or imprisonment for the teenage drug users and for the burglar who killed the woman whose house he was robbing. In the case of the teenagers, *confinement* means any official type of restriction on the 16 year olds' freedom, ranging from (a) holding them for a few hours at a police station to (b) committing them to several years in a reformatory. The word *other* refers to any dispositions of the case instead of confinement. Methods included under *other* include letting the pair off with a warning, reporting them to their parents, suspending them from school, and requiring them to perform community service or enroll in a drug-education class.

The percentages of respondents choosing to confine the teenagers reveal a consistent, statistically significant trend across age levels (well beyond .01 for 9 year olds versus the older groups). The younger the respondent, the more likely he or she would imprison or detain the drug users. The older the respondent, the more likely he or she would recommend counseling, community service, drug abuse education, or parental guidance for the youths. Among interviewees who suggested other options, the two reasons most often offered for rejecting incarceration were that confinement in juvenile hall was too harsh a punishment for a first drug offense or that a period in juvenile hall would produce no constructive change in the youths' behavior.

In contrast to the case of the drug users, respondents' sanctions for the burglar/killer showed no age trends. The two principal alternatives that students offered were to confine the felon or to execute him. (As noted in Chapter 11, a few participants would leave the decision about sanctions up to God; however, for the immediate purpose of protecting the public, even those respondents would restrain the offender at least temporarily.) The only notable deviation

Table 12-1
Confinement Versus Other Options
(in percentages)

	Age	*9*	*14*	*17*	*21*	*All*
	N	*33*	*36*	*34*	*33*	*136*
Drug Users & Peddlers						
Imprison		88	56	44	34	56
Other options		12	44	56	66	44
Burglar/Killer						
Imprison		91	94	79	91	89
Execute		9	6	21	9	11

over age levels in the disposition of the burglar occurred among the 17 year olds: 21% (7 of the 34 respondents) of the 17 year olds would put the man to death, whereas no more than 9% in the other age groups would do so.

In the total sample of 136 participants, 60% of females and 52% of males would confine the teenagers, while 94% of females and 83% of males would lock up the burglar. In neither the drug use case or nor the burglary case did these differences between males and females approach statistical significance at even the .05 level.

Whose Welfare Is Served by Imprisonment?

Slightly less than half of the interviewees (65 out of 136) suggested who would likely profit from confining the teenagers in the drug case. Far more participants (111 out of 136) proposed whose well-being would be served by incarcerating the burglar. As noted earlier, these opinions could be located under three categories: (a) the offenders' welfare, (b) the general public's good, and (c) the well-being of both the general public and the offenders. The numbers of people at each age level who expressed such opinions are shown in Table 12-2.

Although the numbers are too small to apply a useful test of statistical significance, the trends would appear to warrant extending the investigation to larger samples of young people to learn if the observed trends are found among others of similar age. For instance, more younger than older students believed that the teenage drug traders would profit from a period of confinement and that locking them up for a while would also contribute to the public good. In contrast, there was essentially no disagreement across ages about what might be expected from imprisoning the burglar/killer. By far the largest number of respondents in all age groups believed that confining the felon would promote the public good. Few thought imprisonment would improve the man's welfare.

Females and males were essentially alike in their notions of who profited from confining the offenders.

How Imprisonment Is Perceived

Related to the matter of whose welfare is served are respondents' perceptions of what goes on in juvenile halls and prisons, the influence of such facilities on inmates, and how well confinement suits the nature of an offender's misconduct. Age group figures bearing on these questions are offered in Tables 12-3 and 12-4. The numbers of students in each cell of Table 12-3 are too small to offer any secure basis for drawing generalizations about adolescents other than those in the present study. Yet the overall pattern suggests that older students, compared to younger ones, are less convinced that juvenile detention facilities have a positive effect on adolescents' lives. Table 12-4 reports students' views of imprisoning the 23-year-old burglar. Not only are the numbers in each cell quite small, but there is no suggestion of differences of opinion about imprisonment across ages. Furthermore, females and males were similar in the ways they perceived imprisonment in each of the cases.

What Length of Sentence Is Appropriate

Most of the interviewees who recommended confining the teenage drug users or the burglar were willing to suggest how long their confinement should be. Table 12-5 summarizes the suggestions by age level. As noted earlier, in both cases there were dramatic differences between the shortest and longest sentences proposed. For the two teenagers, the shortest recommended confinement was one day and the longest 15 years. For the burglar, the shortest was a few months and the longest was his entire life.

To manage such extremes within a brief table, we grouped the suggestions into irregular categories, then calculated averages (means) and standard deviations from the midpoints of the categories. For purposes of computation, categories in each portion of the table were converted to a common currency, which was *days* in the case of the drug users and *years* in the case of the burglar.

As shown in the upper half of the table, a few respondents in each age group declined to cite a specific length of sentence but, rather, recommended that the teenagers be confined until they appeared cured of their drug habit or otherwise earned parole. In addition, a few participants at ages 14, 17, and 21 failed to state how long confinement should last, but they did say six months was excessive.

Table 12-2
Who Profits from Imprisonment
(in numbers of respondents)

Age		*9*	*14*	*17*	*21*	*All*
Drug Users	N	28	19	9	8	65
Offenders' Welfare		10	4	6	2	22
Public's Welfare		6	2	2	1	11
Offenders & the Public		12	13	1	5	32
Total		28	19	9	8	65

Age		*9*	*14*	*17*	*21*	*All*
Burglar/Killer	N	27	33	23	28	111
Offender's Welfare		0	1	1	0	2
Public's Welfare		21	22	14	18	75
Offenders & the Public		6	10	8	10	34
Total		29	33	23	28	111

Table 12-3
Perceptions of Imprisonment—Teenagers
(in numbers of respondents)

Age	9	14	17	21	All
N	33	34	32	33	132

Imprisonment is too harsh a penalty for the nature of the offense.

	2	12	14	7	35

Juvenile hall has a destructive effect on youths—bad models and bitterness.

	0	3	9	9	21

Juvenile hall leaves offenders unchanged.

	2	1	3	8	14

Juvenile hall helps offenders become more law abiding because:
—they fear future punishment.

	17	9	1	9	36

—they reform—adopt more constructive values and behavior.

	2	1	2	0	5

—they learn to avoid drugs.

	10	8	3	0	21

Table 12-4
Perceptions of Imprisonment—Burglar/Killer
(in numbers of respondents)

Age	9	14	17	21	All
N	24	26	24	27	101

Prison has a destructive effect on inmates—bad models and bitterness.

	0	1	1	1	3

Prison leaves offenders unchanged.

	3	4	4	2	13

Prison helps offenders become more law abiding because:
—they fear future punishment.

	8	2	4	2	16

—they reform—adopt more constructive values and behavior.

	1	12	8	8	29

(Reformation is a desirable goal but is rarely if ever achieved.)

	(3	2	6	10	21)

—they learn to abide by the law.

	9	5	1	4	19

Table 12-5
Suitable Sentence Length
(in numbers of respondents)

	Age	9	14	17	21	All
Drug Users	N	32	24	13	12	81
1-2 days		2	2	1	4	9
3-6 days			1		1	2
1-2 weeks		1	1	2		4
1-5 months		6		1	2	9
6 months		10	5	3	1	19
1-4 years		8	1			9
5-15 years		3				3
Until cured or paroled		2	7	1	1	11
6 months is too long			7	5	3	15
Mean years		1.9	.5	.3	.13	
Standard deviation (years)		2.9	.7	2.2	.17	
Burglar/Killer	N	29	34	23	27	113
Less than 1 year		3			1	4
1-2 years		6	1	2		9
3-9 years		5		1	2	8
10-19 years		1	4	6	3	14
20+ (short of lifetime)		3	8	2	6	19
Entire lifetime		6	16	3	5	30
Until cured or paroled		5	5	9	10	29
Mean years		20.4	39.6	22.8	30.4	
Standard deviation (years)		19.4	14.1	17.2	16.9	

The average (mean) length of confinement recommended for the pair of teenagers decreased as respondents grew older. The average of 2.9 years proposed by 9 year olds is significantly longer (.02) than the average in any of the other three groups.

In the case of the burglar/killer, the pattern of averages is quite different. The 14 year olds recommended sentences nearly twice the length of the ones proposed by either the 9 or 17 year olds, a difference significant beyond the .001 level. The recommendations of the 21 year olds (30.4 years) fell about midway between the suggestions of the 9 and 14 year olds.

Females and males were nearly identical in the length of time they would confine the offenders in both the drug case and the burglary. The slightly longer time that females would lock up the burglar did not approach statistical significance at even a .10 level.

CONCLUSION

In this chapter, interviewees' attitudes about the effects of imprisonment on offenders and about suitable lengths of confinement were quite as varied as the opinions regarding God's role in administering justice and the propriety of the death penalty reported in Chapter 11. In effect, marked diversity in sanctions, aims, and supporting rationales was a principal feature of students' conceptions of imprisonment. Such diversity was displayed within each age group and within each gender group. Each group included students who viewed the effects of confinement as constructive, ones who saw it as exerting no influence on offenders' future behavior, and ones who thought it would harm the wrongdoers. Furthermore, when two interviewees agreed on a particular proposal regarding imprisonment, they often differed in the line of reasoning leading to their proposal. In effect, simply knowing that a respondent would send the teenagers to juvenile hall did not reveal whose welfare the respondent thought would be served or what moral values lay behind that recommendation.

There was far greater agreement about imprisonment as an appropriate sanction for the burglar/killer than for the teenage drug users. Although the great majority of respondents would imprison the burglar, less than half would detain the teenagers. The aim that most students hoped to achieve by locking up the burglar was that of protecting the public. In contrast, the principal goal to be reached by confining the 16 year olds was to promote those youths' future welfare by teaching them to obey the drug laws. Unlike the burglar, the drug traders were usually not considered a threat to the public good.

No differences appeared between age groups on the issue of locking up the 23-year-old burglar. However, there was a significant age trend in students' intention to confine the 16 year olds; the younger the respondent, the more willing he or she would be to sentence the adolescent drug users to a term in juvenile hall. This trend seemed to result chiefly from different attitudes within the four age cohorts (a) about whether drug use constituted serious wrongdoing and (b) about the sorts of sanctions that might contribute most constructively toward the offenders' well-being. (In Chapter 14, attitudes toward drug use are analyzed in considerable detail.) In contrast to the age trends, no significant differences regarding the treatment of the 16 year olds were found between female and male respondents.

13

Empathy and Sympathy

The original intent of this study did not include assessing the empathic and sympathetic responses of the individuals who were interviewed. However, the responses of some interviewees to certain questions led us to a closer examination of empathy and sympathy, particularly as related to age and gender differences and to matters of fright and public exposure of an offender's wrongdoing. For example, one 9 year old, in answer to the question about giving the fifth-grade math test cheater a good scare, said,

> "No! Who would want to be scared? I get scared very easy. When my cousin jumps out of the bushes when I'm walking by, I know he's there but I don't know where he's going to jump out. It just gives you a . . . well, I just would not like to be scared at school." [9]

Another child, when asked whether other people should be told about the boy and girl who were caught trading drugs for concert tickets, answered,

> "I don't think they should tell it to everybody because it might hurt their feelings or they might get embarrassed that they were doing all that stuff. They might get embarrassed by their teacher." [9]

This kind of response demonstrated that, in some instances, the interviewees were feeling *for* the individuals in the cases, and at other times they were feeling *with* them, placing themselves in the situation when evaluating the desirability of a proposed sanction. Thus, we posed the following questions which are addressed in this chapter:

—Are there either gender or age differences among respondents in terms of spontaneously generated empathic and sympathetic statements?
—Are there differences among respondents based on the severity of the wrongdoing?

—What were stated reasons and conditions for expressing empathic and
   sympathetic responses?

The presentation opens with definitions of empathy and sympathy, then
continues with comparisons of empathic and sympathetic reactions.

EMPATHY AND SYMPATHY DEFINED

The terms *empathy* and *sympathy*, though closely related, are often
differentiated, as is the case in the present chapter.

Not all authors agree on what constitutes empathy. For instance, in an
historical review of how the term has been used, Goldstein and Michaels (1985)
identified 16 different meanings. For present purposes, we adopted a definition
that combines several features implied in a number of the ways the word has
been applied. Thus, we define empathy as "the act of putting oneself in the
other's place, or entering the other's mind" (Demos, 1984, p. 9)—an act that
involves "sharing the perceived emotion of another—'feeling with' another"
(Eisenberg & Strayer, 1987, p. 5). Displaying empathy is not merely an
emotional reaction; it also involves cognition, particularly in an individual's
ability to differentiate between self and others and to take on the roles of others
(Eisenberg & Strayer, 1987, p. 8).

We are assuming that empathy develops from the time of infancy and is
affected by children's life experiences, their rate of cognitive development, their
capacity to differentiate self from others, their role-taking skills, and their ability
in the early stages of growth to perceive similarities between themselves and the
person with whom they are empathizing. Empathy depends on people's being
able to project themselves into others' lives and imaginatively share their
experiences. For example, in the case of the burglar killing the householder, a
17-year-old respondent projected herself into a similar situation during the
process of suggesting an appropriate sanction.

"I know I'd be very upset if someone came and robbed my house and killed my
mom. I'd definitely want to see that person put in jail for a long time." [17]

In contrast to empathic responses that involved projection—in the sense of
imagining another's experience—some respondents placed themselves in the role
of the other through the use of their personal history, linking the case of
wrongdoing to a similar event in their own life. In reaction to the case of the
fifth-grade girl who copied math test answers, a 21-year-old respondent said,

"Because I did go through that. I was verbally assaulted when I was in the
fourth grade. My teacher every day made me ashamed of who I am. So I am very
strong on that. I do not believe children should be made to feel ashamed about
anything they do." [21]

Now we progress to the meaning of *sympathy*. For present purposes,
sympathy relies on individuals feeling *for* another person without using either

projection (imagining they are in the same position) or personal history (citing an experience in their own life). In our study, sympathetic responses were ones in which participants expressed concern for the well-being of individuals in the three cases and about the effects that a given sanction might have on those individuals, but without the respondents placing themselves in the roles of the individuals by means of projection or personal history. To illustrate, when asked if it would be a good idea to give the fifth-grade girl a good scare for copying test answers, one student stated,

> "It would just scare her and make her think that everyone's against her, and so she might do worse. She might not copy anymore, but she might not do any of her work anymore either. She might not want to be involved in school." [14]

As a reaction to the same case, another participant said,

> "Making her feel ashamed would be detrimental to her later." [21]

In sum, respondents who were credited with making sympathetic statements were those who evaluated the impact of a particular sanction on the individual without projecting themselves into the role or recounting similar incidents in their own history as the basis for their decisions.

COMPARISONS OF EMPATHIC REACTIONS

We interpreted interviewees' empathic responses from four perspectives: type of case, type of empathy, age, and gender.

Type of Case

In Table 13-1, as shown by the row entitled *F-M Total*, 32% of the inter-viewees (females and male combined) expressed empathy when judging the case of the 9-year-old girl who had copied math answers. Less than half as many (14%) included empathic comments about the teenage drug users, whereas 20% showed empathy in the case of the 23-year-old murderer. However, the first two cases differed from the third in terms of who was the object of empathy. In the first two cases, empathy focused on the offenders—the girl who copied and the teenagers who were caught trading drugs.

> "I know personally that when I was that age, I used to hate spanking, so you should only do stuff to others that you'd want done to yourself." [14]
> "Being the kind of person I am, it's kind of hard to sit in judgment on the ones who had the drugs." [17]

Whereas empathy in the first two cases focused on the offenders, in the third case the empathy of nearly all 20% of the respondents expressed concern for indirect victims of the burglary-murder, that is, for relatives of the dead woman.

Table 13-1
Empathic Reactions to Three Cases of Wrongdoing
(n=136, in percentages)

Age Group	Case 1 math test		Case 2 drugs		Case 3 rob & kill	
	Female	Male	Female	Male	Female	Male
9	2	2	0	0	1	1
14	7	4	1	3	2	2
17	7	3	4	2	6	2
21	5	2	2	2	4	2
Total	21	11	7	7	13	7
F-M total	32		14		20	

"Because I've been in that situation before. My uncle killed my cousin, and he only got put in prison for four years, and I think he should be in there for the rest of his life, and I hope he lives with it forever that he killed my little cousin. If he were there for life, it would make me feel so much better to know he wasn't out and around, but I think it does give the family satisfaction when the person is punished." [17]

Only one 9 year old displayed concern for the relatives both of the dead woman and of the murderer who might be executed for the crime.

"The other people that were in his family, they would be missing a person, but it would be the same thing as for the woman's family." [9]

Several interviewees who focused their empathic feelings on indirect victims implied that they would not wish to take responsibility for ending the life of the felon, a reaction that might be interpreted as either a mild form of empathy or else an unwillingness to take drastic action affecting others' lives.

"What if he was in my house and killed my parents or something. You think that person should be put to death because they don't deserve to live. But it's like I wouldn't want to be the one in charge of pulling the [electric-chair] switch or be on the jury that convicted him, so I don't know if I can say [he deserves the death penalty] without saying that I'd do it." [21]

We estimated that the reason the largest amount of empathy occurred in the first case was that the girl's cheating in math was the only incident from the three cases that was well within the direct life experience of every respondent. As a result, copying from a classmate would be the event most likely to draw an empathic reaction from all age groups.

The drug case elicited the least empathy. No 9 year old expressed empathy for the teenagers. Perhaps this was partly because these particular 9 year olds were routinely involved in drug awareness programs at their elementary schools, so their responses appeared to reflect the messages they were being given in school that using drugs was wrong and harmful. In contrast, older respondents seemed to identify with the drug case, presumably because their life experience had more often involved experimentation with drugs, either personally or by relatives or friends.

"When I was a rebel, the only thing that got me out was Jesus Christ." [17]
"I went to a drug rehabilitation program when I was 13, and it didn't do anything." [21]
"There are lots of kids who were really into drugs when they were younger and then they came out of it, and they don't want to hear about that anymore." [21]

The students were least likely to have had direct experience with burglary and murder. However, it was clear that many could imagine how they might feel at having a relative or friend suffer at the hands of a lawbreaker.

Type of Empathy

Nearly all empathic responses were one of three types (A, B, and C) or, in a few instances, of two types combined.

In Type A, the student assessed the efficacy of a sanction as based on that student's past experience. The sanction was evaluated as either effective or ineffective for convincing an offender to avoid similar misbehavior in the future.

"I've been spanked before when I was a little kid, and that's not what I remember most. It's my parents' telling me what I was doing and stuff like that, or it was when I was thinking about what I was doing wrong that made me shape up. It wasn't because I got spanked or anything. That's not why I stopped." [17]
"I've known friends who went to juvenile hall, and they came out just as bad or the same as when they went in." [21]
"If I did something like that, I know juvenile hall wouldn't help me a bit." [17]
"Yeah, going to jail would deter me." [21]

Type B responses featured the emotional content of an empathic reaction.

"If they just gave me a zero on the test, I wouldn't be afraid." [14]
"I'm 21 years old, and I still hate it when my teachers make an example of me. It's very degrading." [21]
"I was lucky. I was only spanked once as a child." [21]
"If I had a daughter and someone killed my daughter, I'd want the person dead. I understand what [the family is] feeling, but you just can't go out and say, 'I want to kill him.'" [17]

Type C reactions simply involved recounting a relevant past experience without either assessing the efficacy of a sanction or expressing emotion.

> "We were brought up at a school where if you got sent to the principal's office and your parents said it was okay to get spanked, then you got spanked." [21]
>
> "I know from personal experience." [14]
>
> "I don't really know, because I was never spanked in my entire life." [9]
>
> "I'm just trying to put myself in her place." [17]

Types A and B were the most frequent, represented in almost equal amounts among answers at all age levels. Type C was considerably less common. Responses that combined two types were very rare, such as those involving both an efficacy assessment and emotional content.

> "When I was younger, I used to get spankings, and it really didn't do anything for me. It would just make me upset or mad. I'd want to go out and again do whatever I did or even something worse." [17]

Age and Gender

Table 13-2 summarizes the incidence of empathic statements across all three cases by age and gender.

As the percentages indicate, 17 year olds offered the greatest number of empathic comments and 9 year olds the fewest, with the 14 and 21 year olds in between. The difference between the 9 year olds and the other three groups did not reach statistical significance at even the .10 level. Yet it is still in keeping with Hoffman's (1987) description of stages in children's development of empathy in which he describes the last period as occurring when children perceive the long-term nature of a person's or a group's distress, a stage more common in adolescence and early adulthood than in late childhood. An additional

Table 13-2

Empathic Reactions Across All Three Cases
by Age and Gender
(N = 136, in percentages)

Age	Female	Male	Total
9	1.0	1.0	3.0
13	3.3	3.0	6.3
17	5.7	2.3	8.0
21	3.7	2.0	5.7
Total	13.7	8.3	22.0

possible factor in the lower rate of empathic responses among 9 year olds may have been their shorter history of life experiences. The 9 year olds would likely have had fewer opportunities than the other participants to encounter, either directly or vicariously, the drug use and burglary-murder incidents.

These observed trends appear worthy of further investigation with larger age samples than those in the present study to determine if they are found within other groups that range in age from late childhood to the early adult years.

In the gender comparison, 13.7% of the empathic statements were offered by females and 8.3% by males, a difference significant beyond the .10 level but not at the .05 level. This hint of a trend is in keeping with Gilligan's (1982) contention that females and males differ in the principles on which they base their moral decisions, with females founding their beliefs on compassionate caring and males on even-handed justice. However, it seems important to note that empathic responses do not necessarily mean that females in this study actually demonstrated more caring in the sanctions they proposed than did the males. A return to our definition of empathy helps to clarify this observation. The females more often either placed themselves in a situation like the one described in the case or they recounted what appeared to be a similar personal incident. Thus, the results here indicate only that the females more often displayed projection and the use of personal experience in the rationale for their decision, not that they generally demonstrated more compassion or caring than did the males. As noted in Chapter 8, whereas more males that females would execute the burglar who had killed the householder, in the main the females and males in our study were essentially alike in the sanctions they suggested.

COMPARISONS OF SYMPATHETIC REACTIONS

As in the analysis of empathy, we interpreted respondents' sympathetic reactions from four perspectives: type of case, type of sympathy, age, and gender.

Type of Case

One-fifth more expressions of sympathy (105) than of empathy (86) were offered across the three cases. As shown in Table 13-3, sympathy was expressed most often in the first case, less than half as frequently in the second, and hardly one-fifth as often in the third. Such a pattern again suggests that the interviewees were more likely to associate emotionally with incidents closely related to their own experiences. The sympathetic reactions differed from empathic responses in that the students neither overtly projected themselves into the roles of people in the case nor recounted a similar experience in their own lives. Instead, they appeared to be feeling *for* rather than feeling *with* the individuals in the cases.

Type of Sympathy

The respondents' remarks implied that their sympathy was motivated by one or more of five principal aims or types of concern, those of (1) avoiding embarrassment and shame for the offenders, (2) protecting offenders from psychological and social damage, (3) protecting offenders from unreasonable physical harm, (4) averting undesired reactions on the part of offenders, and (5) enabling victims' relatives to feel that justice had been served.

The most frequent motive (in nearly one-third of the reactions) was to shield the fifth-grade girl and the teenage drug users from embarrassment and shame.

"They shouldn't try to scare the girl. She shouldn't feel afraid and ashamed at school. It's going to hurt her." [9]

"Spanking would cause her to feel even more ashamed to ask for help. I don't think that's a good thing for something that is probably a symptom of a much bigger problem." [21]

"It's downgrading to use a person as an example." [21]

"The point isn't to embarrass them. It's to punish them." [14]

"I don't think a minor person should be paraded around for using drugs and stuff like that because it's embarrassing. It's not really right because they are still children." [17]

"They'd have to go back to school, and it'd be embarrassing and stuff." [9]

The aim of averting psychological and social damage to the offenders was reflected in such remarks as the following:

Table 13-3
Sympathetic Reactions to Three Cases of Wrongdoing
(N = 136, in percentages)

Age Group	Case 1 math test		Case 2 drugs		Case 3 rob & kill	
	Female	Male	Female	Male	Female	Male
9	4	2	2	2	2	1
14	5	5	4	4	1	0
17	7	3	4	2	2	1
21	10	7	6	2	1	1
Total	26	17	16	10	6	3
F-M total	43		26		9	

"I don't think it would be good to scare her because she could have nightmares." [9]

"It would make her feel not as smart as the other students. It might just scare her and make her think that everyone's against her and she might do worse. She might not copy anymore, but she might not do any of her work anymore. She might not want to be involved in school." [14]

"Hitting a child, you're just going to make it more afraid." [21]

"If everybody knew the boy and girl had been using drugs, they wouldn't have any more friends." [9]

"You should never do anything to bring down a person's morale and self-esteem." [21]

Sympathetic objections were also raised over the likelihood that the offenders would suffer undeserved physical harm.

"Spanking only gets someone hurt, and you shouldn't want to hurt your own children." [9]

"You could be beat up in jail or juvenile hall, and the guards wouldn't know it until morning, and you could be dead." [9]

"Executing the killer is not something civilized people should be doing. If they caught him, they should be going, 'Okay. He's caught. Hopefully, we can do something with him.' It shouldn't be, 'Ha-ha, he's caught. We're going to kill him.' That's turning the criminal into the victim." [17]

Several interviewees feared that a proposed sanction would result in future undesirable behavior on the part of the offender.

"Spanking causes resentment within the child toward whoever was doing it, and later in life that's going to trip her up somehow." [17]

"She might just totally withdraw." [17]

"If you get somebody ashamed like that, she might want to run away or hide from her friends." [14]

"Making her feel ashamed would be detrimental to her later." [21]

In the third case, most sympathetic reactions concerned the dead householder's family members, particularly as related to the question of whether sanctions should aim at giving satisfaction to the family of the victim.

"I'll bet her family feel bad." [9]

"If he went free, that would feel really awful for the family, knowing they lost a daughter and nothing was being done about it." [17]

"I certainly have more sympathy for them than for the killer." [21]

"They've lost somebody very dear to them, and they should be repaid for someone's death in their family when that person didn't really die naturally. Everyone should be able to die a natural death, not somebody killing them." [9]

One further sympathetic remark was made about the burglar in reaction to the proposal that he be executed.

"It's not to give the family satisfaction. Nothing's going to bring her back.
The burglar needs help now." [14]

In summary, the interviewees provided sympathetic responses chiefly out of
concern that a particular sanction could have negative repercussions for the
wrongdoer, a concern that tempered the sanctions that would be acceptable.

Age and Gender

As shown in Table 13-4, the largest percentage of sympathetic remarks across
all three cases were made by 21 year olds and the smallest percentage by 9 year
olds, with the 14 and 17 year olds in between.   None of the differences
between age groups approaches statistical significance at the .05 level.
However, since the trend was similar to that for empathy, perhaps the younger
students' shorter history of life experiences may have rendered them less prepared
to sympathize with other people's situations than did the older students' greater
experience.

Once more, as with empathy, females expressed sympathy more often than did
males, but this gender difference fails to reach a .05 level of significance.
Nevertheless, the trend again offers possible support for Gilligan's belief that
females, more often than males, base moral decisions on compassion.

CONCLUSION

Across the three cases of wrongdoing, 22% of the 136 interviewees' reactions
included expressions of empathy, whereas 26% included expressions of
sympathy. The 9 year olds made fewer empathic and sympathetic comments
than did the 14, 17, or 21 year olds, although the differences between groups
failed to reach a .05 level of significance. Females more frequently than males

Table 13-4
Sympathetic Reactions Across All Three Cases
by Age and Gender
(N = 136, in percentages)

Age	Female	Male	Total
9	2.7	1.7	4.4
14	3.3	3.0	6.3
17	4.3	2.0	6.3
21	5.7	3.3	9.0
Total	16.0	10.0	26.0

expressed both empathy and sympathy. But again, these differences were not significant at the .05 level. Nevertheless, the consistency of such trends suggests that the observed tendencies warrant investigation with larger samples of respondents to determine whether these results might obtain generally across age and gender groups and thus be socially important.

The three types of empathic comments among a total of 86 expressions of empathy involved (1) estimating the efficacy of a proposed sanction for achieving a particular aim, (2) reacting emotionally to a sanction, or (3) recounting a relevant past experience in the respondent's life without either an assessment of the efficacy of a sanction or an expression of emotion. The 105 sympathetic remarks were categorized under five types that reflected inter-viewees' desire to (1) avoid embarrassment and shame for the offenders, (2) protect offenders from psychological and social damage, (3) protect offenders from unreasonable physical harm, (4) avert undesired reactions on the part of offenders, or (5) enable victims' relatives to feel that justice had been served.

A comparison of the three kinds of wrongdoing that our cases involved showed that the greatest number of empathic (32%) and sympathetic (43%) comments were made about the girl who had copied test answers, perhaps because the math test situation was well within the life experience of all interviewees. The case of the adolescents who traded drugs drew fewer expressions of empathy (14%) and sympathy (26%). The types of life experiences of the respondents might have been a factor differentiating one age group from another, since the 17 and 21 year olds empathized and sympathized more often with the teenage drug users than did the 9 year olds. The fewest empathic (9%) and sympathetic (20%) remarks were offered in the case of the burglar who killed the householder. The great majority of those remarks involved concern for the feelings of the victim's family rather than for the fate of the killer.

14

Drugs and the Law

In Chapter 6 we noted that adolescence has often been depicted as a period of rebellion against societal values and adult authority. We also suggested that such a broad generalization conveys an unduly simplistic view of the teen years, obscuring the true complexity of that time of life. We then proposed that the results of the present study might contribute toward understanding the nature of adolescent rebelliousness through showing how closely the opinions of our 136 interviewees deviated from, or agreed with, what we have called *societal standards*. Applying those standards means judging people's behavior in terms of the adult society's dominant laws, regulations, or widespread customs. Under this definition, the behavior of the central characters in all three of the cases used in our study was wrong. That is, most American adults would judge copying other pupils' test answers to be cheating and, as such, immoral. Ingesting illicit drugs or peddling them to others is—as indicated by the term *illicit*—against the law. So also are burglary and murder. Therefore, adolescent rebelliousness might be measured by the extent to which adolescents disagreed with adults in considering such behaviors as wrongdoing.

We have relegated the discussion of adolescent rebelliousness to this chapter because only in the case of the drug trading 16 year olds was there evidence that any notable number of our interviewees rejected, or even questioned, societal standards. Without exception, all 136 regarded the 9 year old's copying test answers as wrongdoing. In a similar manner, all respondents condemned the 23 year old's burglary and his killing the householder as serious crimes. However, while most respondents identified drug trading and drug use as wrongdoing, some said there was no harm in trading drugs, and even more believed that using illegal drugs was not wrong but, rather, was simply a matter of personal choice.

The intent of this chapter is to inspect the drug trading case in some detail so as to display the diversity of moral value positions reflected in our interviewees' responses and to suggest what our results may mean for understanding the nature of teenage rebelliousness. The presentation begins with an overview of diverse viewpoints that students displayed, then continues with a description of age and gender trends, and finishes with an interpretation of the rebellious adolescent.

A VARIETY OF OPINIONS

The responses of the 136 participants in the drug trading case reflected a variety of attitudes toward illegal drugs and toward the law as it relates to drugs. The following paragraphs first describe perceptions of the law found in the interviews and, second, identify types of opinion about the use and trading of drugs.

Attitudes Toward the Law

Six attitudes toward the law that were implied in participants' remarks represent viewpoints founded on social concern, selective control, prudence (penalty avoidance), interim compliance, risk of apprehension, and selective compliance. Illustrations of the six appear in the segments of interviews quoted under each type.

Social Concern. People who base their respect for the law on social concern believe that the law furnishes the necessary framework within which a society can operate in a predictable, peaceful, and productive manner. The law should always be obeyed. Failing to do so courts social chaos.

"The boy and girl broke the law, and that's wrong. The reason for laws is to protect people from hurting themselves or others." [14]

"They were caught in possession of illegal drugs, which is commonly known to be a crime, and they admitted to using drugs, so both those things are wrong." [17]

Selective Control. A variant of social concern is the opinion that the law should seek to control access to drugs but, in doing so, it should differentiate among the types of people who are permitted the freedom to choose whether or not to use drugs. The purpose of such legislation would be to protect youngsters from inadvertently coming to harm through the use of drugs because they have not yet reached "the age of reason and responsibility." Just as the legal age for imbibing alcohol has been set by the U.S. government at age 21, so also a legal age should be established for using other substances that currently are forbidden by law. Or perhaps there should be some way other than by a person's age to decide which people are capable of using drugs responsibly.

"Young kids should be prevented from getting hold of drugs, since they really don't know what they're doing. That's where the laws should come in." [17]

"I'm not an advocate of drug use, but I think drug use is a real tricky thing. I would love to leave it up to people's own personal judgment about whether they would use drugs. Theoretically, I wish it could be like that. But unfortunately there's a lot of misunderstanding and a lack of knowledge about the effects of drugs. I believe there should be some control until such a time that people are better educated about the really harmful effects of drugs." [21]

Penalty Avoidance. People operating from a penalty avoidance perspective contend that it is prudent to comply with the law in order to stay out of trouble. Getting caught breaking the law results in punishment and inconvenience, which interfere with people's freedom to conduct their lives as they wish. Hence, it is in one's own best interest to comply with the law.

"Of course what they did was wrong. It was stupid. Why put yourself in the position of having the police catch you? It just wasn't smart." [17]

Risk of Apprehension. According to the risk-of-apprehension policy, if people feel they are likely to be caught breaking the law, then they should not break it. In other words, the decision about whether or not to obey the law should be based on an estimate of the probability of being apprehended. Thus, it is appropriate to comply with the law only if there is a high probability of getting caught.

Respondent: "The boy and girl used drugs as money to buy tickets. If they'd used money, this wouldn't have happened. So what they did wrong was getting caught with the drugs. They weren't careful."

Interviewer: "You don't see anything inherently wrong with exchanging drugs for tickets. What you see as wrong is that they got caught at it?"

Respondent: "That's right. The act wasn't wrong; it was how society perceived the act." [17]

Interim Compliance. Supporters of this position hold that even though people may disagree with a law, they still should obey it until it is officially amended or replaced. If people adopted the habit of refusing to comply with whatever laws happened to displease them, society would be in constant turmoil. Consequently, everyone should continue to obey any and all laws while, at the same time, working to have unsatisfactory legislation revised or eliminated.

"I don't think the drug laws are all that great. But you still ought to follow them while you're trying to get them changed into something better." [17]

Selective Compliance. Advocates of selective compliance argue that people should obey only those laws which, in their own opinion, are proper. Laws should not be regarded as objective, absolute standards of conduct that are necessarily correct. Instead, laws are simply rules created by people who are trying to impose their values on the general populace. Often the rule-makers' primary intent is to further their own interests rather than to promote the general good.

"You shouldn't tell the kids that all laws should be obeyed. If a law comes along that shouldn't be agreed with, that's just blatant manipulation of the people, then you can't tell kids to just be passive. You've got to tell them to believe in what they believe in. And you can't scare them away from that. I think that better than to obey the law is to try not to obstruct the social stream, but be your own person. I'm not talking communism, but you can't go out of your way to make other people miserable in this life." [21]

Attitudes Toward Illicit Drugs

In the present study, respondents' notions about using and trading illegal drugs were manifold, varied, and frequently complex. As a way of systematizing such a mixed bag of opinions, we have ordered the interviewees' opinions in the form of a list that advances from (a) strong condemnation of both drug use and drug trading to (b) open approval of both drug use and drug trading. The presentation of each position includes a description of the perspective and one or more quotations from interviews illustrating that position.

Legality. The law defines which drugs should be avoided. Since those drugs are prohibited by law, people should not use them.

"They were caught in possession of illegal drugs, which is commonly known to be a crime, and they admitted to using drugs. And that's wrong." [17]

"I think they did wrong because our law is against drugs. So it was wrong, both using drugs and trading them to someone else. Our society gives very harsh penalties for drugs. In this case, the boy and girl were wrong according to the law, but obviously they aren't aware of the harshness of the penalties. I think they should be punished, because if they're not, they'll continue to be involved in those situations—since drugs make them feel good." [21]

General Harmfulness. Illicit drugs should not be used, since they do both physical and psychological damage.

Interviewer: "Did the teenagers do anything wrong?"
Respondent: "Of course. Medical research and everything have shown that drugs are bad and addictive. They sure shouldn't be using drugs." [21]

Legal Distinctions. Some drugs are relatively harmless, while others are quite harmful, leading to addiction, to incapacitation, and to behaviors that may harm self and others. People should have the choice of using the relatively harmless drugs, particularly if they use them only socially and are not addicted in ways that their drug use interferes with their fulfilling responsibilities.

"I separate certain drugs from other drugs. Like alcohol we accept as being okay whereas something like cocaine we don't. So society makes that distinction—and like marijuana is very big around here but it's illegal. I really think our government is much too strict in their punishment." [21]

Effect on Self, Effect on Others. It is wrong to contribute to other people's drug use, either by introducing them to drugs or by supplying them with drugs to maintain an existing habit. However, if they choose to indulge in drugs themselves, they should have the right to do so.

Respondent: "Giving the drugs to their friend was wrong, but if they want to ruin their lives and kill themselves by taking drugs, that's not my problem."

Interviewer: "So it was wrong to give drugs to their friend, but it was okay for them to take drugs themselves?"

Respondent: "Well, not really, but if that's what they want to do, it's okay with me." [9]

Interviewer: "Did either the boy or the girl do anything wrong? And if so, what was it?"

Respondent: "Well, what they did wrong was to exchange the drugs for the tickets. If it was only the boy and girl who were involved, then the drugs might have hurt them, but they wouldn't have been hurting someone else. But trading drugs to someone else could hurt them, and that was what was bad." [14]

Normal/Natural Development. Youths who try drugs should not be dealt with harshly because doing such things is just a natural part of growing up. It is no more than a social experience that contributes to becoming an informed, mature person.

"I think those kids did wrong because our law is against drugs. But I think that experimenting with drugs is all part of growing up. I mean, well, it's difficult to say anything without incriminating myself." [21]

Direct Experience. People are not qualified to make judgments about matters which they have not personally experienced. The only way people can accurately understand the advantages and disadvantages of drugs is through sampling those substances.

"Those people who are so against getting caught using drugs have never tried it before, because there's a lack of understanding of what it is. I almost feel that people should try things like drugs at least once." [21]

Selective Use. People should be selective in terms of the substances they use and the conditions under which they try them. Drugs should not be consumed under conditions that may cause the user serious harm or may negatively affect the lives of others.

"Using some kinds of drugs can cause permanent damage, and it can affect your work performance. But using drugs in your leisure time when you have nothing to do, I have no problem with that." [17]

Character Configuration. If people who use drugs are, in other respects, admirable individuals, then using drugs must not be a bad thing. In other words, using drugs may be just one aspect of the general character configuration of someone who is quite a good person.

> "I really didn't like what the questions about the two teenagers seemed to imply. It's because kids that I've hung around with seem like good people and they use drugs—not hard drugs—but like dope." [17]

Informed Choice. People can be trusted to use drugs responsibly—that is, to avoid drugs entirely or use them in nonharmful ways—if they are properly informed about the effects of different types of drugs and of different methods of using them.

> "What you need to do in a drug-education program for kids who want to experiment with drugs is to inform them about the drugs, about what is going to happen to you if you do drugs. 'This is going to happen to you if you do heroin, this is going to happen to you if you do cocaine, this is going to happen to you if you do LSD. You can expect certain results.' You can also show that it varies with the individual. Tell the kids what it's about instead of trying to say it's bad and leave it at that unquestionably. If you inform them, they can make wiser decisions." [21]

> "I don't think the teenagers should be put in a drug rehabilitation program. It doesn't sound like they're addicted. I think rehab is for extreme cases who can't handle drugs on their own. But there are people who can handle drugs casually instead of addictively. The best thing would be to put the 16 year olds in a drug education program, not a rehabilitation program, because a rehabilitation program would be to get at the underlying problem—whatever the user is trying to repress or escape. In the drug education program they need to learn what drugs can do. Teach them about different kinds of drugs and what they do to a person, physically and psychologically. Tell them the structure of the drug, how it binds with the receptors in your neurons and what happens to them cognitively and behaviorally and what can happen addictively. Tell them the steps to take to avoid addiction. Just as there is safe sex, there is safe experimentation with drugs; so they should know how to keep control. They have sex education in the schools, so drug education should be next. Just as everybody needs to know how to use a condom, so with drugs they should also learn how to use a pipe safely, how to use a syringe safely. If they're going to experiment, they should do it safely." [21]

Arbitrary Lawmaking. The laws bearing on substance use are inconsistent and contradictory. How can you expect people to respect laws which make illogical distinctions among substances?

> "The law is really freakish, since some damaging drugs—particularly alcohol—are legal and widely advertised, while others that aren't bad—like marijuana and LSD—are illegal and can get you into prison." [17]

Individual Rights. Even if drugs are not good for people's health and for the conduct of their lives in a responsible manner, it is still the individual's right to decide whether to use drugs. It is the individual's choice, not the business of the government. There should be no laws proscribing drug use.

> *Respondent*: "The main harm that drugs cause in society is their being declared illegal, so people commit crimes to get them." [21]

> *Interviewer*: "Did either the boy or the girl do anything wrong?"
> *Respondent*: "No. I don't think either of them did anything wrong."
> *Interviewer*: "What should happen to the boy in the case?"
> *Respondent*: "Nothing should happen to him. He didn't do anything wrong."
> *Interviewer*: "What about the girl?"
> *Respondent*: "Same thing. Girls use drugs just as much as guys."
> *Interviewer*: "Would you want the boy and girl to learn to obey the law?"
> *Respondent*: "Definitely not." [17]

ATTITUDES BY AGE AND GENDER

With the foregoing assortment of opinions in mind, we next consider how such attitudes were distributed across age and gender groups.

When respondents were asked whether the teenagers had done anything wrong, the majority at each age level disapproved of trading or giving drugs to someone else (Table 14-1). Considerably smaller percentages also cited the youths' use of drugs as wrongdoing. Possibly more than that number disapproved of drug use but, when asked what the teenagers had done wrong, they may have focused attention primarily on the drug trading as the greater misdeed. In any event, trading rather than use was more prominent in the students' opinions. An additional few at ages 14, 17, and 21 mentioned that the drug was illegal, the boy and girl had it in their possession, and that they had broken the law. A small number contended that there was no wrongdoing in the case—that using drugs was simply a matter of personal choice or that the fault was with having laws that proscribed drug use.

Throughout Table 14-1 consistent age trends are evident. Younger respondents in significantly larger numbers disapproved of both drug trading and drug use (difference between 9 and 21 year olds >.01). Furthermore, when asked whether one of their aims in the drug case would be to see that the law was enforced, the majority of students at each age level said yes. However, the proportions that desired to see drug laws obeyed decreased with age. All 9 year olds advocated enforcing the law, although 9% felt that such an aim was really not feasible since "You couldn't guarantee it" and "Somebody would have to be watching them all the time." Respondents at other age levels gave a variety of reasons that the goal of enforcing the law might be a good idea but was not very practical.

"How do you enforce it? Kids will do those things anyway." [17]
"That's a good idea, but what really concerns me is what happens to the boy and girl." [17]

Table 14-1
Attitudes Toward the Drug Case by Age
(in percentages)

Age	9	14	17	21	All
N	33	36	34	33	136
What was the nature of the wrongdoing?					
Traded or sold drugs	94	89	79	67	82
Used drugs	67	42	38	33	45
Possessed illegal drugs		6	15	21	10
Broke the law		6	9	12	7
The drug was illegal		6	9	21	10
There was no wrongdoing.			6	9	4
Using drugs is just a matter of personal choice, so it was the teenagers' own right to use drugs.		6	9	12	7
The laws are wrong. There shouldn't be any drug laws.			3	9	3
Would one of your aims be to enforce the law?					
Yes	91	89	74	73	82
No		3	20	27	12
That's not very feasible	9	8	6		6

In like manner, students who rejected the aim of enforcing the law buttressed their opinions with diverse rationales.

"Some laws aren't logical. People need to make decisions for themselves about what is right. Counseling could help free those kids from drugs." [17]

"We should be more concerned about the individuals involved—worry more about people not getting hurt by using and trading drugs." [17]

"Enforcing the law is the police's job, not mine."

"There are lots of bad laws, like the ones against drugs." [21]

"Instead of using the law, I'd have the boy and girl be given a good scare about drugs. They should be 'scared straight.'" [21]

"Some laws shouldn't be observed. Instead, you need to teach kids to function properly in society but to question unfit laws. Get them off drugs by education and rehabilitation, not laws." [21]

In Chapter 6 we noted that Piaget (1932/1948) distinguished between heteronomy and autonomy in children's moral reasoning. In his view, a heteronomous perspective accords unilateral respect for authorities and the rules or laws they prescribe. In contrast, people displaying an autonomous viewpoint base their moral judgments on mutual regard among peers or equals and respect for the rules that guide their interaction. Whereas heteronomous morality requires obedience to authority and to authority-produced laws, autonomous morality is based on reciprocity and equality among peers. Piaget suggested that development in reasoning tended to progress from heteronomous morality to autonomous morality. In a limited sense, the age trends reflected in Table 14-1 could be interpreted as evidence of Piaget's proposal. More younger than older students agreed with the drug laws, whereas older students tended to express greater originality in their reactions to the case of the teenagers. However, it could be argued that older respondents who felt there was no wrongdoing in the case were expressing a "reciprocity and equality among peers" that was hedonistic and self-indulgent rather than morally responsible in terms of the general welfare of society.

Table 14-2 compares gender attitudes in the drug trading case. As in the age comparisons, a clear majority of both females and males disapproved of the youths' supplying drugs to a companion, whereas substantially smaller numbers

Table 14-2
Attitudes Toward the Drug Case by Gender
(in percentages)

	Female	Male	All
N	69	67	136
What was the nature of the wrongdoing?			
Traded or sold drugs	90	73	82
Used drugs	58	31	45
Possessed illegal drugs	6	15	10
Broke the law	23	24	24
The drug was illegal	10	16	13
There was no wrongdoing.			
Using drugs is just a matter of personal choice, so it was the teenagers' own right to use drugs.	1	9	7
The laws are wrong. There shouldn't be any drug laws.		6	3
Would one of your aims be to enforce the law?			
Yes	88	75	82
No	6	19	12
That's not very feasible	6	6	6

mentioned drug use as wrongdoing. Significantly larger (.01) numbers of females than males opposed both drug trading and drug use. The difference in the proportion of females (88%) and males (75%) who would enforce the law was significant at the .05 level.

ADOLESCENT REBELLIOUSNESS

The question now is: How should this chapter's results be viewed in relation to the notion that adolescence is a period of rebellion? By comparing how the interviewees perceived wrongdoing in the three cases, we perhaps can estimate the extent and nature of rebelliousness.

First, it is important to recognize that a large majority of both females and males at all four age levels concurred with adult rules about cheating, trading drugs, burglary, and murder. In effect, most respondents believed that the rules should be obeyed. Thus, a great many of the 136 participants displayed no rebellion against the society's standards for the types of behavior represented in our three cases. The only noteworthy disagreement with such standards appeared in the drug case; that very modest suggestion of rebellion appeared primarily among older students, especially among males.

In an effort to interpret such results, we propose that a combination of three factors might be responsible for the evidence of rebellion: (a) estimated risk of harm, (b) lack of victims, and (c) a need for ego defense.

Risk of Harm. A first factor may be the belief held by certain older youths about what harm, if any, drugs may do to those who use them. Three characteristics of drug use that serve to confuse the issue are these—the extent of damage suffered can vary from one type of drug to another, from one dosage to another, and from one individual to another. The sort of information, or misinformation, that adolescents accept about such matters can affect their view of the harmfulness of drugs. As Kleiman (1992, 253–255) has explained:

> Aside from the almost self-evident proposition that smoking anything is probably bad for the lungs, the quarter century since large numbers of Americans began to use marijuana has produced remarkably little laboratory or epidemiological evidence of serious health damage done by the drug. . . . Still, marijuana is a powerful intoxicant, and it can generate a powerful bad habit. Crude and necessarily imprecise calculation suggests that, as measured by hours spent in a state of diminished self-command, marijuana contributes about as much to the total intoxication burden on the American mind as alcohol, and far more than cocaine. In addition, marijuana intoxication is qualitatively different from intoxication with the widely used depressants and stimulants, including alcohol and cocaine, in that it involves more complicated and profound subjective effects, in some ways similar to those of the psychedelics. . . . Marijuana is forbidden, despite its limited potential to create measurable health damage and its lower rate of compulsive use, because it produces an "altered state of consciousness."

Evidence that respondents held diverse beliefs about potential damage from drugs appeared in such an assortment of comments as:

"Drugs are bad for you." [14]

"When you do drugs, you just hurt yourself." [17]

"Drugs can kill you. Give them to others, you can kill them, too." [9]

"In doing drugs, you risk your life." [9]

"Drugs aren't ideal, but it's not much of an offense." [21]

"Drugs are for personal use only and shouldn't be traded to other people." [17]

"Pot's [marijuana] not bad. It depends on the kind of drug to say it's the wrong thing to do." [14]

"Pot's okay. It just makes you feel good." [21]

"There's nothing wrong with drugs if you use them just for recreation—it's like social drinking—and if you don't get addicted." [17]

In sum, youths who thought that little if any damage would be suffered from drugs could be expected to propose that there was nothing wrong with using and trading them.

Victimless Misdeeds. A second factor is a person's belief about who is harmed by drug use. One variety of such belief is referred to as the victimless crime concept, which holds that no sanctions need be imposed for acts that do not harm other people. Such seemed to be the attitude of a 9 year old we quoted earlier:

Interviewer: "So it was wrong to give drugs to their friend, but it was okay for them to take drugs themselves?"

Respondent: "Well, not really, but if that's what they want to do, it's okay with me." [9]

Whether or not a person's behavior significantly harms others can be a matter of considerable debate. Increasing amounts of evidence suggest that drug use and drug peddling result in far more damage than many youths have imagined. Women who use alcohol while pregnant are at risk for delivering a child who suffers from fetal alcohol syndrome. Young people who encourage companions to try cocaine may be leading their companions into a life of addiction. Robbery or burglary committed to obtain money for purchasing illicit drugs is not without its victims.

In effect, people who believe that the use of drugs is "their own business and shouldn't concern anyone else" can defend their own drug use as a victimless act that does not deserve to be censured.

Ego Defense. A third possible reason for rebelliousness derives from the proposition that it is natural for humans to see themselves as decent, worthy individuals. Thus, in order to maintain a positive image of themselves, they try to cast questionable segments of their behavior in as favorable a light as possible. Therefore, youths could be expected to rationalize any of their self-indulgent personal habits as being quite acceptable or at least "not all that bad."

CONCLUSION

Our three cases of misdeeds have been used in this chapter as a vehicle for assessing the traditional view of adolescence as a period of rebellion against rules of adult society. Rebelliousness has been measured here by the extent to which the behavior of the main characters in the three cases was judged by interviewees to be wrongdoing. Because all three cases involved acts that by law or custom would clearly be improper, respondents would be considered rebelling if they either failed to deem the acts wrong or they diminished the commonly accepted seriousness of the deeds. When the 136 participants are judged by this criterion, none can be viewed as defiant in their responses to the math test and burglary cases, and only a small proportion of them would be considered rebellious in their reactions to the drug case. In brief, very little of the putative teenage rebelliousness was reflected in the students' views of the three cases. This absence of defiance is in concert with the survey studies cited in Chapter 6.

The modest amount of deviation from societal standards shown in the drug case was age related. The older the respondent, the greater the tendency to regard drug dealing—and particular drug use—as acceptable behavior. These data are at odds with Nicholi's (1988) suggestion in Chapter 6 that defiant teenage behavior is at its height during ages 12 to 14. Perhaps the age at which youth tend to reject adult standards varies with the aspect of life under review. Longing to garb oneself in ways regarded as odd by adults may peak at one age, whereas yearning to ingest forbidden substances may become more pronounced at a different age.

The observed deviation from societal standards was also slightly gender related, with more males than females identifying illicit drug trading and use as acceptable. Such a result is in keeping with the culture's widespread folk stereotype which pictures boys as more rambunctious and fractious than girls.

The chapter's findings led us to speculate that youths more likely approve of behavior that deviates from societal standards if that behavior (a) entails little or no risk of harm to others, (b) does little harm to oneself, compared to the pleasure gained, and (c) is an established habit that the individual does not wish to—or cannot—break and is therefore rationalized as acceptable, leaving one's self-esteem intact.

15

Views of Retribution

Here is a question students were asked about the sanctions they proposed in the case of the burglar who had killed a householder: "Would one of your aims be to give the family of the dead woman the satisfaction of having her killer punished?"

In the total sample of 136 students, 68% said yes, they would indeed endorse such an aim. The remaining 32% said they would not. The following analysis of these reactions first describes the assortment of reasons students gave in support of their position and then reports the results by age and by gender.

REASONS FOR AND AGAINST RETRIBUTION

Interviewees interpreted the word *satisfaction* in a number of ways. Some believed the family members had a right to the comfort they would derive from knowing that the felon was punished. In other words, they argued from the position of *retribution* as promoting victims' welfare by means of personal recompense for recipients of wrongdoing. From this perspective, the aim of a sanction can properly be to soothe, pacify, mollify, or conciliate those offended by the misdeed. However, other interviewees interpreted satisfaction as *revenge, vengeance,* or *payback,* and they thought the family had no right to try avenging the murder.

Over the centuries, there has been strong support for vengeance as an suitable reaction to wrongdoing. Religious doctrine in the Judeo-Christian-Islamic tradition repeatedly endorses vengeance as an instrument of morality. God is quoted as saying, "Vengeance belongeth unto me, and I will recompense" (*Holy Bible,* 1611, Hebrews 10:30). The psalmist acknowledged this claim by imploring, "Oh, Lord God, to whom vengeance belongeth, show thyself" (*Holy Bible,* 1611, Psalms 94:1). In contrast to the frequent appearance of vengeance in the Christian Bible (chiefly in the Judaic Old Testament) is the rarer mention of rejecting vengeance in favor of forgiveness and of turning the other cheek, which are features of the New Testament. According to the disciple Matthew, Jesus advised:

> Love your enemies, bless them that curse you, do good to them that hate you, and pray for them which deceitfully use you and persecute you. (*Holy Bible*, 1611, Matthew 5:44)

Recent decades have witnessed the continuation of this controversy about whether vengeance is a morally acceptable aim of sanctions. And if acceptable, under what conditions is it justified? An example of the debate is found in the 1987 U.S. Supreme Court 5–4 split decision in the case of *Booth vs. Maryland*. The judgment concerned the conviction of a John Booth for committing a gruesome double murder during his attempt to rob a home. The issue at hand was whether testimony by members of a murder victim's family regarding harm they suffered should be admissible in determining society's reaction to the crime. Five Supreme Court justices decided that such testimony was not acceptable because it shifted the focus away from the blameworthiness of the defendant. However, four dissenting justices deemed that family testimony should indeed be considered in deciding the offender's fate. They contended that pain suffered by victims deserves in some way to be satisfied by the sentence meted out to the transgressor (Boudreaux, 1989). This lack of agreement on the Supreme Court about the proper place of vengeance in the administration of justice is a reflection of a similar lack of consensus within the general citizenry and within our collection of 136 interviewees (Smith & Wooton, 1994; Stewart, 1992; Wilson, 1994).

Reasons for Satisfying the Victim's Family

The rationales offered by the two-thirds of our sample who endorsed retribution were directed at five purposes, those of providing (1) emotional comfort, (2) payback gratification, (3) rightful compensation, (4) participation in setting sanctions, and (5) future safety. Some participants also saw retribution as either (6) a natural desire or (7) a concomitant outcome of sanctions.

Emotional Comfort. The belief here is that family members are indirect victims and deserve some sort of spiritual recompense for their loss.

"It'd make the woman's relatives feel better." [9]
"The family definitely needs to see something happen to the killer." [17]
"The family would be sad and want him punished." [9]
"Knowing that the killer is punished helps the family in getting closure over their relative's murder. The family needs to be appeased." [21]
"People close to the woman need rest of mind." [14]
"Making him spend life in prison would give me personal satisfaction." [14]

Payback Gratification. Several students focused attention on the kind of the punishment that would provide the family gratification.

"Her family would get satisfaction if he was put to death." [9]

"The electric chair would take care of their satisfaction." [17]

"He killed a woman, so he should be killed." [9]

"The family lost someone, so the killer should die." [17]

"The family has suffered, so they should be allowed to see the burglar suffer, too." [9]

"The family needs to see him suffer." [17]

Rightful Compensation. The conviction that family members deserved some sort of reimbursement for their relative's death was expressed in several forms.

"The family should be repaid some way, because they lost someone very dear to them." [9]

"Having him punished would help the family see that justice has been done." [14]

Participation in Setting Sanctions. Some respondents believed that family members should have a hand in determining what punishment was deserved.

"If the woman was married, I'd let the husband choose what happens to the killer." [9]

Future Safety. Numbers of participants based their support of the *satisfaction* aim on the assurance that imprisonment or death would keep family members safe from the killer in the years to come.

"If the man's punished, the family wouldn't have to worry about other family members being killed by him." [9]

Natural Desire. Certain students did not seek to rationalize a desire for retribution but simply accepted it as a normal human trait.

"It's only natural for them to want him punished." [21]

"Humans like revenge." [14]

Concomitant Outcome. There were also respondents who saw family satisfaction as a subsidiary, natural result of punishment that need not to be a stated aim of the people who impose the sanctions.

"It wouldn't be my main purpose, but it would happen—they'd get satisfaction." [14]

"It's a good purpose, but it shouldn't be the main reason the man should be punished." [14]

"The family's satisfaction shouldn't be the only reason, but it would be an indirect benefit of punishing him." [21]

"Some form of revenge is included in sentences." [14]

Reasons for Repudiating Revenge

In rejecting the aim of providing satisfaction for members of the murder victim's family, the people composing one-third of our sample defended their stance with reasons focusing on (a) revenge as a motive, (b) the appropriate purpose of sanctions, (c) victims' unreasonable emotional condition, and (d) the futility of revenge.

Revenge as a Motive. Many of the dissenters repudiated revenge as a motive for consequences imposed on wrongdoers.

> "If they're happy to see the man punished, then they're just as bad as him." [9]
> "What? He's already done too much bad without the family adding more." [21]
> "I don't believe in that revenge stuff, like all that karma—what goes around, comes around." [14]
> "I don't think the family should get pleasure from seeing him punished in return." [14]
> "People shouldn't get satisfaction from the punishment of others." [17]
> "Revenge is a bad purpose. We need to forgive wrongdoers." [17]
> "People should be forgiving and act out of love, not out of bitterness, anger, and revenge." [17]
> "That family would have to be sick to want revenge." [17]

Proper Purposes of Sanctions. Several participants identified purposes other than vengeance as the rightful, more reasonable objectives of sanctions.

> "Revenge is irrational."
> "We need to focus on the killer's problems, not on the family's revenge." [21]
> "Nothing's going to bring the woman back. What the man needs is help. He probably can't be reformed, but he should be helped to realize why he did it." [14]
> "He should be punished for doing something bad, not for revenge." [14]
> "The burglar should get what he deserves, but not to satisfy the family." [14]
> "The proper purpose is to keep society safe." [21]
> "Personal revenge is not a good motive. Punishment needs to be directed at helping the entire community." [17]

Victims' Emotional State. A variety of respondents implied that direct or indirect victims of crime would be in a poor emotional condition to suggest reasoned, constructive consequences for their offenders.

> "The family's not in a right frame of mind to make a fair decision." [17]
> "The man's life should not be in the family members' hands. The law needs to deal with him." [17]
> "The family probably hates him, so they might want to have him killed, and that's not right." [14]

Futility of Revenge. Several interviewees believed the goal of offering family members satisfaction would simply be fruitless.

"Punishing him isn't going to bring the murdered family member back." [21]

"How could the family feel satisfied, since the woman is already dead?" [21]

"The family's not going to get any lasting pleasure for such short-lived, cheap satisfaction." [21]

Summary

The above review of diverse rationales illustrates once again an observation offered in earlier chapters of Part II; it is that simply hearing the aim a person hopes to achieve by a particular sanction does not identify the moral values behind that aim. In order to understand a person's values, it is necessary not only to learn the aim to be achieved, but also the line of reasoning that relates the aim to the proposed sanctions. As the foregoing examples showed, some students who wished to provide satisfaction for family members sought to do so by having the offender suffer; in contrast, others wished to preserve the family members' future safety. Furthermore, some who rejected satisfaction as an aim were concerned with solving the offender's problems. Others were opposed to the whole idea of revenge; and some believed the family could gain no lasting comfort by punishing the offender, since the murdered woman was dead and gone forever.

AGE AND GENDER COMPARISONS

As shown in Table 15-1, the proportion of students who endorsed the aim of giving the family satisfaction diminished regularly with increasing age. Although the percentage differences between adjacent age groups are not statistically significant at even a .05 level, the trend of diminishing support for revenge with increase in age is consistent; and the difference between the extreme ages 9 and 21 is significant well beyond the .001 level. On the other hand, there was no significant difference between genders. Only four percentage points separated the numbers of males (66%) and females (70%) who supported the aim of satisfying the family; such a slight difference cannot be considered important.

In our effort to interpret the age trends, we can draw on a pair of explanations deriving from Piaget's and Kohlberg's work.

Piaget's theory of intellectual development pictures the child as advancing from egocentricity toward an increasingly realistic or allocentric condition.

At the egocentric stage in the logic of feeling, the self becomes the single dimension around which feelings and social interaction revolve. . . . [However], the allocentric stage is multidimensional, like formal operations: the individualcan construe himself as a dimension in a matrix, including abstract principles and social norms as other dimensions. (Biggs, 1976, p. 157)

Table 15-1
Attitudes Toward Revenge by Age
(in percentages)

"Would one of your aims be to give the family of the dead woman the
satisfaction of having her killer punished?"

Age	9	14	17	21	All
N	33	36	34	33	136
YES	91	75	58	48	68
NO	9	25	42	52	32

We might propose, then, that respondents who wanted to have punishment provide satisfaction for the victim's family were imagining themselves in the role of family members and thus were reacting in an egocentric manner to the question of sanction aims. ("Making him spend life in prison would give me personally satisfaction" [14].) We might further suggest that respondents who rejected revenge as a motive were viewing the murder from a multifaceted allocentric perspective, thereby weighing more societal factors in their decision than just the feelings of the family. ("Personal revenge is not a good motive. Punishment needs to be directed at helping the entire community" [17].) In advancing such an explanation, we can account for the age trends by contending that lingering egocentrism among younger students accounted for their subscribing to retribution in greater numbers than did older students.

An interpretation extracted from Kohlberg's theory closely follows Piaget's egocentric-allocentric theme. As noted in Chapter 6, within Kohlberg's hierarchy of six stages of moral development, Stage 2 is characterized by morality based on one's own personal welfare. "Since each person's primary aim is to pursue his or her own interests, the perspective is pragmatic—to maximize satisfaction of one's needs and desires while minimizing negative consequences to the self" (Kohlberg, 1984, p. 626). However, when advancing age carries the youth to Stage 4, "The pursuit of individual interests is considered legitimate only when it is consistent with the maintenance of the sociomoral system as a whole. . . . A social structure that includes formal institutions and social roles serves to mediate conflicting claims and promote the common good" (Kohlberg, 1984, p. 631). Thus, by assuming Kohlberg's perspective, we could suggest that the younger the respondent, the more likely he or she would perceive retribution in terms of Stage 2. Conversely, the older the respondent, the more likely he or she would consider retribution in terms of Stage 4.

CONCLUSION

As was true with so many aspects of this study, the question of retribution as a proper aim of sanctions elicited a wide variety of viewpoints from the 136 interviewees. Within the 68% of respondents who approved of such an aim, the values on which they founded their opinions often differed from one person to another. A similar diversity of values was expressed within the 32% of the students who rejected such an aim. Students' answers revealed a consistent age trend, with younger respondents more often approving of retribution than did older ones. No such differences were found in comparing females with males.

16

Lessons Learned

At the time we launched the study reported in this book, we entertained a number of hopes and expectations. The purpose of this final chapter is to identify (1) which of those hopes and expectations were satisfied, (2) which went unfulfilled, and (3) unforeseen ways in which we were enlightened. The chapter, in effect, is an account of lessons learned.

HOPES

What we most hoped to discover were a considerable number of significant differences among age groups in the (a) sanctions students recommended, (b) the aims those sanctions were intended to achieve, and (c) the modes of reasoning students displayed in supporting their decisions. Finding such differences would enable us to draw generalizations about how the advancing years of adolescence produced systematic changes in moral reasoning.

However, the hope of finding "a considerable number" was not well fulfilled. The only noticeable age trends in sanction and aim proposals were in the following instances:

Types of Sanctions. Slightly more older than younger respondents would suggest counseling for the girl who had copied math test answers. Slightly more younger than older students would imprison or detain the teenage drug traders and would delegate to someone other than themselves the authority to impose sanctions on the 23-year-old burglar. None of these possible trends reached statistical significance at the .05 level. (Chapter 8)

Types of Aims. Slightly more younger students would (1) deter the offenders in all three cases from committing further misdeeds, (2) try to reform the 9-year-old test copier's general character, and (3) expect the teenage drug traders to express gratitude for being dissuaded from further drug use. None of these approached .05 statistical significance. (Chapter 8)

Clarity of Explanation. In explaining their conceptions of a possible role played by God in adjudicating cases of wrongdoing, older students (17 and 21) were significantly (.001) more lucid and consistent than younger ones (9 and 14). The way several older respondents declared their lack of belief in God suggested that their conviction was of a thoughtful variety, likely arrived at after their considering the issue at some length. For example, numbers of the older students identified themselves as atheists, not simply as doubters or nonbelievers, thereby indicating that they were aware of how their belief system would be labeled in theological terms. (Chapter 11)

Confining Teenagers. In Case 2, the younger the respondent, the longer the time of detention or imprisonment recommended for the teenage drug traders (.02). This trend seemed to result chiefly from different attitudes among certain members of the four age groups about (a) whether drug use constituted serious wrongdoing and (b) the sorts of sanctions that might contribute most constructively toward the offenders' well-being. Younger students more often than older ones believed that drug use was destructive and that putting the two 16 year olds in a detention facility for a while would teach them not to trade or use drugs in the future. (Chapter 12)

Empathy and Sympathy. Although nine year olds made fewer empathic and sympathetic comments than did members of the other age groups, this tendency fell short of statistical significance at the .05 level. (Chapter 13)

Retribution. Between ages 9 and 21 there was a systematic decrease in the percentage of students who would punish the burglar to provide satisfaction for the family of the murder victim. In effect, younger students more often approved of retribution than did older ones. (Chapter 15)

In summary, these few findings fell far short of satisfying our hope of identifying a significant number of age trends. Out of the 130 different sanction choices expressed by respondents, only 12 (9%) displayed even the slightest hint of an age trend. Among the 162 patterns of aims among the 136 respondents, only 18 (11%) displayed even the least indication of systematic differences across ages. (Chapter 8)

Hence, we were obliged to conclude that the differences across age groups 9 through 21 in choices of sanctions and their aims, as well as in the rationales in support of those choices, were far fewer than the likenesses across groups. In brief, the groups had much in common, and the marked variability of students' opinions within a group was similar from one age level to another. Thus, simply knowing a youth's age would be of little or no help in predicting the sanctions and aims that he or she would advocate.

EXPECTATIONS

One of our most obvious expectations was that respondents would display quite complex sanction/aim patterns of reasoning when we added probing queries to the initial interview questions of (a) what consequences should be assigned to offenders and (b) what aims those consequences would be expected to serve. In each of the three cases of wrongdoing, around 50% of the participants offered only a single sanction and a single aim when first asked what should be done about the offenders. However, when probing questions followed, only 1% of the interviewees retained the single sanction and single aim. The other 99% displayed far more complicated sanction/aim linkages. And if more options had been offered to respondents, it is reasonable to believe that their reasoning patterns would have assumed even more elaborate configurations. (Chapter 9)

We also expected that students' choices of aims and sanctions might confirm (a) Piaget's idea of development from heteronomous to autonomous morality, (b) Kohlberg's corrective justice levels, (c) Lewin's life-space differentiation and expansion, and (d) a developmental advance from fanciful to realistic sanction recommendations. Although our results furnished no support for either Piaget's or Kohlberg's proposals, the data did offer some confirmation of Lewin's concepts of differentiation and expansion of youths' moral reasoning, with the most notable advance toward more differentiated and expanded thought coming during early adolescence. In addition, respondents' sanction choices in the drug trading and murder cases somewhat corroborated the belief that young people become more realistic over the years of adolescence in the consequences they assign to wrongdoers, with most of the change once again appearing within the 9- to 14-year-old period. Nine year olds, more often than older participants (14, 17, 21), recommended penalties that were unrealistically harsh for the teenage drug users (such as several years in prison) while recommending penalties unrealistically lenient for the burglar who had slain the householder (such as one month or one year in jail). (Chapter 8)

Furthermore, we anticipated that students' answers would often reflect their conceptions of reality and their moral values. This expectation was well satisfied, as illustrated in Chapter 11's analysis of responses to a pair of probing questions about the case of the burglar. The question about God's role in punishing misdeeds led to our inspecting students' beliefs about whether there really was such an entity as God and, if so, what sorts of attributes characterized that entity. The question of whether the burglar/murderer should be executed led to the analysis of respondents' values regarding the sanctity of human life and their beliefs about the conditions under which that sanctity should be honored. Although we chose to use the questions about God and the death penalty for illustrating how answers reflected ideas about reality and moral values, other portions of the interviews would have served this purpose equally well. That is, students' value systems were revealed in each of the aims and rationales they offered to support why sanctions should or should not be endorsed. Likewise, their beliefs about reality were reflected in the consequences they hoped would result from the sanctions they weighed during the process of arriving at their decisions.

Another expectation was that some measure of teenage rebelliousness might show up in the students' opinions. However, the only evidence of even slight rebellion against main-line societal standards appeared in the drug trading case. The older the respondent, the greater the tendency to regard drug dealing—and particularly drug use—as acceptable behavior, with the greatest deviation from standards appearing at the 17- and 21-year-old levels. (Chapter 14)

In recognition of Gilligan's (1982) proposal that females tend to differ from males in the bases of their moral judgments, we expected that some gender differences might appear in the youths' attitudes. Although most of the comparisons throughout the study showed no differences between males and females, our expectation was fulfilled in a few instances. More females than males:

> (*a*) opposed both drug trading and drug use (.01). (Chapter 14)
> (*b*) would counsel the teenage drug traders (.001). (Chapter 8)
> (*c*) would imprison rather than execute the burglar/killer (.014) and would furnish counseling for him (.001). (Chapter 8)
> (*d*) expressed empathy and sympathy, though the difference between the gender groups fell short of the .05 level. (Chapter 13)

ENLIGHTENMENT

In the present context, *enlightenment* refers to insights that were not actually surprising but were ones that proved more intricate and elaborate than we had originally imagined.

We were most impressed by the great diversity in the ways the 136 youths spoke about both sanctions and aims. A remarkable degree of individualism in overt moral reasoning appeared, with that individualism no more pronounced in one age or gender group than in another. In other words, marked variability in modes of thought was equally evident in all groups. Although we had expected to find individual differences among respondents, we had not expected the differences to be as great as they were. While a few students might reason in a rather similar fashion about one case, when their answers across two cases were analyzed, it became clear that their reasoning in the pair of cases combined was quite different. Such an outcome warned us that knowing the age and gender of a youth during the years 9 through 21 is essentially useless for predicting how that individual's views of sanctions and aims would compare with the views of any other youth in that same age bracket. A 9 year old was as likely to favor the death penalty for heinous crimes as a 21 year old. A 14 year old was as apt to doubt God's adjudicating earthly wrongdoing as was a 9 or 21 year old. Hence, to learn a given teenager's mode of moral reasoning, it would be necessary to study that individual's particular beliefs about aims and sanctions as expressed about a variety of cases of misdeeds.

Although we concluded that age and gender were not trustworthy indicators of youths' reasoning about wrongdoing, this does not mean we consider the results of the study useless for predicting how young people in general think about such matters. Indeed, we consider the results for the 136 respondents as a whole to be quite informative. For instance, we found it helpful to learn that:

(a) Over half (53%) of the students conceived of God as a real entity, but few (4%) thought God imposed sanctions on offenders during the offenders' lifetime rather than only after death (17%).

(b) Nearly two-thirds (61%) would favor executing murderers under at least some circumstances, whereas slightly over one-third (36%) would never favor execution; and a few (3%) could not make up their minds about the issue.

(c) Nearly all (91%) would reject corporal punishment (spanking) for the girl who had copied test answers.

(d) Three-quarters (75%) would recommend personal counseling for the teen-age drug traders, with counseling often combined with another sanction.

(e) The great majority (84%) would reject the notion of publicizing the teenagers' drug use.

We consider these sorts of data beneficial for estimating what other adolescents might believe about such matters.

Another example of enlightenment is found in the set of conclusions we extracted from examining the styles of response that determined the length of students' interviews. Although for 9 year olds, 17 year olds, and 21 year olds the average length of interviews was quite similar, the characteristics of style that determined that length appeared to differ between the 9s and the two older groups. Rather lengthy discourse among 9s was frequently caused by a hesitant and halting delivery (diffidence and a need to have questions explained), whereas among 17s and 21s a lengthy interview more often resulted from elaborated and proliferated answers. The 14 year olds, whose interviews were significantly shorter on average from those of the other three groups, tended to offer simpler, more concise answers than did the 17s and 21s. (Chapter 10).

Further enlightenment resulted from the task in Chapter 11 ("Conceptions of God and the Sanctity of Life") of analyzing students' conceptions of God and attitudes toward human life. The task required that we classify respondents' answers in ways that permitted concise age and gender comparisons. Creating the classification systems involved an inductive process—examining the entire set of responses to the particular question and deciding what sorts of categories might reveal interesting likenesses and differences in participants' beliefs about reality and values. This process proved enlightening since it guided us to new insights about how the youths' responses could be patterned. Equally informative were the tasks of developing schemes for classifying views of imprisonment (Chapter 12), empathy and sympathy (Chapter 13), drugs and the law (Chapter 14), and attitudes toward retribution (Chapter 15).

UNFINISHED BUSINESS

The archetypal closing remark that can be appended to the end of virtually every research report goes something like this:

Although satisfactory answers were found for certain of the key questions that this study addressed, it is apparent that the investigation generated more questions than it answered. More research is necessary.

The following are among the "more questions" that call for attention.

How will the results of the present study compare with the results of the same sort of study conducted with other samples of young people?

How will the use of types of wrongdoing other than test cheating, drug trading, and burglary/murder affect the generalizations about adolescence drawn from the present study?

What array of cases of wrongdoing will be most effective for revealing the complex patterning of an individual youth's mode of moral reasoning?

What sorts of cases about wrongdoing might clarify issues of adolescent rebelliousness more adequately than the cases used in the present study?

How readily will individuals abandon their initial sanction or aim proposals when confronted with arguments that favor other options? Are there age or gender differences in this willingness to be influenced by suggested alternatives? What factors influence an individual's willingness to change?

How consistent from one case of wrongdoing to another are the moral principles underlying young people's recommendations of sanctions and aims? Are there age trends in consistency?

What more satisfactory criteria than chronological age can be used to judge young people's development in reasoning about sanctions and aims?

Could Piaget's or Kohlberg's proposals be confirmed if children younger than age nine were included along with adolescents in such a study as the one reported in this book?

References

Andrews, D. A., Zinger, I., Hoge, R. D., Bonta, J., Gendreau, P., & Cullen, F. (1990). Does correctional treatment work? A clinically relevant and psychologically informed meta-analysis. *Criminology*, 28 (3), pp. 369–404.

Barker, R. G., Dembo, T., & Lewin, K. (1943). Frustration and regression. In R. G. Barker, J. S. Kounin, & H. F. Wright (Eds.). *Child behavior and development*. New York: McGaw-Hill.

Biggs, J. B. (1976). Schooling and moral development. In V. P. Varna & P. Williams (Eds.). *Piaget, psychology, and education*. Ithaca, IL: F. E. Peacock.

Black, H. C. (1951). *Black's law dictionary*. St. Paul, MN: West.

Boudreaux, P. (1989). Booth vs. Maryland and the individual vengeance rationale for criminal punishment. *The Journal of Criminal Law & Crimnology*, 80 (1), 177–196.

Calligan, M. E. (Ed.). (1992) *1992 penal code: Abridged California edition*. San Clemente, CA: Qwik-Code Publications.

Carp, R. A., & Stidham, R. (1990). *Judicial process in America*. Washington, DC: CQ Press.

Colby, A., Kohlberg, L., Gibbs, J., & Lieberman, M. (1983) *A longitudinal study of moral judgment*. Monographs of the Society for Research in Child Development, Serial No. 200, Vol. 48, Nos. 1–2. Chicago: Society for Research in Child Development.

Demos, V. (1984). Empathy and affect: Reflections on infant experience. In J. Lichtenberg, M. Bornstein, & D. Silver (Eds.). *Empathy II*. Hillsdale, NJ: Analytic Press.

Douvan, E., & Adelson, J. (1966). *The adolescent experience*. New York: Wiley.

Eisenberg, N., & Strayer, J. (Eds.). (1987). *Empathy and its development*. Cambridge: Cambridge University Press.

Feld, B. C. (1987). The juvenile court meets the principle of the offense: Legislative changes in juvenile waiver statutes. *Journal of Criminal Law & Criminology,* 78 (3), pp. 471-533.

————. (1990). The punitive juvenile court and the quality of procedural justice: Disjunctions between rhetoric and reality. *Crime & Delinquency,* 36 (4), pp. 443–466.

Flexner, S. B. (Ed.) (1987). *Random house dictionary of the English language.* New York: Random House.

Freiberg, A. (1987). Reconceptualizing sanctions. *Criminology,* 25 (2), pp. 223–255.

Freud, A. (1958). Adolescence. *Psychoanalytic study of the child,* 13, pp. 255–278.

Gert, B. (1970). The moral rules—A new rational foundation for morality. New York: Harper & Row.

Gilligan, C. (1982). *In a different voice.* Cambridge, MA: Harvard University Press.

Gilligan, C., Ward, J. V., & Taylor, J. M. (Eds.). (1988). *Mapping the moral domain.* Cambridge, MA: Harvard University Press.

Goldstein, A. P., & Michaels, G. Y. (1985). *Empathy: Development, training, and consequences.* Hillsdale, NJ: Erlbaum.

Henry, R. M. (1983). *The psychodynamic foundations of morality.* Basel, Switzerland: Karger.

Hoffman, M. L. (1987). The contribution of empathy to justice and moral development. In N. Eisenberg & J. Strayer (Eds.). *Empathy and its development.* Cambridge: Cambridge University Press.

Holy Bible. (1611). (King James authorized version) Philadelphia: John C. Winston, 1930.

Kegan, R. (1982). *The evolving self.* Cambridge, MA: Harvard University Press.

Kleiman, M. A. R. (1992). *Against excess: Drug policy for results.* New York: Basic Books.

Kohlberg, L. (1984). *The psychology of moral development.* San Francisco: Harper & Row.

Kuhn, D., Langer, J., Kohlberg, L., & Haan, N. S. (1977). The development of formal operations in logical and moral judgment. *Genetic Psychology Monographs,* 95, pp. 97–188.

Lab, S. P., & Whitehead, J. T. (1990). From "nothing works" to "the appropriate works": The latest stop on the search for the secular grail. *Criminology,* 28 (3), pp. 405–417.

Matthews, R., & Young, J. (1992). Reflections on realism. In J. Young & R. Matthews. *Rethinking criminology: The realist debate.* Newbury Park, CA: Sage.

Morley, C. (Ed.) (1948). *Familiar quotations.* Boston: Little, Brown, and Co.

Nicholi, A. M., Jr. (1988). The adolescent. In A. M. Nicholi, Jr. (Ed). *The new Harvard guide to psychiatry* (pp. 637–884). Cambridge, MA: Harvard University Press.

Offer, D. (1969). *The psychological world of the teenager: A study of normal adolescent boys.* New York: Basic Books.

Offer, D., & Church, R. B. (1991). Turmoil, adolescent. In R. M. Lerner, A. C. Petersen, & J. Brooks-Gunn (eds.). *Encyclopedia of adolescence* (Vol. 1, pp. 1148–1152). New York: Garland.

Offer, D., & Offer, J. L. (1968). Profiles of normal adolescent girls. *Archives of General Psychiatry*, 19, pp. 513–122.

Pelikan, J. (1979). Sin. In P. K. Meagher, T. C. O'Brien, & C. S. Aherne. *Encyclopedic dictionary of religion* (Vol. 3, pp. 3307–3308). Washington, DC: Corpus Publications.

Piaget, J. (1932/1948). *The moral judgment of the child.* Glencoe, IL: Free Press.

Piaget, J., & Inhelder, B. (1969). *The psychology of the child.* New York: Basic Books.

Smith, W., & Wooton, J. (1994). Jailhouse blues: Federal judges seem infinitely solicitous of the inmates of state prisons, and nearly indifferent to the victims, past and future. How can law-abiding citizens begin to redress the balance? *National Review,* 46 (11), pp. 40–44.

Stewart, D. O. (1992). Prisoner rights rebound. *ABA Journal*, 78 (May), pp. 48–50.

Sutherland, E. H., & Cressey, D. R. (1970). *Criminology.* Philadelphia: J. B. Lippincott.

Thomas, R. M. (1995). *Classifying reactions to wrongdoing.* Westport, CN: Greenwood.

Webster's encyclopedic unabridged dictionary of the English language. (1989) New York: Portland House.

Werner, H. (1961). *Comparative psychology of mental development.* New York: Science Editions.

Werner, H., & Kaplan, B. (1963). *Symbol formation—An organismic-developmental approach to language and the expression of thought.* New York: Wiley.

Whitehead, J. T., & Lab, S. P.(1989). A meta-analysis of juvenile correctional treatment. *Journal of Research in Crime and Delinquency*, 26, pp. 276–295.

Wilson, J. C. (1994). Inmates' license to sue. *Corrections Today*, 56 (4), pp. 150–152.

Appendix:
The Interview Guidesheet

The two authors and the six graduate students who interviewed young people for this project were guided in their effort by the following set of instructions.

PREPARING FOR THE INTERVIEW

Permission Sheet: Several days prior to the conduct of an interview, the Parent's Permission Sheet (for participants ages 9, 13, and 17) should be sent to the intended interviewee's parents or guardians. In the case of 21 year olds, the sheet should be signed by the interviewee rather than a parent, and this can be done at the outset of the interview. The signed sheet must be in the interviewer's possession before the interview begins.

Time and Place. The date, time of day, and location of the interview need to be settled several days prior to the interview, and the interviewee should be reminded of these matters prior to the interview.

EQUIPMENT AND SETTING

Equipment. Every interview needs to be recorded on audiotape. Therefore, a tape recorder and an extra tape should be available at the time of the interview. The *Interview Guidesheet—Short Version* should be in hand, along with a notebook in which information relevant to the interview can be written.

Setting. Every interview should be conducted with only the individual interviewee present rather than in a setting that includes other people who might distract the interviewee. Whenever feasible, the interviewer and the participant can sit at a desk or table with the tape recorder between them.

INTRODUCING THE TASK

The following script illustrates the way the task should be introduced:

Interviewer: "We're trying to learn how young people of different ages think about the consequences people should face when they've done something wrong. So we are asking you to help us as one of the (age) year olds that we are interviewing. Here's the way it goes. I'll read you a short description of a case of somebody doing something wrong, and then I'll ask a few questions about the case. This isn't some kind of test. It's just a way to collect people's opinions, so you can say whatever you think. We just want your opinion.

"I'll tape-record what you and I say so that later I can write down your exact ideas and not make any mistakes. We won't be using your name, so you can feel free to say anything you like and not be worried about who might hear it.

"Do you have any questions about how this goes?"

(*Interviewer answers subject's questions, then turns on tape recorder and provides the following information: the interview number and the age and gender of the interviewee. Examples:* "This is interview number 12 with a 9-year-old boy." "This is interview 93 with a 21-year-old woman.")

THE SEQUENCE OF STEPS IN PRESENTING EACH CASE

Case 1

1. (*Interviewer presents the case.*) "I'll read you the first case:
"A 9-year-old, fourth-grade girl was caught copying another pupil's answers on a mathematics test. This was the third time in the past two months that she had copied someone else's work and handed it in as her own. Among her classmates, this girl had a reputation for telling lies.
"So that's what happened. Now I'll ask some questions to get your ideas about the case."
2. "First question: Do you think the girl did anything wrong? If so, what was it?"
3. "All right, here's another question. What do you think should be done about the girl? I mean, what should happen to her?" (*Interviewer awaits answer. If the subject appears not to understand the question, it can be rephrased, such as:*) "What consequences do you think the girl should face? Or how do you think the girl should be treated?"
4. "Now, the next question. You've suggested that (*interviewer repeats consequence the subject suggested*). How do you think that would help? I mean, what good do you think that might do?" (*Interviewer awaits answer. If the subject appears not to understand the question, it can be rephrased, such as:*) "What would be the purpose or the aim of (*interviewer mentions the consequence that the subject proposed*)?"
5. "Two of the other people we interviewed had different ideas about what should happen to the girl. I'll read each of their suggestions, and you can tell me if you think either of these is as good as the suggestion you gave."

(*Interviewer reads the first of the options:*)

> 5-1. "She should be given a good spanking."

(*After reading the first option, interviewer asks:*) "What do you think about that? How do you like that suggestion compared to your own?"

(*Interviewer listens to the response, then asks:*) "Why do you feel your suggestion is better than this other one?" (*Or if the subject favors the first option over his or her own, the interviewer asks:*) "Why do you feel this other suggestion is as good as your own?" (*or*) ". . . is better than yours?"

(*The same procedure used with the first option is repeated with the second option, which is:*)

> 5-2. "Now here's the other suggestion: She should be warned by the teacher not to cheat and lie again or she then would be in very serious trouble."

(*Note: If the respondent has already proposed one of these two options as his or her own suggestion, then the following option should be substituted for the option that the respondent had spontaneously proposed.*)

> 5-3. "She should have to stay after school every day for a week and write 'I will not cheat again' 500 times each day."

6. "When I asked you what good you thought your suggestion would do, you said (*Interviewer repeats the aim the subject had offered*). But often people have more than one purpose in mind, even though they've mentioned only one. I have four other purposes listed here. In addition to the purpose or aim you mentioned, would any of these four be ones you would agree with?"

"Here's the first one." (*Interviewer reads the first aim, then asks:*) "How about that aim? Would that be a purpose you would include?" (*If the subject says no, the interviewer asks:*) "Why or why not?

(*The procedure used with the first option is then used with the remaining three as well. The four options are as follows:*)

> 6-1. "To teach her not to cheat again."

> 6-2. "To show other pupils what could happen to them if they cheated."

> 6-3. "To give her a good scare. To make her afraid and ashamed."

> 6-4. "To make her pay for what she has done. When you do wrong, you deserve to be punished."

(*Note: If the respondent has already proposed one of these four options as his or her own suggestion, then the following option should be substituted for the option that the respondent had spontaneously proposed.*)

> 6-5. "To make the girl want to be a really good person, to really change her personality."

(Cases 2 and 3 are presented in the same general sequence of 5 steps. The only differences among cases are in (1) the nature of the misdeed, (2) the sanction options, (3) the alternative aims, and (4) Case 2 having two offenders rather than one.)

Case 2

1. (*Interviewer presents the case.*) "I'll read you the second case of wrongdoing:
   "A 16-year-old boy and his girlfriend, who was the same age, were arrested for giving illegal drugs to a high-school friend in exchange for tickets to a rock concert. As far as the police could find out, this was the first time the two teenagers had ever given drugs to someone else, but they did admit that they sometimes used illegal drugs themselves.
   "So that's what happened. Now I'll ask some questions to get your ideas about the case."
2. "First question: Did either the boy or the girl do anything wrong? If so, what was it?"
3. "Now the next question: What do you think should be done about the <u>boy</u> in this case? I mean, what should happen to him?"
   "And what do you think should be done about the <u>girl</u>? What should happen to her?"
   (*If the respondent suggests a different consequence for the boy than for the girl, the interviewer asks:*) "Why should the boy be treated differently than the girl?"
4. "For the <u>boy</u>, you've suggested that (*interviewer repeats consequence the subject suggested*). How do you think that would help? I mean, what good do you think that might do?"
   "For the <u>girl,</u> you've suggested that (*interviewer repeats consequence the subject suggested*). How do you think that would help? What good might it do?"
5. "Two of the other people we interviewed had different ideas about what should happen to both the boy and girl. I'll read each of their suggestions, and you can tell me if you think either of these is as good as the suggestion you gave."
   (*Interviewer reads the first of the options.*)
   > 5-1. "They should be put in a drug rehabilitation program that's supposed to make people quit using drugs."

   (*After reading the first option, interviewer asks:*) "What do you think about that? How do you like that suggestion compared to your own?"
   (*Interviewer listens to the response, then asks:*) "Why do you feel your suggestion is better than this other one?" (*Or if the subject favors the first option over his or her own, the interviewer asks:*) "Why do you feel this other suggestion is as good as your own?" (*or*) ". . . is better than yours?"
   (*The same procedure used with the first option is repeated with the second option, which is:*)
   > 5-2. "Both should be put in juvenile hall for six months."

   (*Note: If the respondent has already proposed one of these two options as his or her own suggestion, then the following option should be substituted for the option that the respondent had spontaneously proposed.*)

5-3. "They should each have to give 100 hours of community service, like maybe doing gardening at a hospital or an old-folks home."

6. "I have four other purposes listed here. In addition to the purpose or aim you mentioned, would any of these four be ones you would agree with?"

(Note: If the respondent has suggested a different aim for the boy than for the girl, then this question should be asked about the boy and about the girl separately. If the respondent's aim has been the same for the boy and girl, then this question can be asked for both of them together.)

"Here's the first one." *(Interviewer reads the first aim, then asks:)* "How about that aim? Would that be a purpose you would include?" *(If the subject says no, the interviewer asks.)* "Why not?"

(The procedure used with the first option is then used with the remaining three as well. The four options are as follows:)

6-1. "To make them stop giving drugs to other people."

6-2. "To make them do something to help the community."

6-3. "To teach them to be responsible for the way they act."

6-4. "To make sure that the law is obeyed."

(Note: If the respondent has already proposed one of these four options as his or her own suggestion, then the following option should be substituted for the option that the respondent had spontaneously proposed.)

6-5. "To let everybody know that the boy and girl were using drugs and trading drugs to other teenagers."

Case 3

(Since Case 3 involves only one offender, it is presented in same basic manner as Case 1.)

1. *(Interviewer presents the case.)* "I'll read you the third case of wrongdoing:

"In a jury trial, a 23-year-old man was convicted of killing a woman when she caught him trying to rob her house in the middle of the night. A police officer who was a witness at the trial reported that the burglar had also been stealing from other homes over the past several months.

"So that's what happened. Now I'll ask some questions to get your ideas about the case."

(Interviewer uses the same approach with items 2, 3, and 4 as in Case 1.)

5. "Two of the other people we interviewed had different ideas about what should happen to the man. I'll read each of their suggestions, and you can tell me if you think either of these is as good as the suggestion you gave."

(Interviewer reads the first of the options:).

5-1. "He should be put to death."

(After reading the first option, interviewer asks:) "What do you think about that? How do you like that suggestion compared to your own?"

(Interviewer listens to the response, then asks:) "Why do you feel your suggestion is better than this other one?" *(Or if the subject favors the first*

option over his or her own, the interviewer asks:) "Why do you feel this other suggestion is as good as your own?" (*or*) "...is better than yours?"

(*The same procedure used with the first option is repeated with the second option, which is*:)

5-2. "I don't have to decide. God will know what to do."

(*Note: If the respondent has already proposed one of these two options as his or her own suggestion, then the following option should be substituted for the option that the respondent had spontaneously proposed.*)

5-3. "He should be put in prison for a year or two."

6. "I have four other purposes listed here. In addition to the purpose or aim you mentioned, would any of these four be ones you would agree with?"

"Here's the first one." (*Interviewer reads the first aim, then asks*:) "How about that aim? Would that be a purpose you would include?" (*If the subject says no, the interviewer asks.*) "Why not?

(*The procedure used with the first option is then used with the remaining three as well. The four options are as follows*:)

6-1. "To fix it so he can't rob or kill again."

6-2. "To teach him to be a better person; I mean, to reform him."

6-3. "To give the family of the dead woman the satisfaction of having the killer punished."

6-4. "To make him do something helpful for the community."

(*Note: If the respondent has already proposed one of these four options as his or her own suggestion, then the following option should be substituted for the option that the respondent had spontaneously proposed.*)

6-5. "To scare other men and woman who think they might like to break into houses and steal things."

TERMINATING THE INTERVIEW

Interviewer: "Well, that's the end of the interview. I want to thank you for all of your help. You really did a nice job. Thanks so much."

Index

Abuse, child, 26
Accountability, 17, 85-87, 89, 92, 112, 114-115
Adultery, 142
Affect, 5, 17, 85-86, 89, 107, 175, 177, 181, 196, 198-199
Age, 5, 62-63, 66-67, 69, 81-83, 90-91, 95, 100-101, 109-110, 113-116, 121, 124-129, 131, 139-140, 148-150, 152-153, 164-171, 173, 176-177, 180-181, 189-191, 195. 199-201, 203-208
Age of reason, 99, 142, 184
Agnostics, 136, 139
Aims, 13, 52-53, 59, 69, 84-92, 94, 170; defined, 24; instrumental, 24-25, 27-31, 108-110; probed, 87-90, 105, 112, 115-116, 119, 204-205; typology, 11, 15-19, 85; ultimate, 24-25, 27-31, 108-110; volunteered, 84-87, 115-116, 119
Alcohol, 28, 186, 193
Allocentrism, 199-200
Apology, 20, 73, 88, 126
Apperceptive mass, 23
Appraisal, unfavorable, 20, 70-72, 80
Aristotle, 49
Assimilation, 23
Atheists, 136, 139, 204

Authority, 48-49, 72, 92, 133-134, 183, 203
Autonomous morality, 48, 92-93, 190-191
Avenge, 19, 86, 88-91, 112, 157

Baldwin, James Mark, 49
Banishment, 4, 20, 53, 70-71, 73, 80, 94
Behavior, alternative, 17
Boundary, 53-54
Burglary, 15, 19, 36, 39, 43, 58, 82-83, 91, 98, 106-107, 111, 115, 117, 119, 122, 125, 132, 134, 136-137, 139-140, 142-145, 153-154, 158, 162, 164-170, 172-175, 177, 177-180-181, 183, 192-201, 208

Capital punishment. *See* Execution.
Causal relations, 23-31, 53, 55, 59, 65, 103-120, 204-205; defined, 23-24
Cause, diagnosing, 85-86
Censuring, 20, 70-71, 100
Chains, 28, 31, 104-105, 118
Character malleability, 106, 108, 111
Cheating, 7, 11, 28, 35, 58, 63, 71-72, 79, 85, 87, 98, 107, 111-

112, 117, 121-122, 125-127,
171, 174, 178, 181, 183, 192,
208
Child rearing, 7, 26
Christ, Jesus, 175, 196
Christianity, 74, 195-196
Clarity, 138-139
Classification systems, 207
Cocaine, 193
Cognitive: development, 113, 123;
sequence, 39-41, 45; style, 13
Commandments, 141-142
Common good, 50, 156, 170, 191
Community service, 9, 19, 30, 35,
40, 66, 73-74, 78, 80-81, 88-89,
161, 165
Compassion, 17, 51, 84, 150, 152,
177, 180
Compensation, 8-10, 18, 20, 31,
43, 51, 70, 73, 80, 86-89, 112,
150, 196-197
Concomitant effects, 64
Confidence, level of, 25, 27, 82
Confinement, 3; solitary, 147, 163
Confiscating, 20, 70, 74-75, 77,
80-81
Confusion, 138-139
Conscience, 137-138
Consensus, 103, 106, 108-119
Conservation, 48
Conviction, ultimate, 43-45, 121,
123, 129
Correction, 153
Cost, 161
Counseling, 21, 26-27, 40, 53, 70-
77, 80-84, 94, 101, 112, 115,
119, 147, 159-163, 165, 190,
203, 206-207
Courts, 30, 41, 43, 76
Crime, 1-3, 51, 62, 112, 184, 189;
defined, 2

Damage, 63, 143, 181, 186, 192
Death penalty. *See* Execution.
Decision-making: discretionary, 6;
moral, 61-62, 84; process, 10, 41
Detaining, 19, 72-73, 80
Detention, 73, 114

Deterrence, 52-53; general, 19, 86-
89, 94, 107, 112, 156-157;
special, 16, 31, 85-92, 109-112,
114, 137, 203
Development: cognitive, 13;
natural, 94; stages of, 47-53
Developmental indicators, 11, 13,
47-58
Diagnosis, cause, 16
Differentiation, 47, 53-54, 58,92,
95-96, 113-114, 205
Disabilities, 18, 86
Disablement. *See* Incapacitate.
Discharging, 19
Dismissal, 19
Diversity, 115,120
Drug education, 73, 97, 107-110-
112, 165, 188, 190
Drugs, 7, 11, 19, 35, 42, 44, 58-
59, 63, 65, 73-75, 79-81, 83-85,
87-88, 90-81, 94, 97-98, 101,
107-112, 117, 119, 125, 153-
155, 159-160, 162, 164-171,
174, 177-178, 181, 183-194,
203-208
Drunkenness, 28

Education, 9, 18-19, 21, 27, 62,
70-71, 73-75,77-78, 86-87, 89,
91, 94, 156, 160-161, 185, 204
Egocentrism, 47, 57, 113, 199-
200
Effects, concomitant, 24-25, 29
Electric chair, 76, 145-146, 164,
174, 197
Embarrassment, 28, 178, 181
Emotions. *See* Affect.
Empathy, 59, 88, 171-177, 180-
181, 204, 207; defined, 172-173
Evaluation, unfavorable. *See*
Appraisal, unfavorable.
Excommunication, 15
Execution, 2, 8-9, 15, 19, 26, 35-
36, 43, 53, 56, 59, 70, 76-78,
80-82, 85, 88,90, 94, 97, 100,
107, 119, 131, 136, 140-152,
157, 163-164-166, 174, 179,
197-198, 205-207

Expansion, 54, 58, 92, 95-96, 113-114, 205
Expectations, 204-206
Expelling, 19
Explaining, 26
Exposing, 20, 53, 88-89, 94, 171

Fact, 53
False witness, 3
Fanciful, 47, 56-57, 92, 96-99
Fans, 28-29, 31, 104-105, 107, 109
Fear, 4, 28, 41, 85, 89, 107, 127, 137, 145, 160, 164, 171, 173, 175, 178-179, 190
Feasibility, 35
Felony, 154
Fetal alcohol syndrome, 193
Fine, monetary, 2, 26, 30, 43, 74-75
Forgiving, 21, 133, 142, 198
Foster home, 35
Framework, interpretive, 13
Freud, Anna, 57
Fright. *See* Fear.

Gender, 63, 69, 83-84, 91-92, 100-101, 115, 121, 124, 129-131, 139, 141, 150-153, 164-171, 173, 176-177, 180, 189, 191-192, 195, 199, 201, 206-208
Gilligan, Carol, 150, 152, 177, 180, 206
God, 2, 9, 37, 40, 59, 78, 80-81, 131-140, 148, 151-152, 165, 170, 195, 204-207
Grounding, 73-75, 80, 84
Guilt, 40, 85, 138

Habermas, Jurgen, 49
Handicaps. *See* Disabilities.
Harm, 19, 63, 159-160, 170, 175, 178-179, 181, 184, 186-188, 190, 192, 194, 196
Herbart, Johann, 23
Heteronomous morality, 48-49, 92-93, 190-191
Hopes, 203-204

Human: dignity, 50, 52; nature, 147; rights, 50
Hypotheses, 101

Idealism, 47, 132, 137-138
Idolatry, 3
Imprisonment, 2, 19, 53, 56, 59, 70, 73-74, 76-78, 80, 82-85, 90, 94, 97, 100-101, 107-112, 114, 134, 150, 153-170, 203-207
Incapacitation, 16, 53, 85-86, 89-90, 94, 107, 112, 142
Incarceration. *See* Imprisonment.
Income tax, 3, 26
Indemnification. *See* Compensation.
Individual differences, 123, 130, 143, 164, 206
Individuality, 103, 108-120, 143, 148, 206
Infraction, 3
Injury, physical, 10
Intelligence, 62
Intention, 52, 142, 147, 156
Interdependence, 47, 53-55, 58
Internal consistency, 139
Interviewers, 66
Interviews, 59, 61-67, 99-100, 213-218
Intuition, 47
Islam, 195-196

Jail, 35, 40, 56, 74-78, 133-135, 137, 146-147, 153-154, 157, 159-164, 175, 179, 205
Judaism, 195-196
Jury, 103, 119-120
Just deserts, 162
Justice, 48-53, 84, 132-133, 178, 197; commutative, 51; corrective, 51-53, 58,92-95; distributive, 51; even-handed, 144, 177; immanent, 52, 132, 162
Juvenile: court, 5; detention center, 28, 66; hall, 27, 74-75, 80-81, 94, 97, 109, 153-155, 158-160, 166, 168, 170, 175, 179

Kant, Immanuel, 49
Killing, 57. *See also* Execution,
   Murder.
Kohlberg, Lawrence, 48-53, 58, 92-
   95, 199-200, 205, 208

Labor assignment, 20, 70, 72, 74,
   76, 78, 80-81, 112, 115
Law, 5, 48, 57, 59, 77, 92, 193-
   194, 198, 207; civil, 2, 119,
   170; criminal, 2-4, 58, 66, 117,
   119, 159, 183-194; enforcement,
   16, 44, 53, 86-89, 92-94, 108,
   109, 111-112, 114-115, 189
Learning process, 41
Leniency, 97-99, 145, 205
Lewin, Kurt, 53-58, 92, 95-96,
   113-114, 205
Life: sanctity of, 37, 59, 131, 140-
   152, 205, 207; space, 53-54, 92,
   95-96, 113-114
Logic, 42, 47-48, 51, 93, 113,
   143, 199
Lovelace, Richard, 4
Lying, 6, 26, 127, 142

Manslaughter, 158
Manson, Charles, 77
Marginal, 55
Marijuana, 27, 192-193
Misbehavior, 3
Misdeeds, 1-3, 15, 33, 62;
   characteristics of, 3
Misdemeanor, 154
Models, 103-108, 162; role, 6, 168
Monitoring, behavior, 6, 20, 30,
   52, 70, 74, 80-81, 108-110
Moral: conditions, 61-62, 64, 133,
   141-146, 148-149, 152; convictions, 120; decisions, 61-62, 84,
   122, 180; development, 49, 95;
   judgments, 33, 48, 92, 106-107,
   111, 142, 150, 191; maturity,
   95, 106-107, 111; principles, 36,
   49, 61, 141-148, 150, 152, 208;
   realism, 49, 113; reasoning, 1,
   11, 13, 33, 37, 39, 42-45, 48,
   51, 93-94, 99-100, 121-130,

142-143, 145, 151, 203, 205,
   208; values, 11, 13, 17, 33, 36-
   37, 77, 86, 94, 131, 140, 143,
   151, 160-161, 170, 183, 199,
   205, 207
Morale, 179
Morality: heteronomous, 49, 52;
   instrumental, 49, 52; normative,
   49-50, 52; social-system, 50, 52;
   social-welfare, 50, 52;
   universalizable, 50-52
Morals, 2, 162
Moses, 141
Motive, 50, 52, 77, 81, 120, 156,
   158, 162, 178
Murder, 3, 7-8, 11, 15, 39-40, 43,
   58, 60, 63-64, 76-77, 81, 83, 85,
   88-89, 91, 98, 106-107, 111,
   117, 122, 125, 132, 134-136,
   138-140, 142, 144, 147-149,
   157, 161, 163-170, 172-175,
   177-179, 181, 183, 192, 195-
   201, 205-207

Networks, 29-31, 104-107, 109,
   118, 120

Obedience, 142
Offenders: rights of, 20, 75; welfare
   of, 155-158, 164, 166, 178
Offense: first, 165; public, 2
Omnipotence, 132-137
Omniscience, 132-137
Ontology, 33
Operations: concrete, 47-49, 113,
   123; formal, 47-49, 51, 113, 123
Opportunities, 20
Ostracism, 20, 53, 70, 80, 94

Pace of response, 42, 121-123,
   129
Pain, 3, 26, 142, 196
Parole, 5, 56, 78, 94, 163, 167
Payback, 195-197
Peers, 6-7, 48, 191
Piaget, Jean, 47-49, 51, 57-58, 92-
   93, 99, 113, 123, 190-191, 199-
   200, 205, 208

Postponement, 21
Prediction, 100-101
Prevention, 16, 30, 85
Prison, 4, 9, 19, 30, 37, 43, 80-81, 89, 133, 136, 138, 142-143, 153-155, 158, 160-162, 168, 205-207
See also Imprisonment.
Privileges, 20
Probation, 5, 21, 26, 28, 30, 70, 73-74, 80, 94, 97, 108, 109-111
Problem solving, 18, 47
Progressive Movement, 5
Prompting, 39
Protection, 18, 26, 37, 52-53, 94, 155, 158, 170, 178, 184
Prudence, 184--185
Psychiatry, 26, 77
Psychosis, 77
Psychotherapy, 28
Public offense, 2
Punishment, 1-4, 27, 52, 56, 89, 109, 154, 164; corporal, 19, 53, 71, 79-80, 94, 175-176, 178-179, 207; defined, 3-4

Rape, 4, 144, 157
Rationales, 66, 142-146, 170, 204
Realism, 132, 137-138; consensual, 56-57, 96-99; naive, 56
Realistic, 47, 54, 58, 63, 78, 92, 96-99, 113, 199, 205
Reality, 11, 13, 33-36, 56-57, 131, 136, 151, 207
Reasoning: moral, 10, 33, 51, 99-100, 142-143, 145, 151; overt, 10, 39-45, 59, 110, 118-130, 206; process, 11, 42-43, 71, 118, 120, 129; styles, 36, 59, 101, 107, 121-130, 146, 204
Rebelliousness, 47, 57-58, 183-184, 192-194, 206, 208
Recidivism, 6
Recommendation specificity, 43-45, 121, 123, 129
Recompense, spiritual, 196
Record keeping, 21, 70

Reformation, 5, 9, 17, 26, 35, 53, 75, 77-78, 85-89, 91,94, 108, 112, 133, 148, 150, 157-158, 160-162, 168, 198
Reformatory, 153-154, 156, 165
Region, 53-54
Rehabilitation, 5-6, 19, 40, 66, 76-77, 80, 148, 156-157, 160-161, 175, 188, 190
Reliability, interrater, 92, 121, 124
Religious: conviction, 50; doctrine, 2-3,
Repentance, 107, 143, 148
Response length, 44-45, 121, 124-129
Response type: concise/elaborated, 125-126; decisive/hesitant, 125, 127; fluent/halting, 125, 127-128; simple/multifarious, 125-127
Responsibility, 66, 77, 79, 114, 119, 133-134, 184, 186, 188; delegating, 21-22, 70, 72-73-75, 80, 84, 86, 88-89,100, 112, 155
Restitution, 51
Retribution, 16, 51-53, 60, 86, 94, 195-201, 204
Revenge, 53, 94, 107, 142, 144, 195, 197-200
Reward, 3-5, 7, 21, 135
Rights: human, 50, 143; individual, 188-189; involuntary participants', 51; minority, 50; offenders', 20; victims', 195-196
Robbery, 7-9, 11, 26, 39, 43, 56, 63, 76-77, 81, 85, 88-89, 117, 134, 138, 142, 145, 193, 196
Roles, 132-137, 172-173, 200

Safety, 196-199
Sampling, 114
Sanctions, 5, 53-54, 59, 61, 65, 69-84, 92, 94, 148, 170; defined, 5; originator of, 30-31; probed, 69, 78-81, 112, 115-116, 119, 204-205; tradition, 106-107, 111,117; typology, 11 15, 19-

22, 71; volunteered, 69-78, 104, 115-116, 119
Sanction/aim relationships, 23-31
Scare. *See* Fear.
Scared straight, 158, 190
Schema, schemes, 23
Second chance, 21
Self, 200; confidence, 18, 52, 86, 89; defense, 36, 76-77, 142, 145, 147, 149; effect on, 187; esteem, 7, 179; indulgence, 191
Sensorimotor stage, 47
Sentences, 3-4, 43, 162-164, 167-170, 197; determinate, 6
Severity, 89, 98-99, 145, 171, 205
Shame, 85, 89, 172, 178-179, 181
Significance, statistical, 82, 125, 139-140, 148, 166, 169-170, 177, 180-181, 192, 203-204, 206
Sin, 2-3, 112; defined, 2-3
Singular connections, 27-28, 104-106
Social: adjustment, 18; concern, 184; realities, 47; system, 155
Societal: goals, 16; standard, 58,
Solipsism, 33
Spanking, 79-80, 175-176, 178-179, 207
Spencer, Herbert, 55
Stabbing, 26, 64
Standards, societal, 183, 194, 206
Stealing. *See* Theft.
Stoning, 4
Suckling, John, 4
Suffering, 3, 144-145, 150, 157, 197, 199
Supernatural intervention, 132; conditional, 132; universal, 132
Supervision, 6, 31
Suspension, 20, 70-71, 73, 80-81, 100, 165
Sympathy, 59, 88, 171, 177-181, 204, 207; defined, 172-173

Task repetition, 72-73, 80
Theft, 3, 6, 36, 112, 132, 142, 147

Thought: added, 39; after, 39, 45, 79, 81, 87, 90, 105, 115-116, 119; initial, 39; logical, 49; preoperational, 47-48; probed, 39, 45, 69, 105, 112, 115-116, 119, 204-205; process, 118, 120
Threat, public, 106-107, 111, 170
Threats, 20, 70, 75
Tradition, 16, 86, 106-107, 117
Training. *See* Education.
Transfer, 20, 70-73, 80-81
Treatment, 1-7, 27, 56, 61, 65, 120, 141, 154, 158, 160; defined, 5-6
Trend: evident, 82-83, 90-91; possible, 82-83, 90-91
Trials, 120
Tutoring, 85
Typology, 13, 92, 100; aims, 11 15-19, 85; sanctions, 11, 19-22

Unfeasible options, 35, 97, 113-114
Unworkable options, 35

Values: moral, 11, 13, 17, 33, 36-37, 77, 86, 94, 131, 143, 151, 160-161, 170, 183, 199, 205, 207; societal, 183
Vandalism, 19
Vengeance, 19, 86, 88-91, 112, 137, 157, 195
Victimless misdeeds, 193-194
Victims, 8, 10, 60, 70, 133, 143-144, 147, 152, 174, 178-179, 193, 195-201, 198, 200; protecting, 86, 89; rights of, 163, 195-196; welfare of, 18, 164, 166, 173-174, 181, 198

Warning, 20, 70-71, 73, 75, 79-80, 108-111, 165
Welfare, 52; future, 5; personal, 200; public, 2, 10, 155, 157-158, 170, 191; victims', 18, 181, 195
Werner, Heinz, 55, 57
Work habits, 18, 53

About the Authors

ANN C. DIVER-STAMNES is an associate professor in the teacher education program at Humboldt State University in Arcata, California. She has published in the areas of poverty and its effects on adolescence, ethnicity and human development, peer counseling, urban education, and adolescent development. Her most recent book is *Lives in the Balance: Youth, Poverty, and Education in Watts* (1995).

R. MURRAY THOMAS is a professor emeritus from the Graduate School of Education at the University of California, Santa Barbara. He is the author of more than 300 articles and books on educational psychology, human development, and comparative education. His most recent books include *Classifying Reactions to Wrongdoing* (Greenwood, 1995) and *Comparing Theories of Child Development* (fourth edition, 1995).

ISBN 0-313-29730-4

HARDCOVER BAR CODE